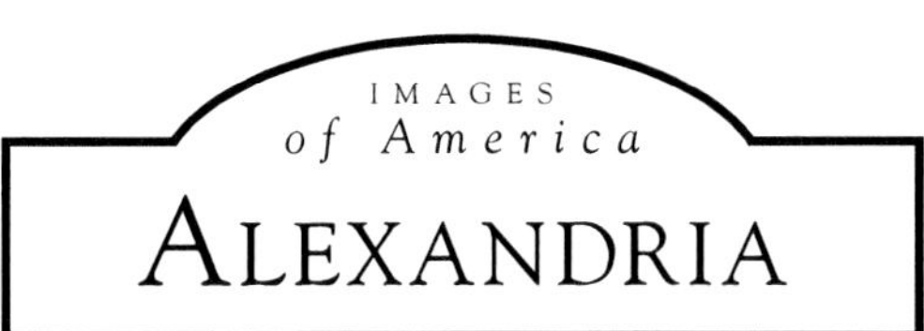
IMAGES
of America
ALEXANDRIA

On the Cover: Local Shriner dignitaries appear around 1912 in a horse-drawn landau before the old Rapides Parish Courthouse as part of a local parade in downtown Alexandria.

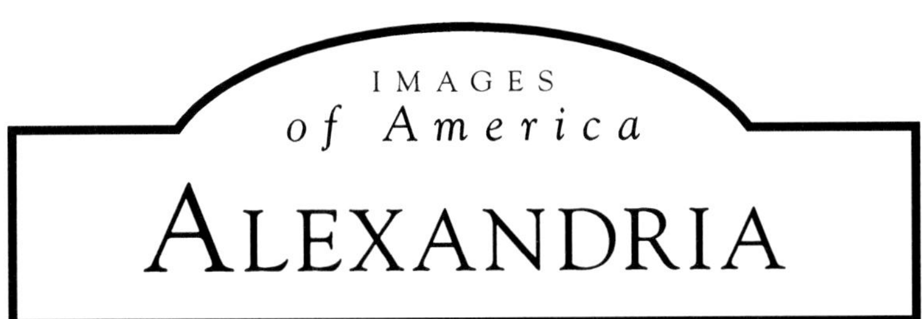

Fr. Chad Partain

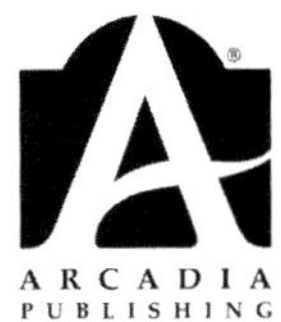

ISBN 978-1-4671-1051-8

Published by Arcadia Publishing
Charleston, South Carolina

Printed in the United States of America

Library of Congress Control Number: 2013933750

For all general information, please contact Arcadia Publishing:
Telephone 843-853-2070
Fax 843-853-0044
E-mail sales@arcadiapublishing.com
For customer service and orders:
Toll-Free 1-888-313-2665

Visit us on the Internet at www.arcadiapublishing.com

This volume is dedicated to my parents, Sam and Jeanette Partain Jr., who shared with me the gift of life and, with love and patience, taught me its meaning and purpose.

CONTENTS

ACKNOWLEDGMENTS

This work honors the many individuals whose love and effort to preserve the history of our community give all of us here in central Louisiana hope for a better tomorrow. In a special way, I would like to highlight the work of Charles Charrier and the members of the Historical Association of Central Louisiana, Alice Scarborough and the members of the Kent Plantation House Board, Dale Genius and the Board of the Louisiana History Museum, Mayor Jacques Roy, Rabbi Arnold Task, Graham Kramer, Mike Jenkins, and countless others who have committed their time and effort to the betterment of this special place we believe to be the true "Heart of Louisiana."

Special thanks to Mary Linn Wernet and the staff of the Cammie Henry Research Center at Northwestern State University for permission to use images from the Delmon Collection and the Newcomb Collection, Dale Genius for permission to use images from his collection and the Louisiana History Museum in Alexandria, Bishop Ronald Herzog for permission to use images from the archives of the Diocese of Alexandria, and all those who contributed images and material for this work.

Introduction

Alexandria's story begins with the story of a river. About 50 miles above the point where the Red River flows into the Mississippi River, a series of irregular ledges of sandstone formed a set of rapids that blocked the channel and made navigation impossible during certain seasons of the year. The site of the rapids lies almost at the geographic center of what is now known as the state of Louisiana, marking a dividing line between the flat, alluvial plains to the south and the pine-covered hills of sand and clay to the north.

In 1714, a French outpost was built among the Natchitoches Indians, and the river became a highway linking New Orleans and French settlers in the interior. A report written in 1722 highlighted the need for a post at the rapids. A French settler named Francois Perrier had been beheaded and his two daughters kidnapped by Chickasaw Indians as he attempted to portage his pirogues over the falls. A post was eventually established on high ground at the site of the present-day Rapides Cemetery under the command of Etienne Marafret Layssard.

The earliest families included the Layssard, Chavalier, Baillio, Deville, Lacaze, LaCour, LaForest, LaSage, Poiret, and Vallery clans. In 1805, Alexander Fulton, an Indian trader and fugitive from the Whiskey Rebellion in Pennsylvania, had a tract of land along the river surveyed. It is on this disputed tract, across the river from the old post site, that Fulton laid out his plans for a settlement that would originally be known as Rapides Parish Courthouse. By 1810, it was known as Alexandria.

After 1815, steamboat service along the Red River made Alexandria's port a center of trade as cotton production soared. Antebellum Alexandria was a place filled with men of business and ambition. Duels over politics, local elections, land speculations, and personal honor frequently polarized the small community. The most famous episode was the "Sandbar Fight" of September 19, 1827.

While cotton brought a wave of prosperity to the region, mortality rates remained high. The Alexandria side of the river was prone to seasonal flooding, and deadly fevers swept the area annually. Despite drought and disease, the population in 1860 had more than doubled since the 1850 census. The bitter presidential campaign of November 1860 and Lincoln's election led to Gov. Thomas Overton Moore's call for secession.

After the formation of the Confederate States of America in 1861, Rapides Parish formed 12 companies of infantry along with two cavalry companies. After the fall of Baton Rouge in 1862, Alexandria became a vital supply depot for the Confederate Army Department of the Trans-Mississippi. On May 7, 1863, Union troops under Gen. Nathaniel P. Banks briefly occupied the town.

Alexandria was again occupied by Union forces during General Banks's disastrous Red River Campaign of 1864. Stunned by Confederate assaults at Mansfield and Pleasant Hill, Banks made the decision to fall back to Alexandria. Harassed by Confederate troops along his line of retreat, Banks's men won the race for Alexandria but not to safety. Less than three feet of water fell over the rapids, trapping Admiral Porter's ironclad fleet.

A solution to the problem was presented by engineer Joseph Bailey of Wisconsin. He had worked in the logging industry before the war, and he proposed the construction of a series of wing dams to create a single deeper channel in the shallow Red River. Three thousand men felled trees and tore apart wharves and warehouses on both sides of the river. By May 12, the fleet was safe in the lower Red.

On Friday, May 13, Union troops appeared, carrying torches and buckets of camphor and turpentine. By 9:00 a.m., the central business district was burning, and a strong spring wind rapidly carried the flames over a 22-block area. The only structures to survive the fire were the brick town hall and the Catholic Church of St. Francis Xavier.

Racked by runaway inflation, harassed by jayhawkers and deserters, and stripped of their labor force, the remaining civilian population tried to survive as best they could in a hostile environment. Confederate forces reoccupied the area, and construction began on two earthworks on the Pineville side of the river: Forts Buhlow and Randolph. A third, Fort Alexandria, was planned but never begun.

In 1866, as part of Reconstruction, Alexandria was again occupied by Union troops under the command of George Armstrong Custer. Tensions flared over the demands of the Freedmen's Bureau. Spring flooding that year ruined crops and the expectations of everyone along the Red River.

A violent yellow fever outbreak in 1867 crushed hopes as well as lives. Troubles surfaced the next year in a different form, when freed African Americans tried to vote in 1868 and were met with armed resistance. Two years later, in 1870, the population of Alexandria stood at just 1,218.

The coming of the railroads in the 1880s made possible the beginning of the timber boom in central Louisiana. Joseph Bentley and other lumbermen made quick fortunes out of the stands of long-leaf pine and hardwoods. In 1899, Alexandria adopted a new city charter, and the town's population numbered 2,800 persons.

From 1901 to 1907, the population tripled in size, and the town itself grew into a more modern, urban environment. Joseph Bentley built the "Biltmore on the Bayou," the Hotel Bentley, which opened on August 10, 1908. In June 1910, the first civic officials moved into a new domed city hall. The structure became an iconic part of the city's downtown landscape. For 52 years, its classical beauty lasted through all the turbulent changes and transitions that saw the small, southern town of Alexandria grow and spread into a modern city.

The end of the World War I brought Prohibition, floods, and falling cotton prices. And, despite Huey Long's Share Our Wealth campaigns, the effects of the Great Depression deepened. In 1930, over 1,200 men were unemployed in Alexandria.

Relief came to the area in 1939 with the arrival of the US Army. The Army General Staff chose central Louisiana to be the base of operations for the huge training maneuvers set for 1940 and 1941. Gen. George Marshall together with his staff, which included men like Patton, Eisenhower, and MacArthur, camped out in the Hotel Bentley while new camps were set up to accommodate over 90,000 men. As troops were deployed for service overseas, their numbers were replaced by Japanese, Italian, and German prisoners of war. The end of the war found a majority of Alexandria's citizens anxious to return to their prewar state. As Frederick Spletstoser wrote, "In essence, Alexandria epitomized the character of its influential citizens. It exuded conservatism and caution was its watchword."

Greater changes came and altered the local landscape after the passing of the Civil Rights Act. The battle for school integration was eventually won when Judge Nauman Scott issued his desegregation order in Rapides Parish on August 10, 1970, mandating the integration of all public schools and bus systems. In 1974, the City of Alexandria voted for a change in its system of self-governance under a new home-rule charter, which called for a mayor and council to work in close collaboration. This change helped to reign in the power of the incumbent mayor, John Snyder, whose outrageous antics, such as filling the municipal swimming pools with catfish, were fast becoming legend. In 1977, the Alexandria Art Museum opened in the former Rapides Bank building, the first step in the establishment of a recognized downtown arts district. The Arna Bontemp Museum became the first African American museum in the state in 1992.

In 1980, the city population peaked at 51,565 persons. During his 20-year tenure as mayor, Ned Randolph helped the city and parish through many difficult transitions, including the closing of the England Air Base in 1992. The dedication of the Riverfront Center and Levee Park helped to highlight the potential of the downtown area. In 2006, the Coughlin-Saunders Performing Arts Center opened its doors.

In 2007, Alexandria celebrated its 200th birthday. In his bicentennial remarks, Mayor Roy recalled the "infectious" excitement that sparked the city's growth around 1907: "Today, we share a similar excitement and enthusiasm . . . the unstoppable growth of our city have all coalesced to make us all, once again, look to Alexandria as a future great."

One

On the Frontier

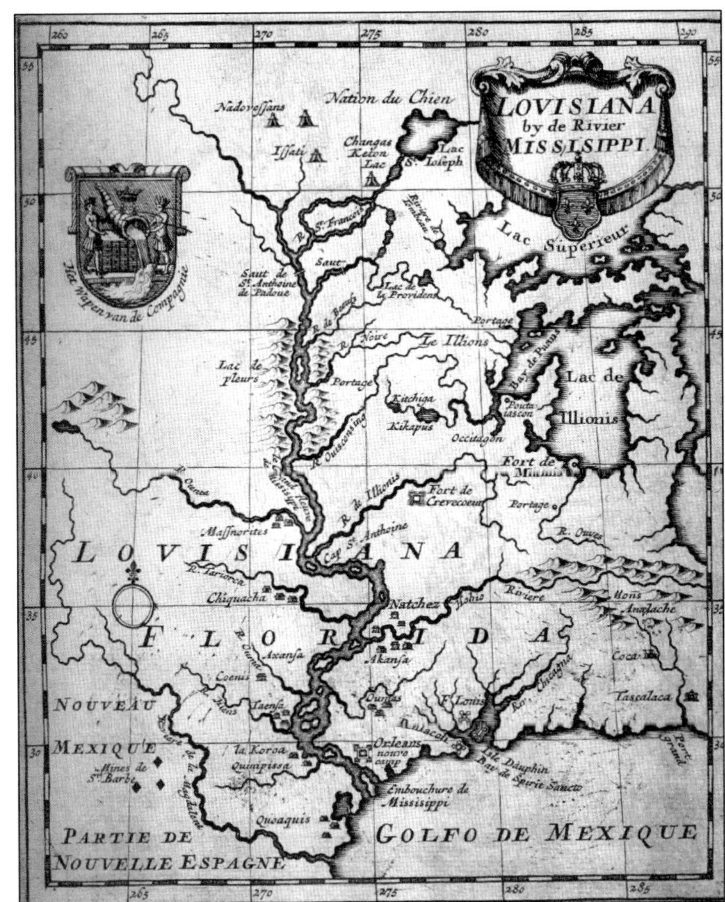

This early French colonial map of the Mississippi River Valley shows the extent of exploration after Robert de La Salle's 1682 descent of the Mississippi. The Red River Valley was explored by the French under Sieur de Bienville in 1700.

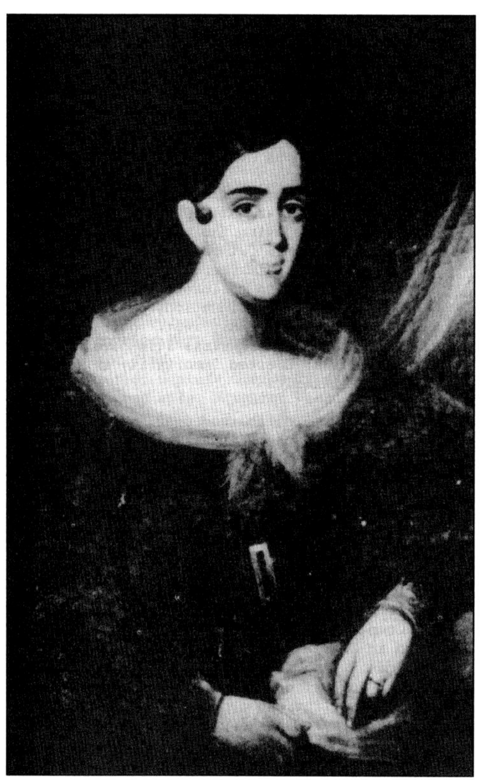

Here is Amelie Baillio, daughter of Pierre Baillio II and Magdelaine Lacour. She later married John Compton, a wealthy Rapides Parish planter.

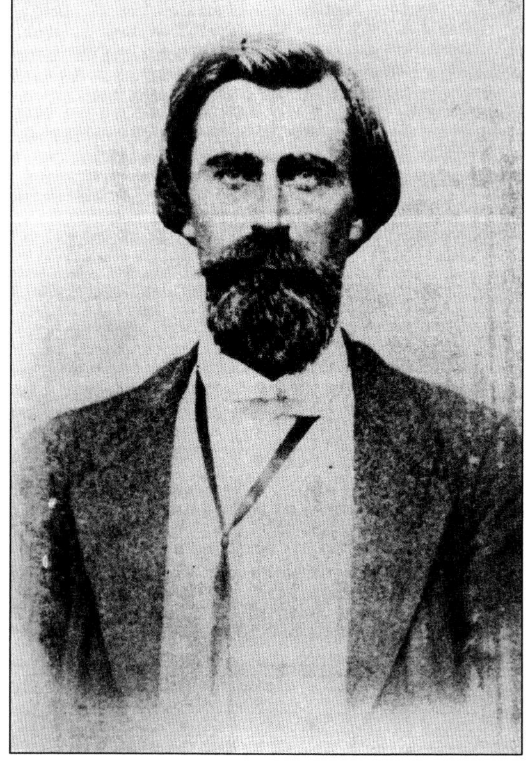

Pictured is Sosthene Auguste Baillio, the son of Pierre Baillio II and Magdelaine Lacour. The master of Flowerton Plantation, Sosthene served as a state representative from Rapides Parish, a trustee of St. Francis Xavier Church, and a member of the board of trustees for Franklin College in St. Landry Parish. He was born in 1800 and died in the yellow fever epidemic of 1853.

Seen here is a c. 1800 survey of early Spanish land grants along the Red River. The site marked "7," designated for Adam Huffman, would become the center of the town of Alexandria.

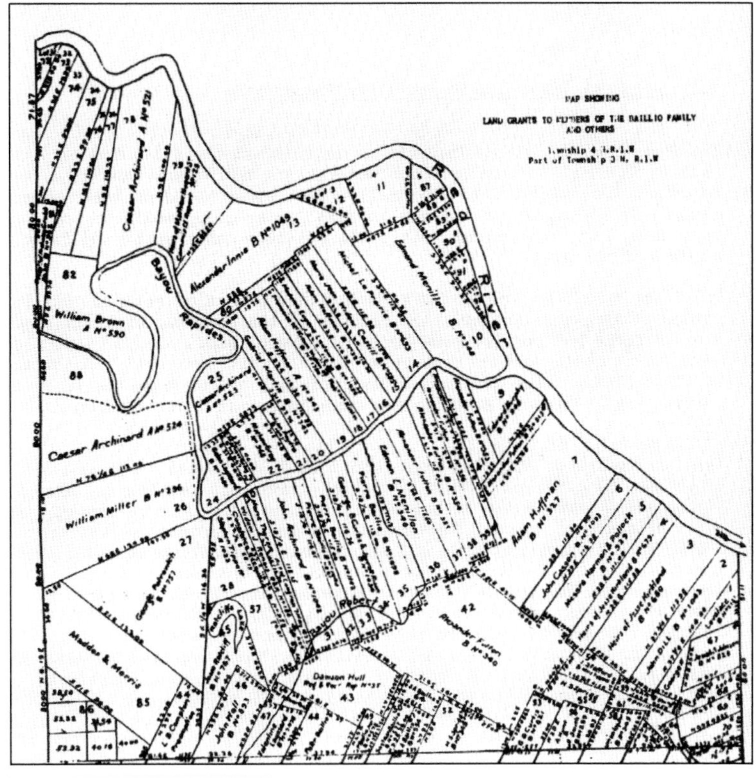

EL BARON DE CARONDELET
CABALLERO DE LA RELIGION DE SAN
Juan, Brigadier de los Reales Exércitos, Gobernador
general, Vice-Patrono de las Provincias de la Luisiana
Florida Occidental, é Inspector de sus Tropas &c.

Hallando por conveniente al servicio del Rey formar una compañia de Milicias en el Puesto del Rapido, y siendolo tambien nombrar para el Empleo de Teniente de ella, persona de valor, zelo y buena conducta, concurriendo estas precisas circunstancias en D.n Belon Leyssard, Por tanto (usando de la facultad que el Rey me tiene concedida) he venido en nombrarlo (como por el presente le nombro) por Teniente de dha. Comp.a y mando á los Ofiz.s, Sarg.s Cabos y Soldados le reconozcan por tal Ten.te obedeciendo las ordenes que por escrito ó de palabra les diere del R.l servicio, guardandole y haciendole guardar, todas las honras fueros y preeminencias que le tocan y pertenecen.

Dado en la N.a Orleans á veinte de Agosto de mil setecientos noventa y quatro

El Baron de Carondelet

Andres Lopez Armesto

V.S. nombra por Ten.te de la Comp.a de Milicias del Rapido a D.n Belon Leyssard

This is an August 20, 1794, appointment letter signed by Baron de Carondelet for Etienne Maraffret "Bolon" Layssard as a lieutenant in the Spanish Army.

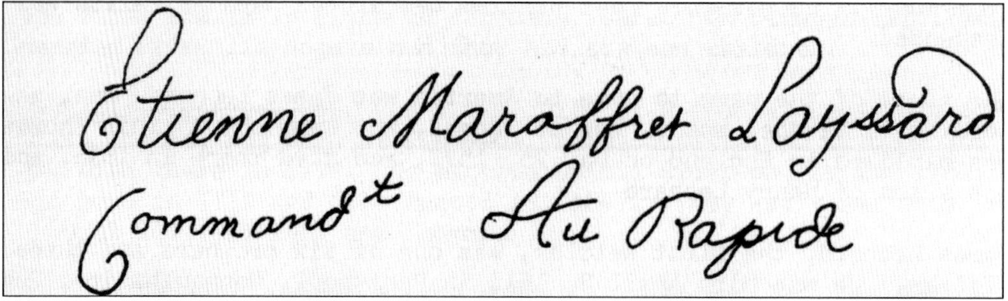

Here is the signature of Etienne Maraffret Layssard, a veteran of the French Army in Arkansas and first commandant of the post at the rapids.

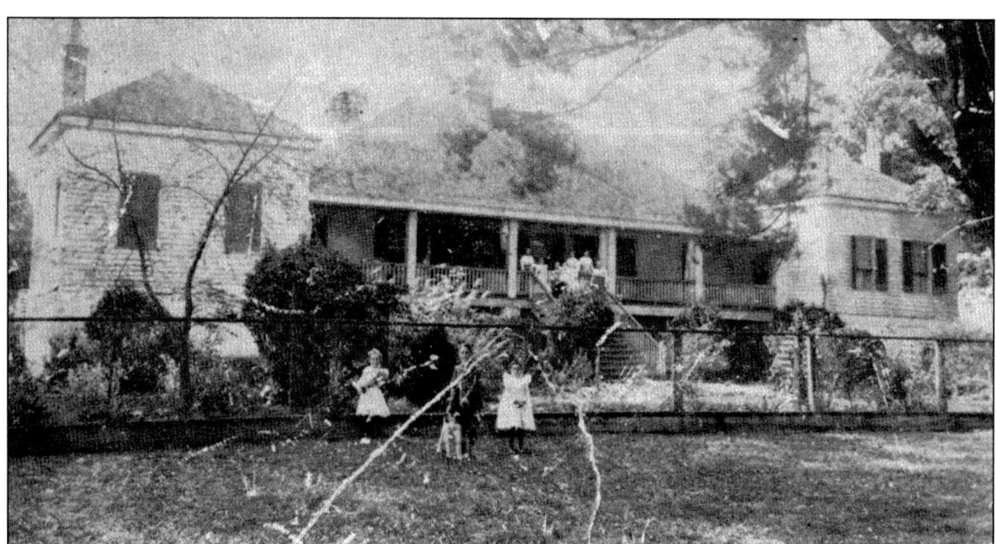

This is an early-1900s photograph of Kent Plantation House at its original site on Rapides Avenue. Built by the Baillio family, the home was eventually sold to Robert Hynson, who added the side rooms seen on either side of the main French colonial structure. The home and surrounding grounds were later acquired by the American Legion in the 1930s.

Pictured is a Spanish land grant to Pierre Baillio III, son of Pierre Baillio II and Magdelaine Emelie Lacour, witnessed by Valentine Layssard, commandant of the El Rapido post from August 25, 1796.

This is the Kent Plantation house as it appeared around 1931. The view shows the original central portion of the house built by Pierre Baillio II and the two side structures added by the Hynson family sometime after 1846.

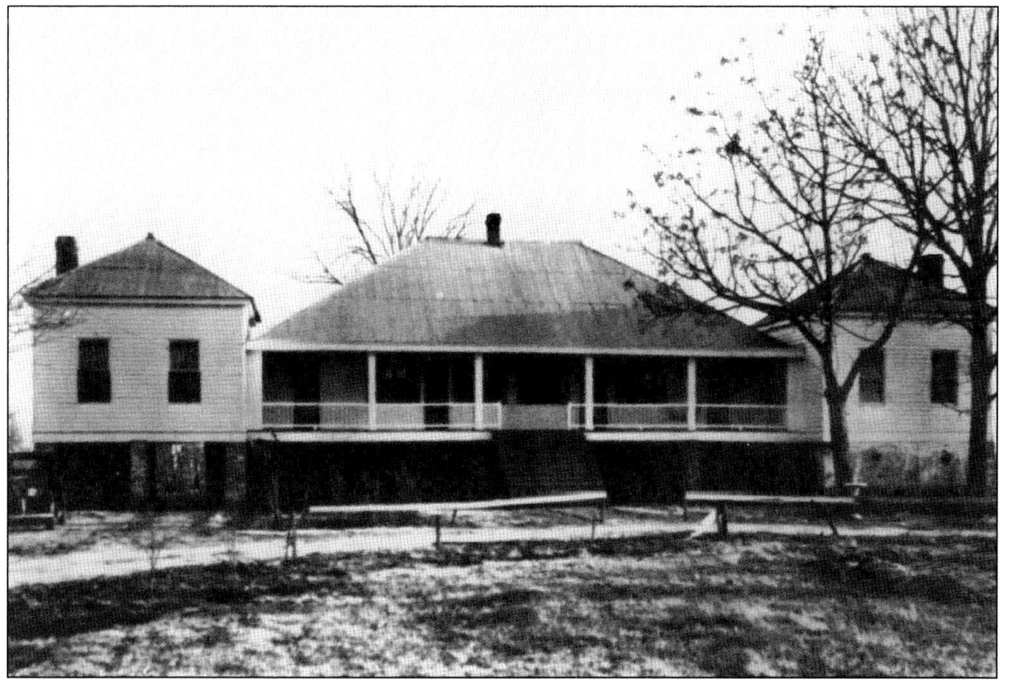

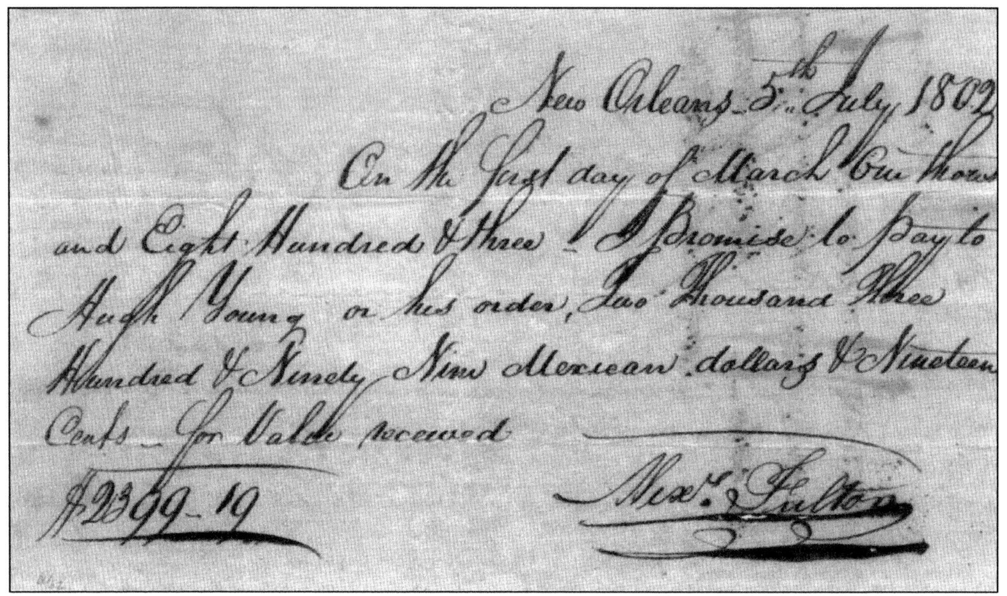

New Orleans 5th July 1802

On the first day of March One thou
and Eight Hundred & three I Promise to pay to
Hugh Young or his order, Two Thousand Three
Hundred & Ninety Nine Mexican dollars & Nineteen
Cents _ For Value received

$2399-19

Alexr. Fulton

This is a promissory note signed by Alexander Fulton, the founder of Alexandria, on July 5, 1802.

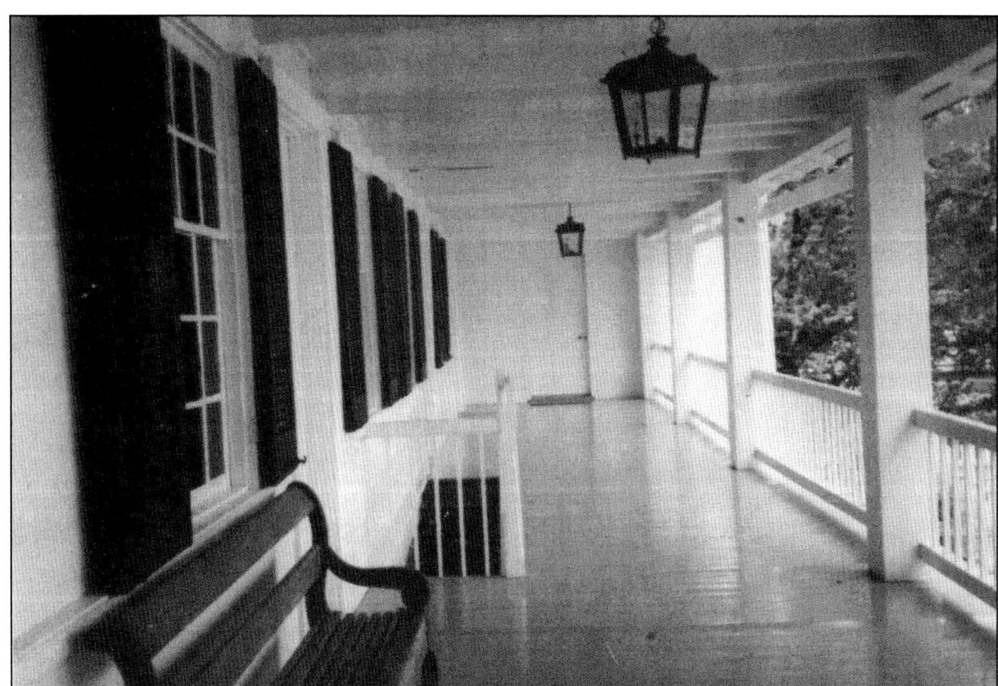

A gallery and stairwell at the Kent Plantation house are pictured here. Built by slaves of Pierre Baillio II on land granted to him by the Spanish Crown, this bousillage structure, dating to 1800, is the oldest surviving structure in central Louisiana and is preserved today as a living history museum.

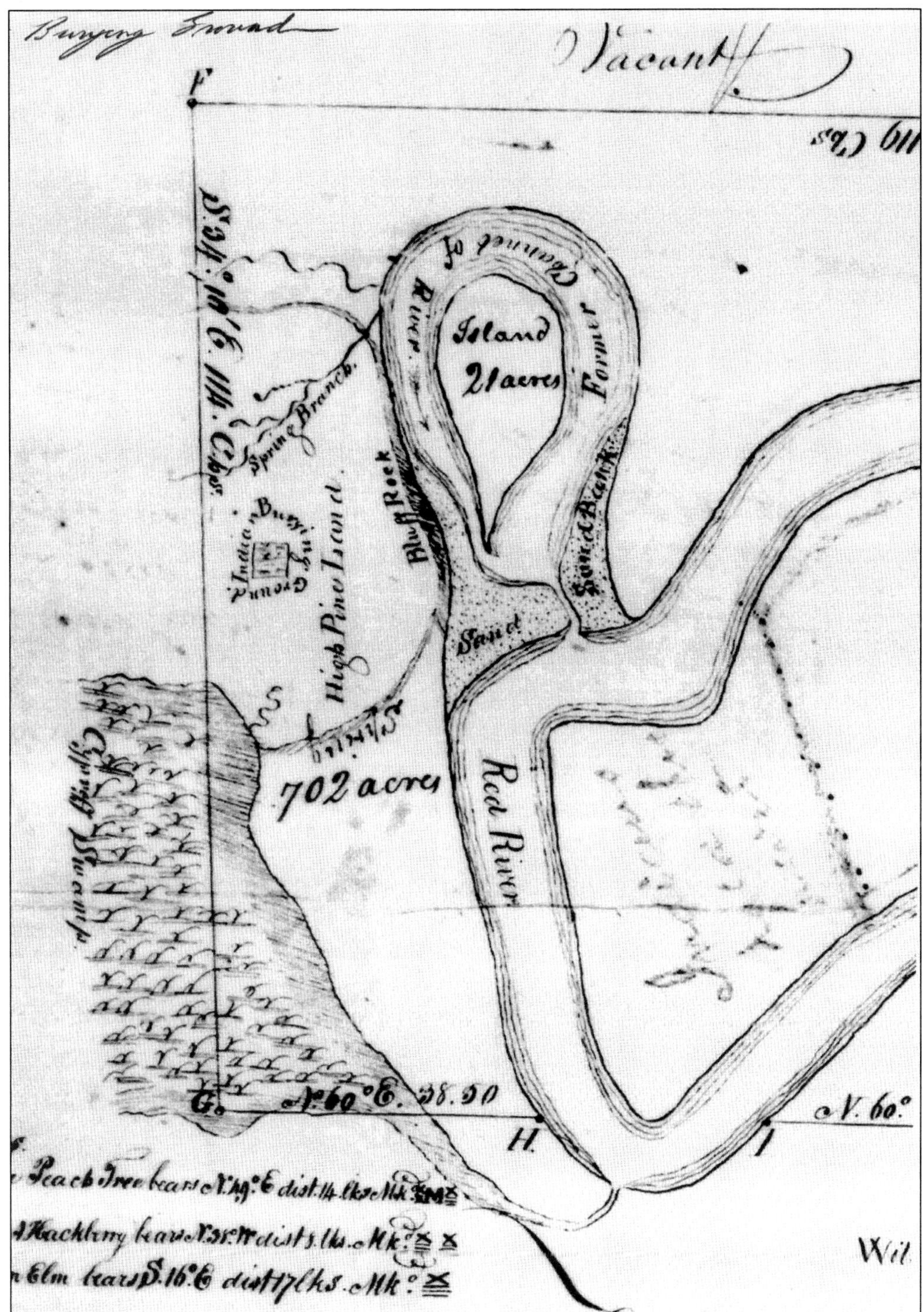

A c. 1819 survey of the Red River shows the location of the Apalachee village and burial ground.

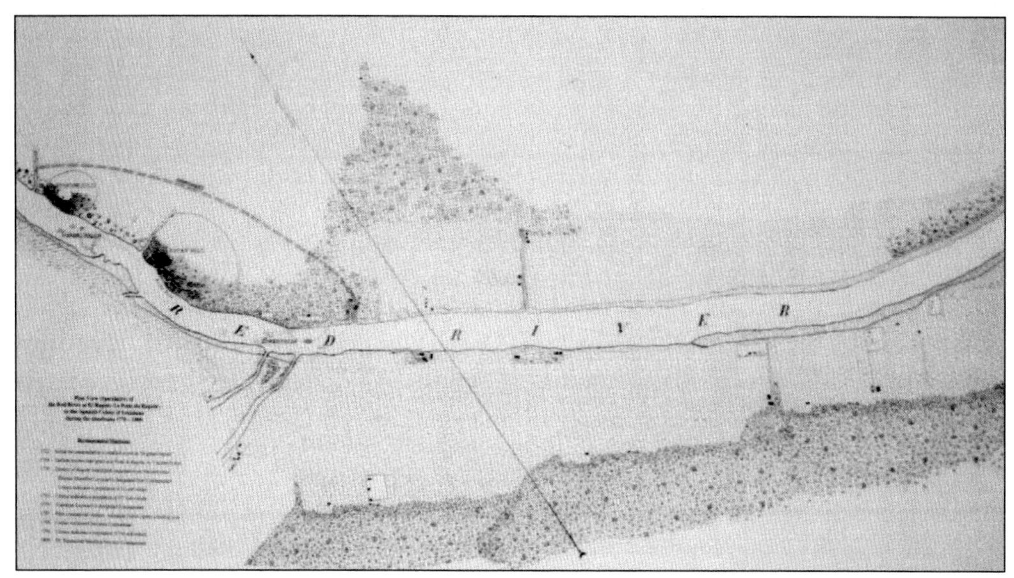

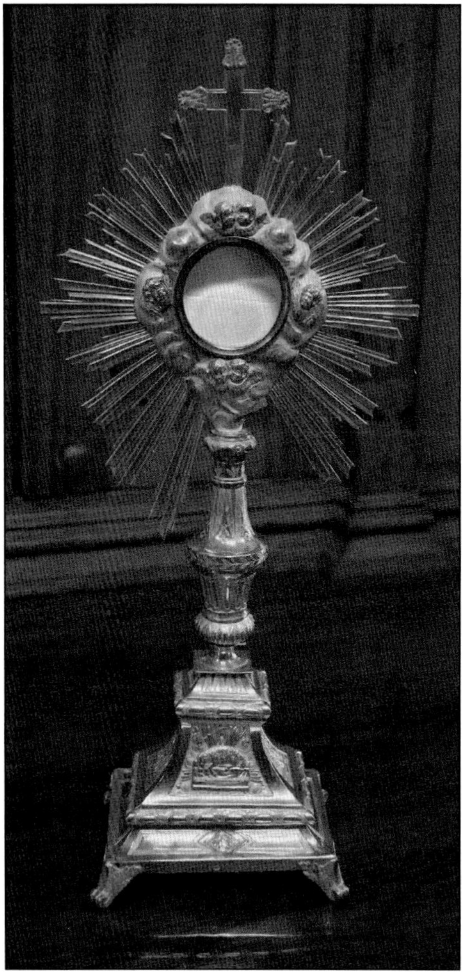

Here is another survey map of the rapids at the Red River and the usual path of portage around the falls. It was on this trail that Francois Perrier was killed by Chickasaw Indians in 1722.

A French monstrance from 1779 is seen here. It was originally used at the Chapel of St. Louis, King of France. It was built by Father Valentin for the Apalachee Indians in March 1764 and now is in the collection of St. Francis Xavier Cathedral in Alexandria.

Two

Antebellum Growth

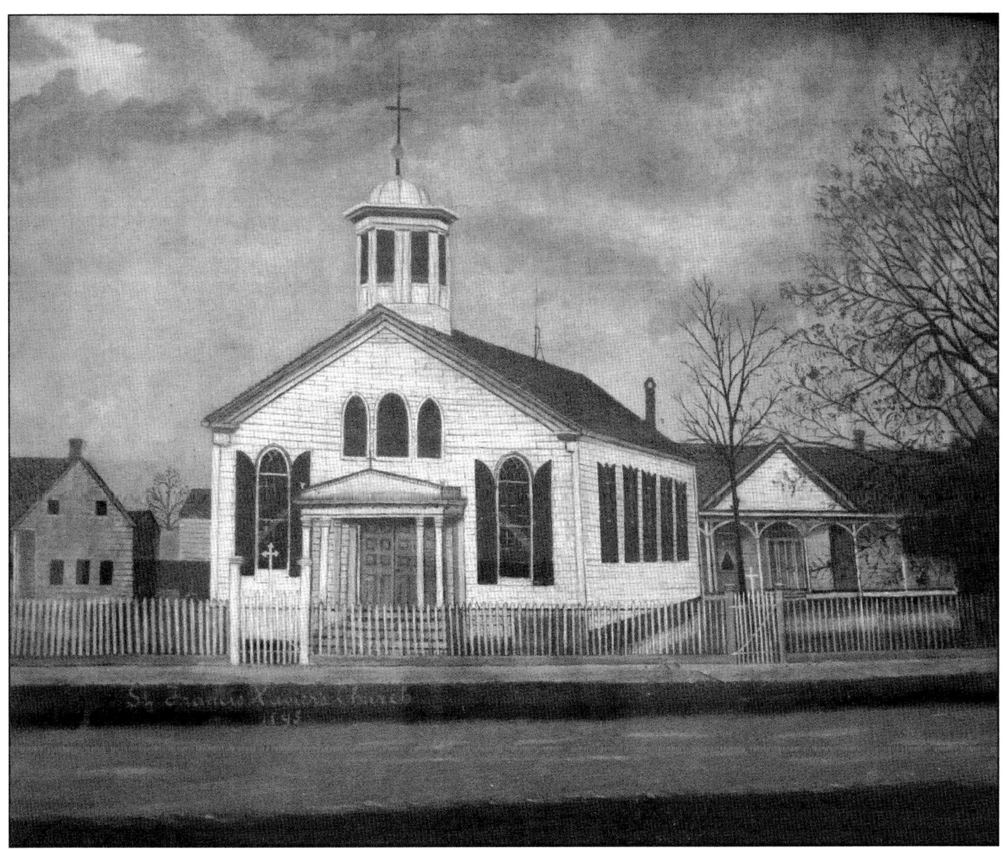

Pictured is St. Francis Xavier Church, built by Theophilius Hilton in 1834. The second Catholic church in Alexandria, this structure replaced an earlier chapel built in 1817. The church survived the fire of May 13, 1864, only to be lost to fire in 1895.

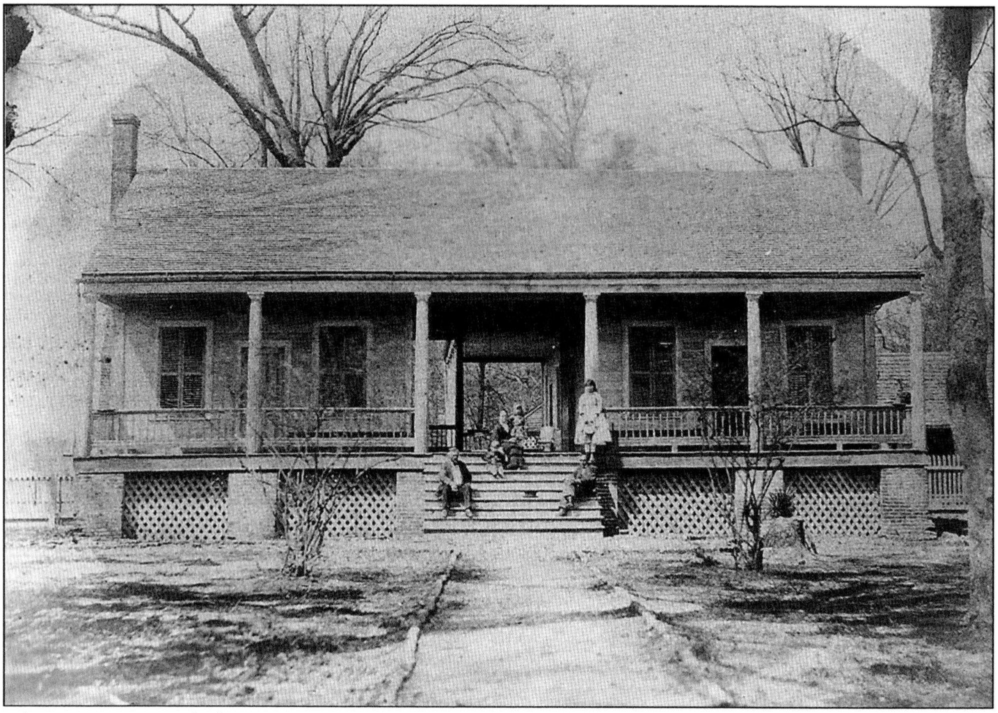

This is Homestead Plantation in 1875. Central Louisiana boasted many fine antebellum homes before the Civil War. Many were lost to fire and the ravages of hard times. A few, like Lloyd's Hall, remain as reminders of past times.

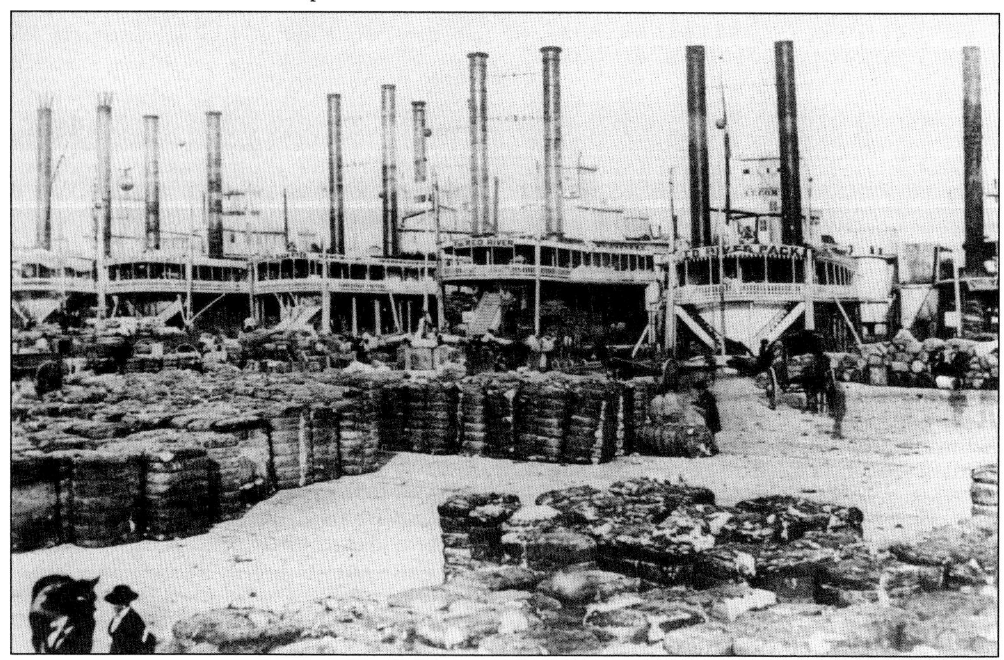

A steamboat on the Red River is loaded with Rapides Parish cotton bound for New Orleans. On average, a typical bale of cotton ready for loading weighed 500 to 800 pounds. Antebellum prices fluctuated between 63¢ and 85¢ cents a pound.

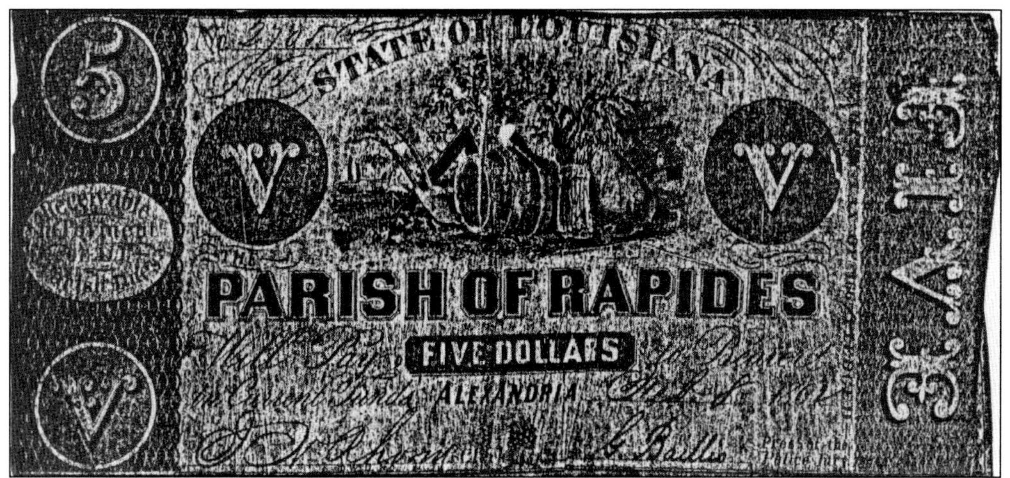

This is an example of local currency printed during the Civil War: a $5 parish note signed by Judge Gervais Baillio.

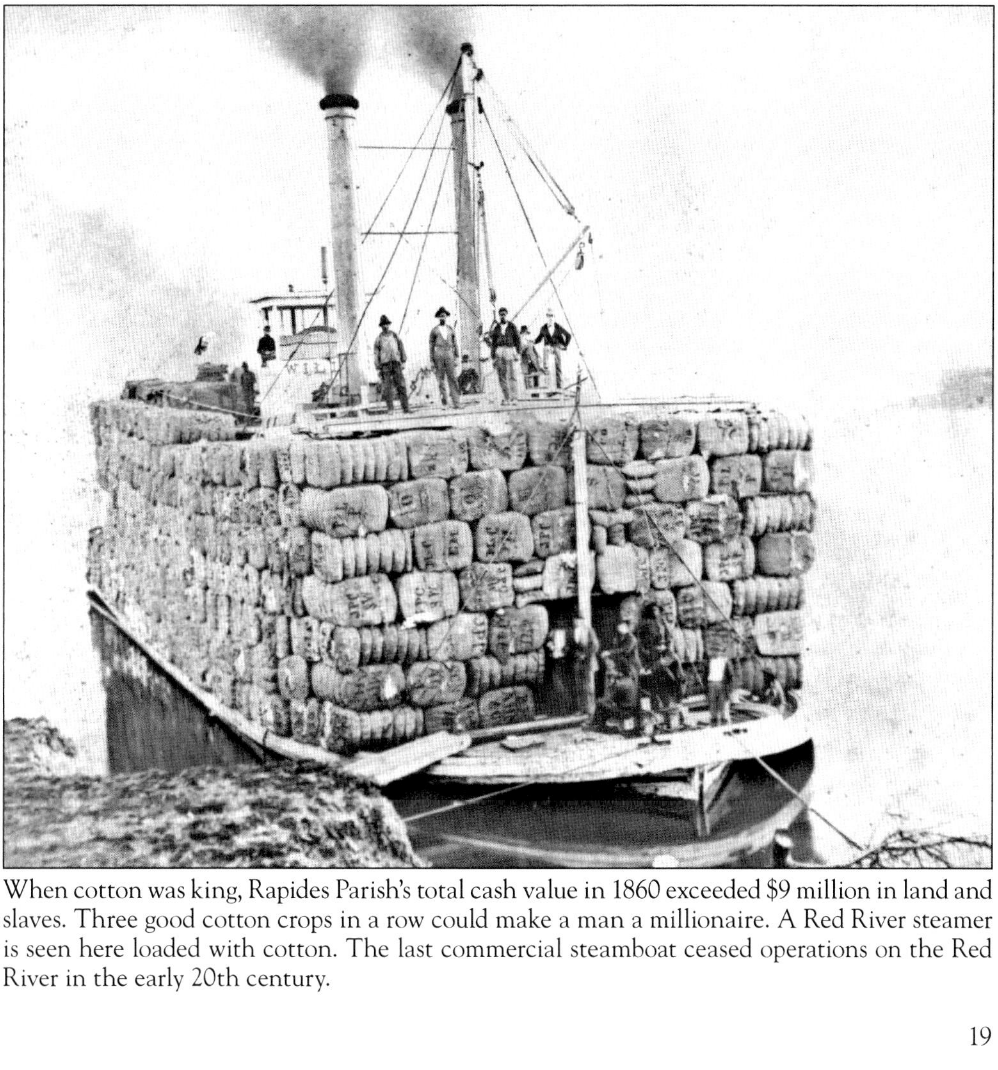

When cotton was king, Rapides Parish's total cash value in 1860 exceeded $9 million in land and slaves. Three good cotton crops in a row could make a man a millionaire. A Red River steamer is seen here loaded with cotton. The last commercial steamboat ceased operations on the Red River in the early 20th century.

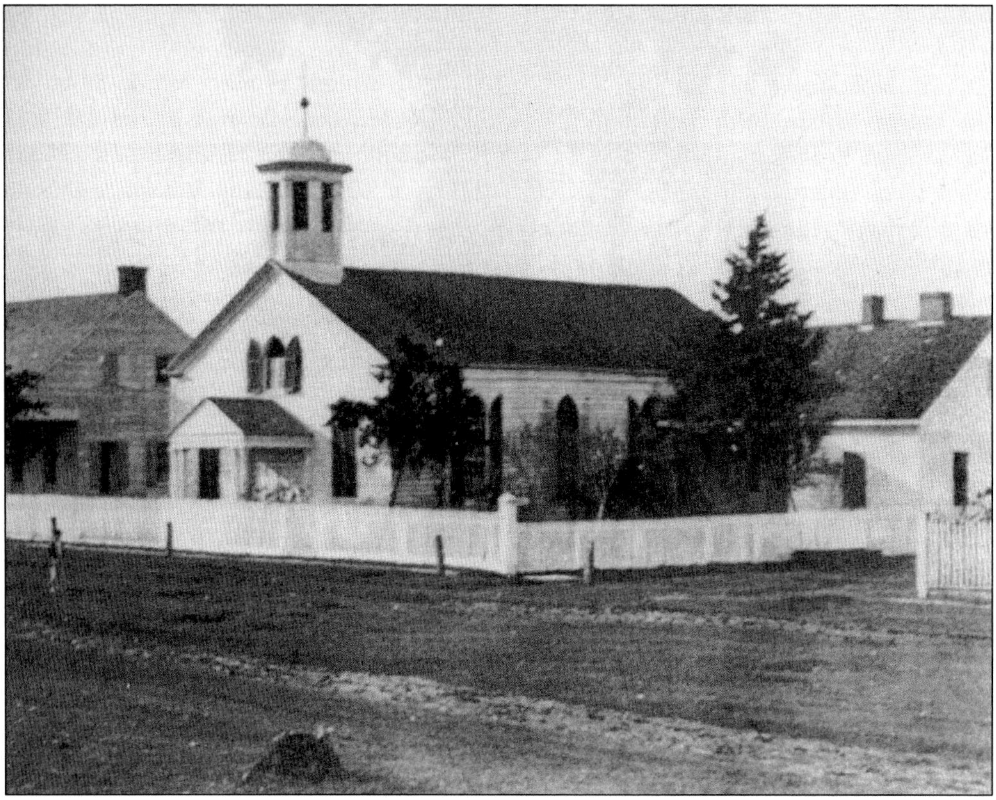

An 1879 photograph shows the St. Francis Xavier Church rectory and convent on Alexandria's famous Front Street.

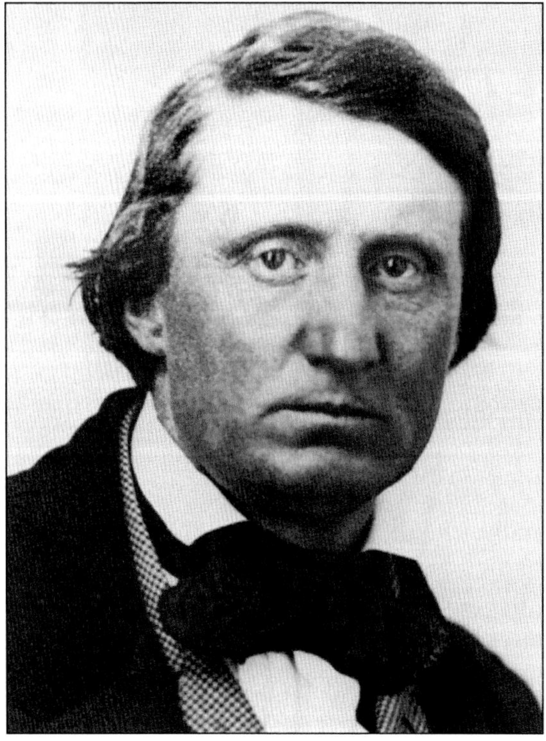

Ralph Smith Smith was antebellum planter and commercial developer. He built the first narrow-gauge railroad west of the Mississippi River to link Lecompte and Alexandria. As the chairman of the Committee of Public Safety for Rapides Parish during the Civil War, his three steamboats served the Confederate cause, carrying men and supplies along the Red River. His boats, as well as his tracks and trains, were destroyed along with his home and depot by Union troops in 1864. He died in 1883.

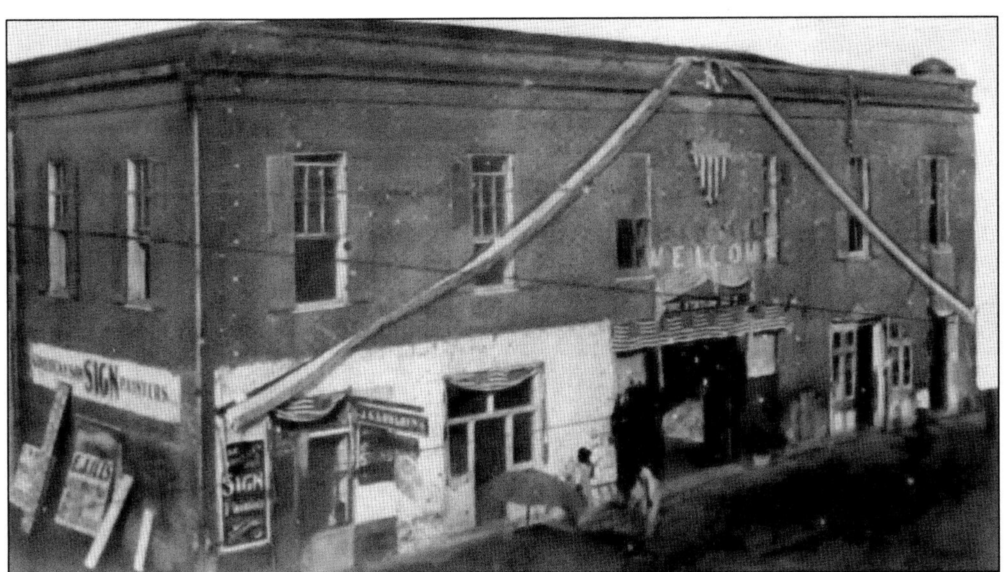

The antebellum city hall, completed in 1860, was damaged during the 1864 fire but was repaired after the war and remained the civic center until construction of a new city hall in 1909.

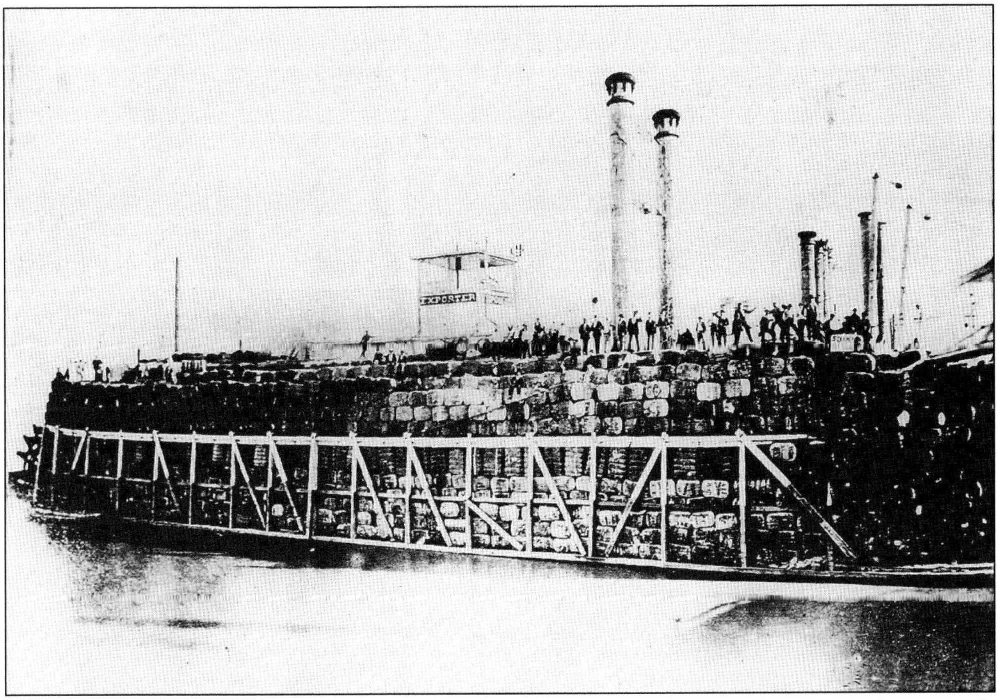

A Red River steamer is docked at a wharf in New Orleans. From 1820 to 1861, steamboats made an average of 500 trips a year between New Orleans and Alexandria. Wrecks and boiler explosions were frequent accidents on the water.

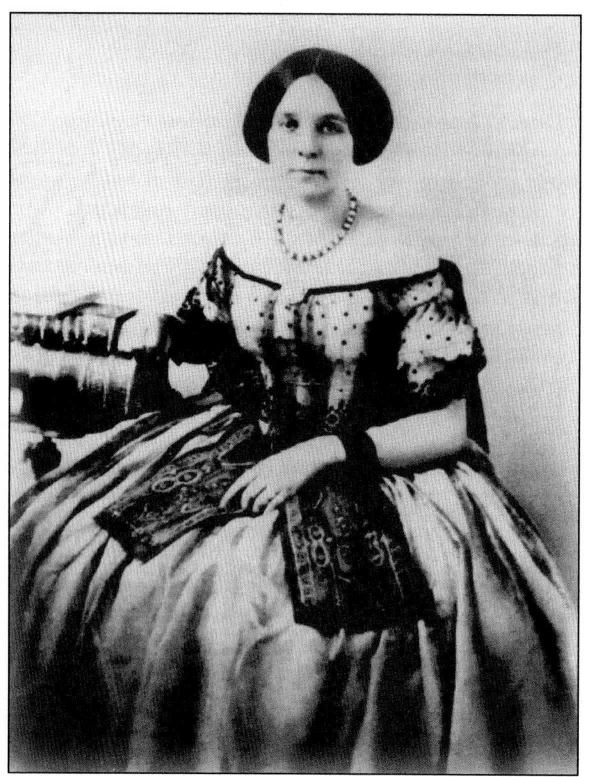

Bethia Johnston Leonard Moore was the wife of Gov. Thomas Overton Moore. The mistress of Mooreland Plantation until the destruction of her home by Union troops in 1864, she survived the war and died in 1880. She is buried beside her husband at Mount Olivet Cemetery in Pineville.

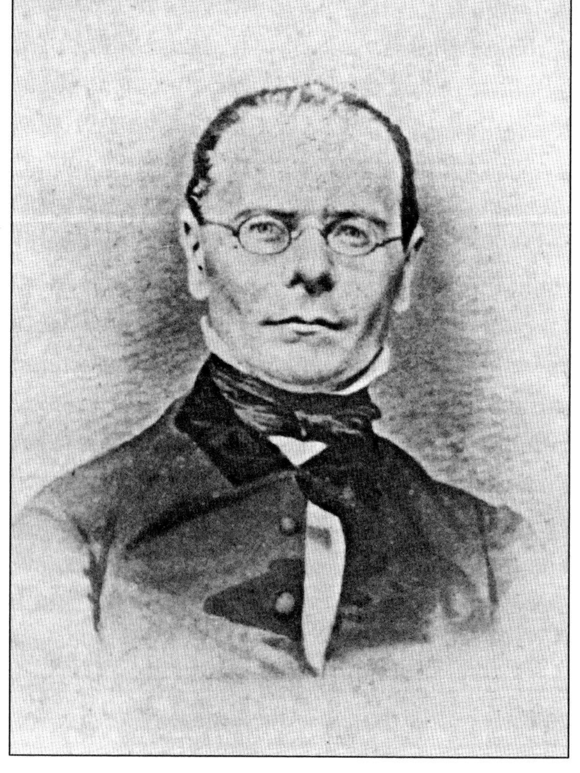

This is Fr. Jean Pierre Bellier, a native of Rennes, Frances, and pastor of St. Francis Xavier Church at the time of the Union invasion in 1864. He saved the church from destruction by threatening to shoot anyone who desecrated the church. Fr. Bellier went on to serve as chaplain and instructor in modern languages at the Louisiana Seminary of Learning in Pineville until his death in 1867.

George Mason Graham was the master of Tyrone Plantation on Bayou Rapides and known as the "Father of LSU." Graham sat as member of the board of supervisors for the Louisiana Institute of Learning in Pineville and worked closely with the first commandant, William T. Sherman of Ohio.

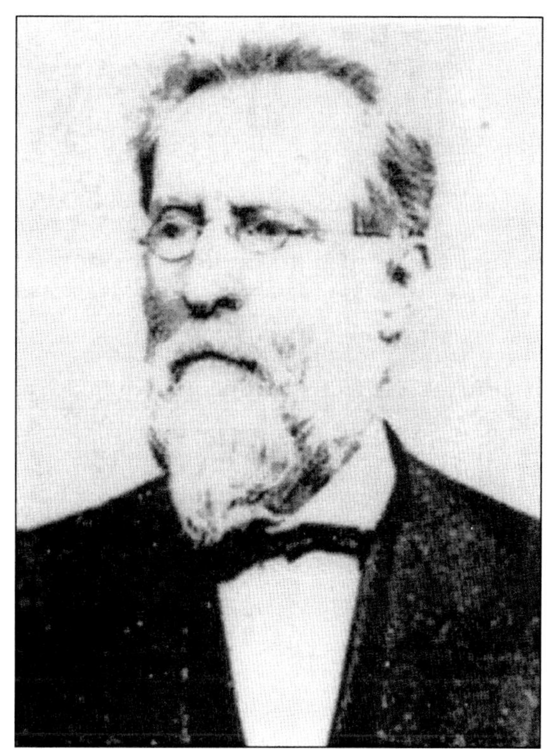

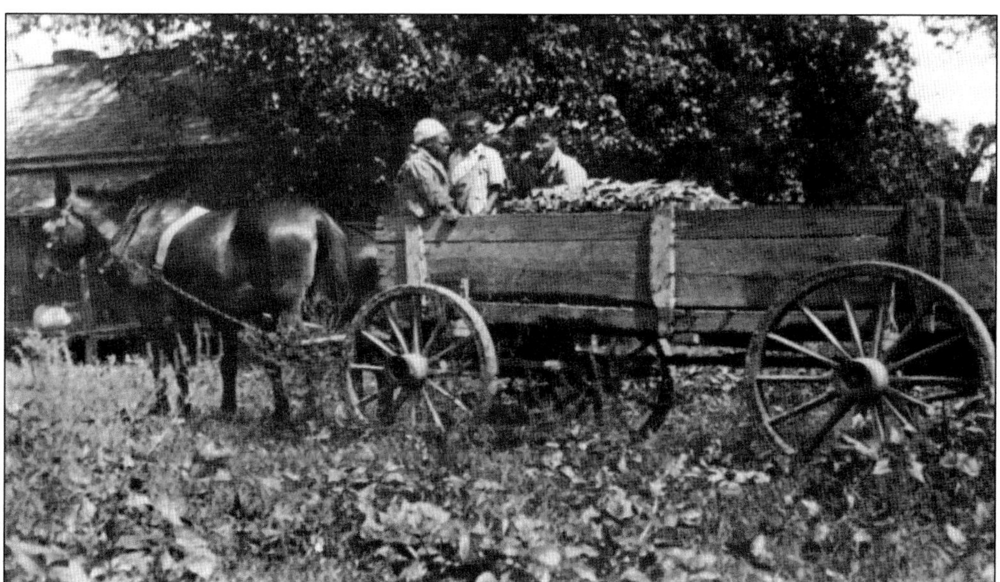

This was a typical scene during harvest time: a mule-drawn wagon in the fields. Central Louisiana's economy remained rooted in cotton production well into the 20th century.

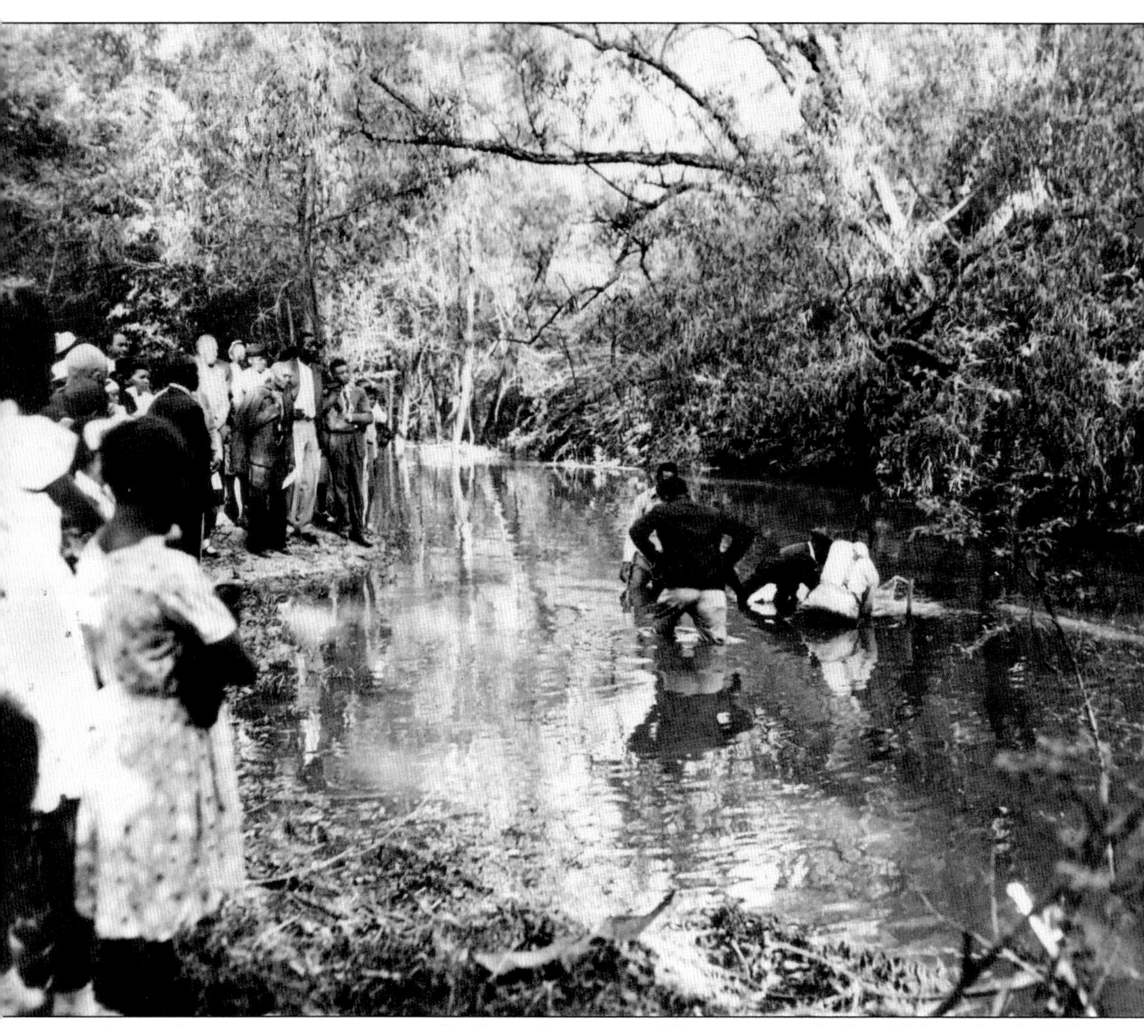

A river baptism was a common sight throughout central Louisiana in the late 19th and early 20th centuries. Under the French and Spanish, Catholicism remained the only recognized religion. After the Louisiana Purchase of 1803, Protestant settlers were free to practice their faith and establish churches.

A group of men stands outside of the B.C. Duke store, located on Front Street in Alexandria.

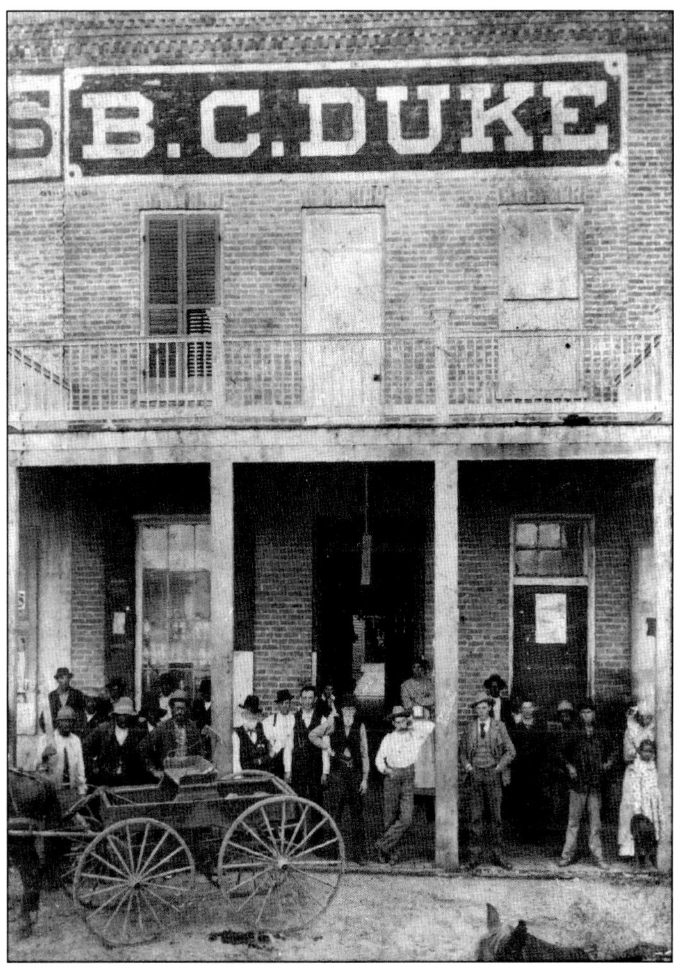

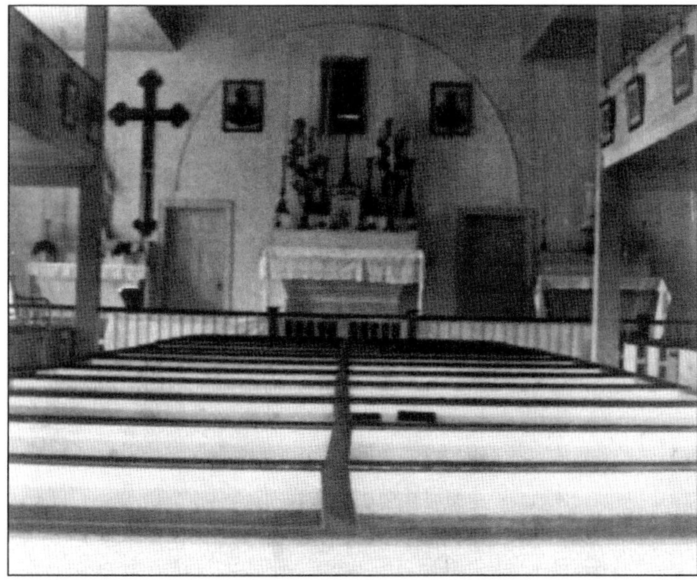

This is a c. 1885 photograph of the interior of St. Francis Xavier Church in Alexandria.

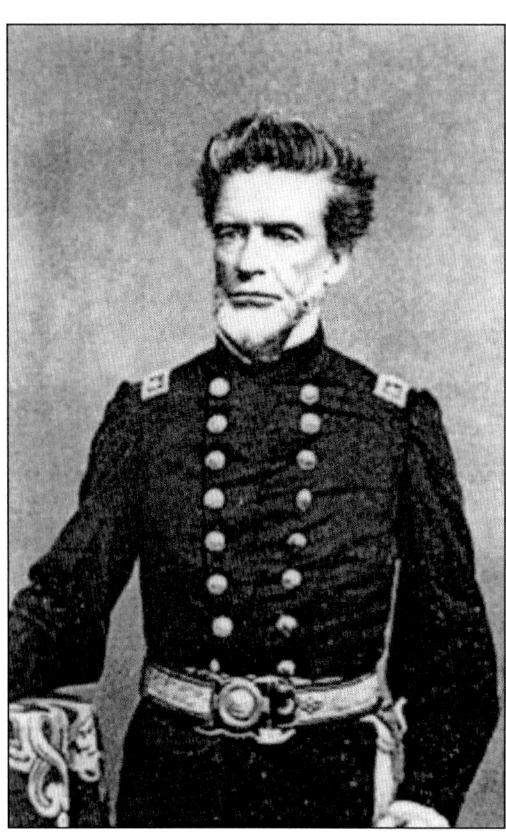

Thomas Overton Moore was a Rapides Parish planter and governor of the state of Louisiana at the time of the secession crisis in 1861.

Pictured is the Tyrone Plantation, the Bayou Rapides home of George Mason Graham. The original antebellum core and 20th-century additions are clearly visible.

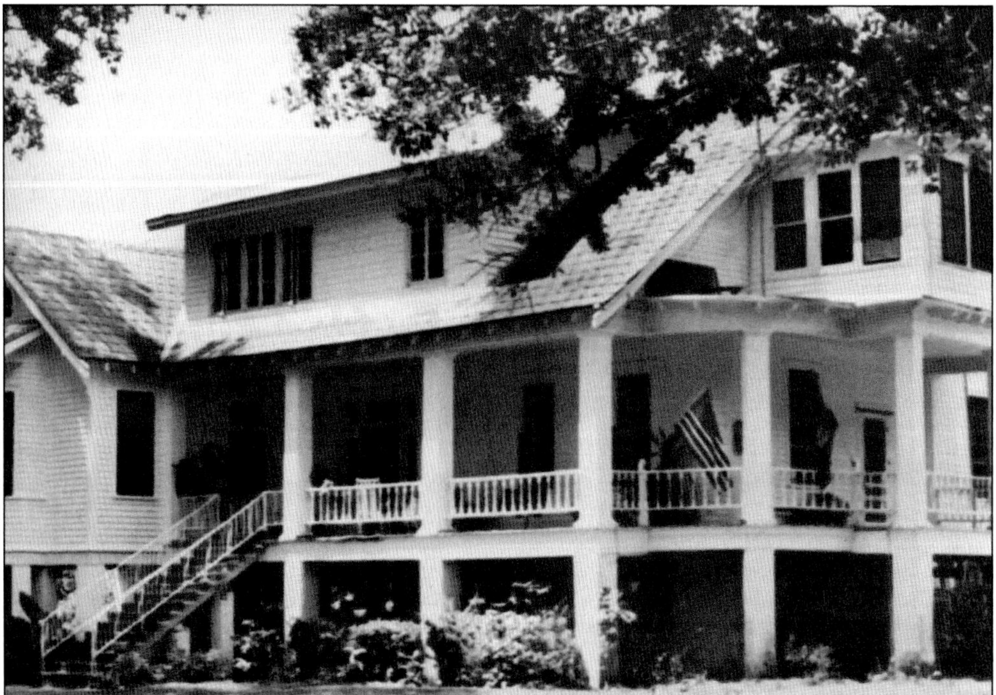

Three

War and Reconstruction

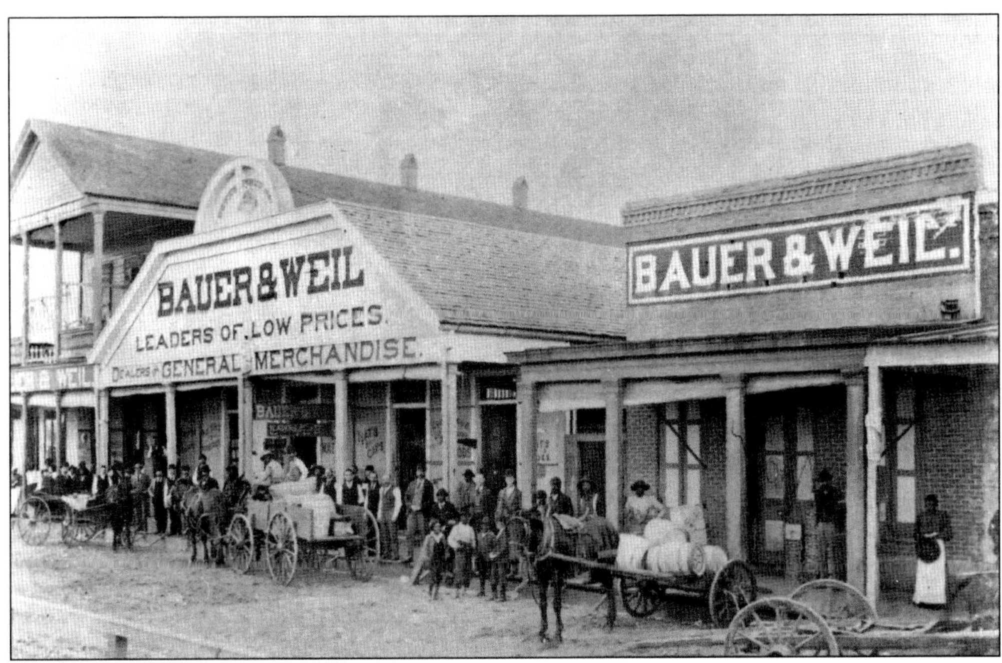

This is the Bauer and Weil General Merchandise in 1886 on Front Street between DeSoto and Murray Streets in Alexandria. Jewish immigration to central Louisiana began during the antebellum period, and their contribution to the region's culture and commerce has been significant.

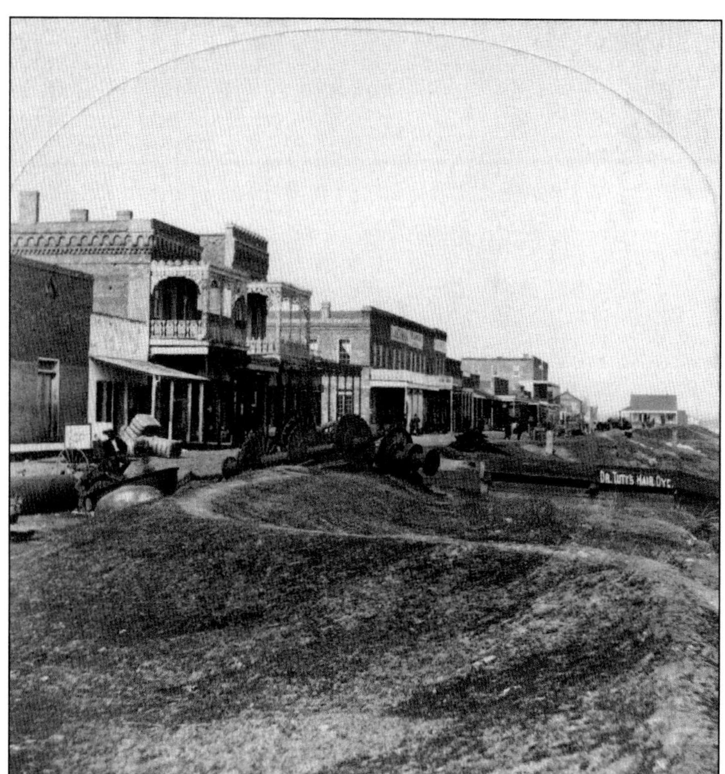

Pictured is Alexandria's Front Street around 1885. The photograph, taken before the first railroad construction, shows the absence of any protective levee along the Red River.

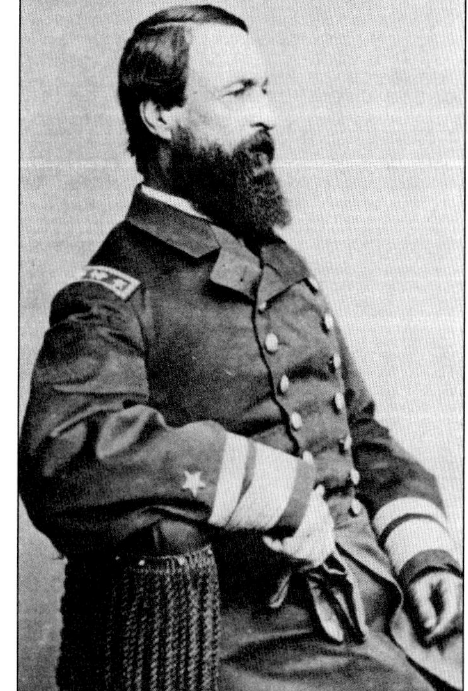

Commanding naval operations during the Red River Campaign, Adm. David Porter was considered flamboyant, scheming, and anxious to confiscate the abundant stores of cotton along the Red River for the booty.

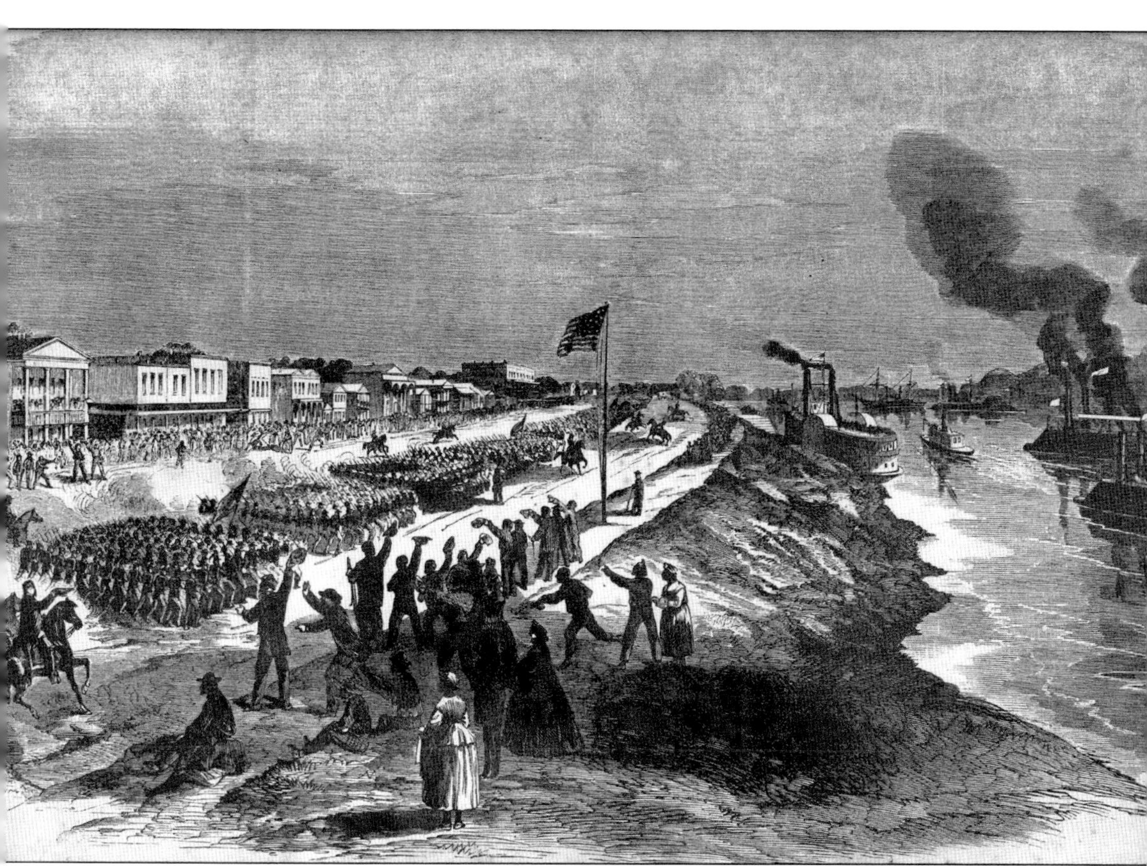

An 1863 *Harper's Weekly* engraving depicts General Banks's army entering Alexandria. The town was briefly occupied by Union troops before Banks was forced to march on Port Hudson. The Union would reoccupy the town the following year.

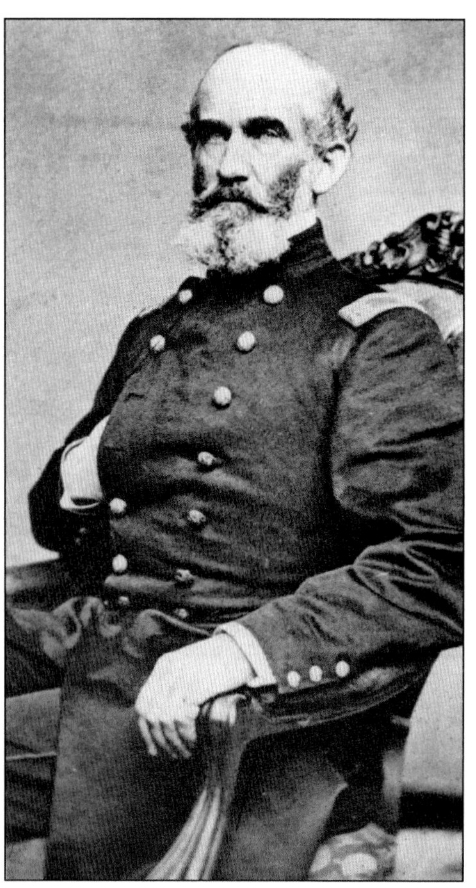

Brig. Gen. A.J. Smith was ordered by his chief, William. T. Sherman, to cooperate with General Banks during the Red River Campaign. Never popular with his own men, he despised General Banks and suggested arresting him for incompetence after his failure to capture Shreveport.

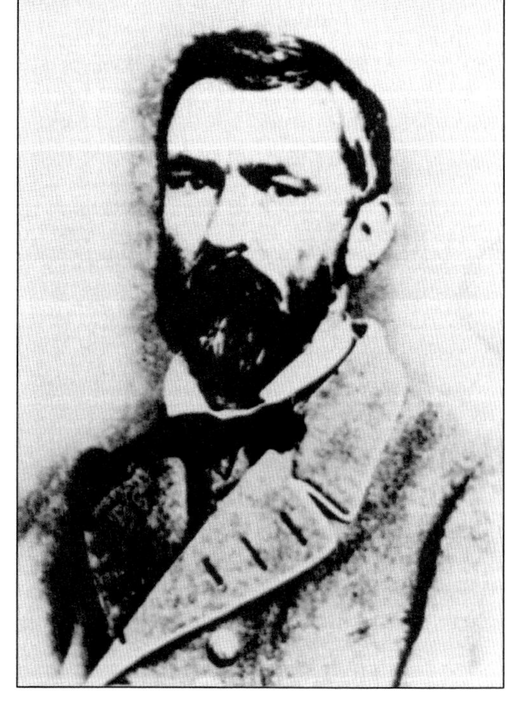

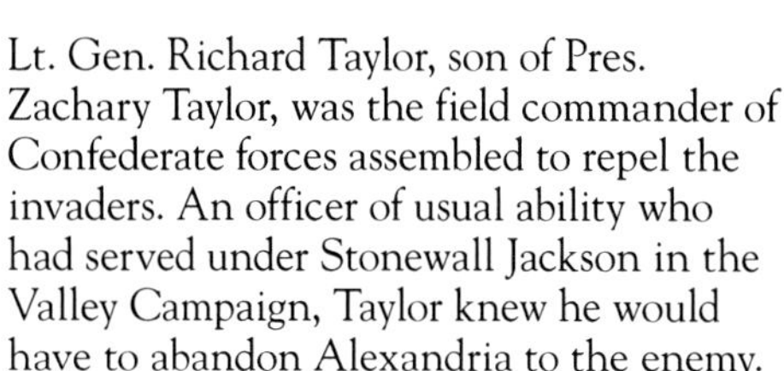

Lt. Gen. Richard Taylor, son of Pres. Zachary Taylor, was the field commander of Confederate forces assembled to repel the invaders. An officer of usual ability who had served under Stonewall Jackson in the Valley Campaign, Taylor knew he would have to abandon Alexandria to the enemy.

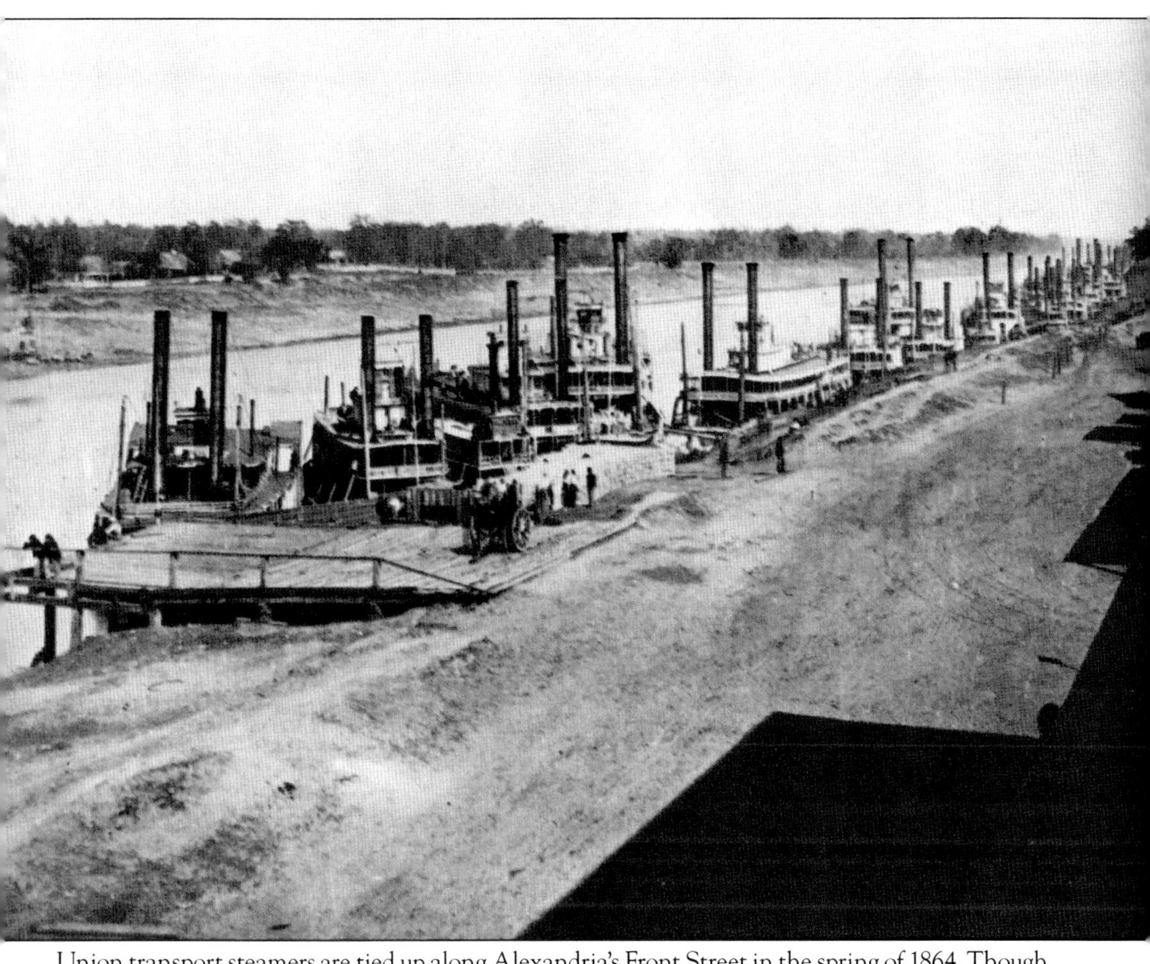

Union transport steamers are tied up along Alexandria's Front Street in the spring of 1864. Though the wharf shown here gives no indication, the river's rapids near the town were so low that only four to five inches of water stood in place, effectively trapping the fleet.

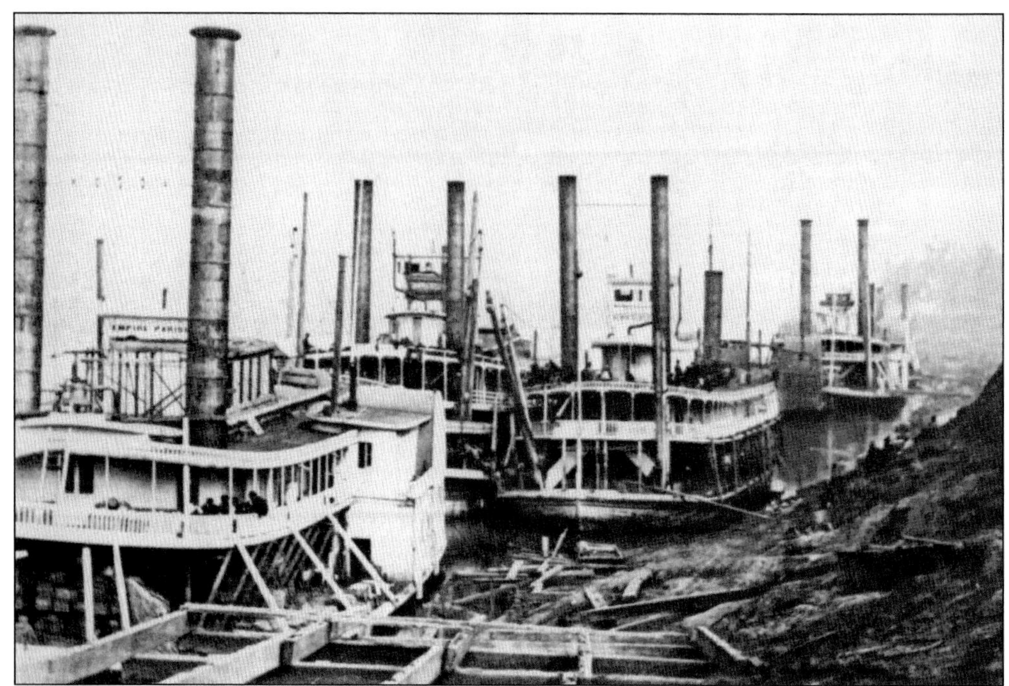

Here, Union steamers and transports are tied to the shore at Alexandria. The wharves have been torn apart by workers scavenging for lumber to build a series of wing dams in an effort to raise the water level over the rapids.

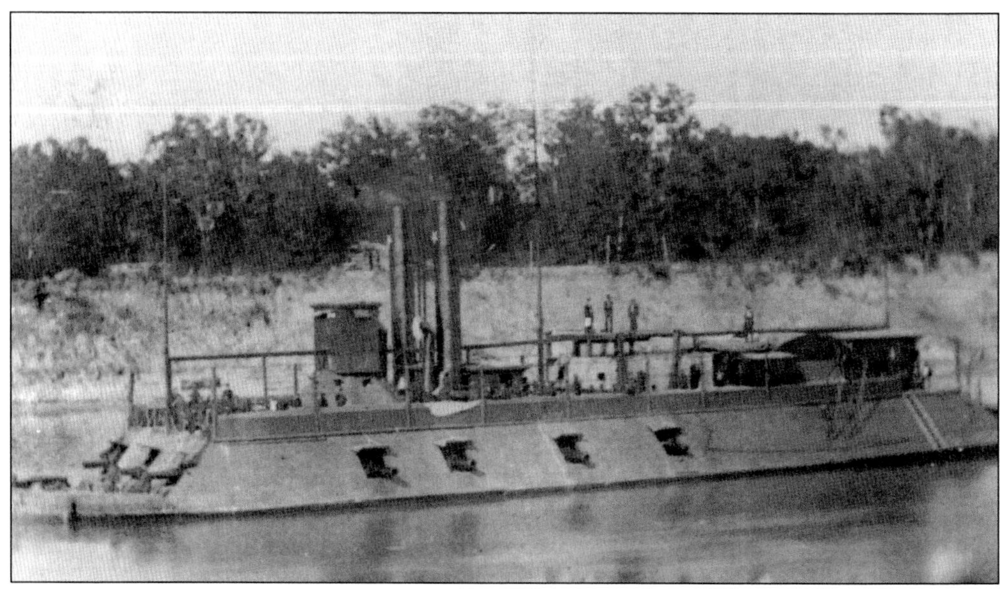

The Union ironclad USS *Mound City* is seen in the upper Red River. It was photographed on the river at Alexandria while waiting for the water to rise or the Confederates to close in.

Col. Joseph Bailey of Wisconsin, a Union staff officer and engineer, proposed a series of wing dams to raise the river and save the fleet. For his efforts, he was promoted to brigadier general and awarded the Medal of Honor.

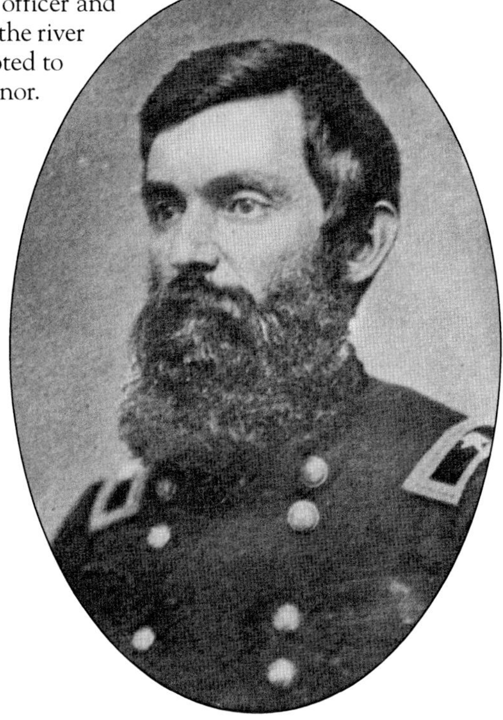

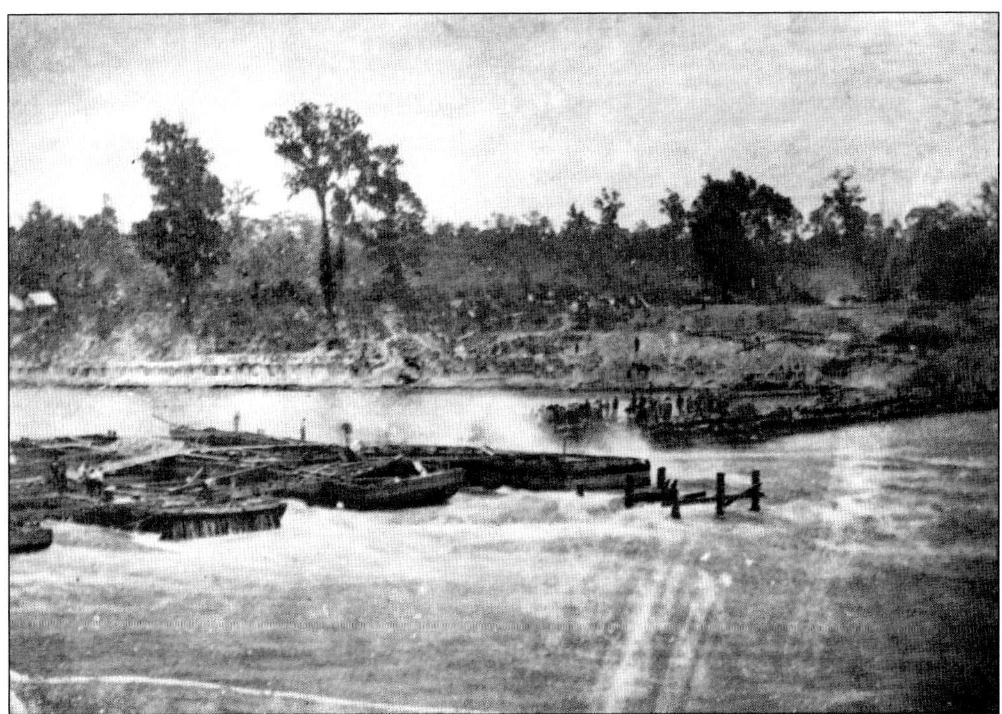

Photographers McPherson and Oliver captured the scene as Bailey's Dam approached completion. Spanning the width of the river (over 750 feet), the dam left just enough room between its wings for ships to pass.

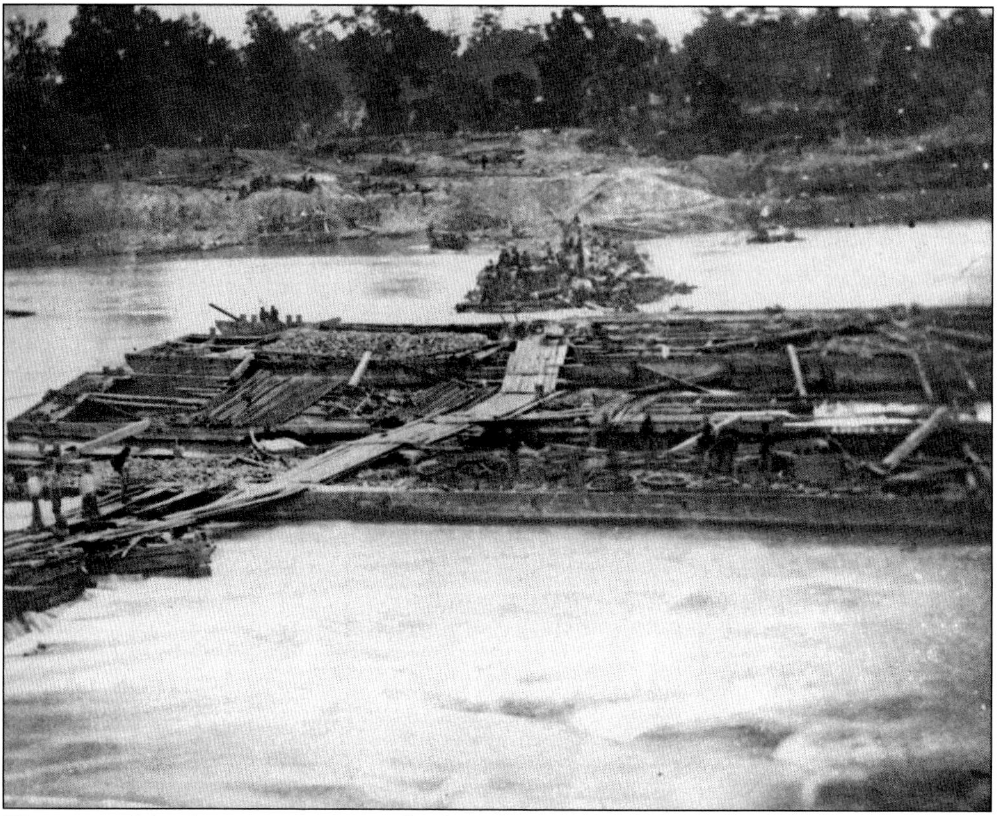

The wings of the dam were constructed as large barges and filled with bricks, felled lumber, and even the tracks and engines from the old Ralph Smith-Smith railroad. Three thousand men, lumberjacks from Maine and freed slaves, felled trees and tore apart wharves and warehouses on both sides of the river to complete the work in a matter of days.

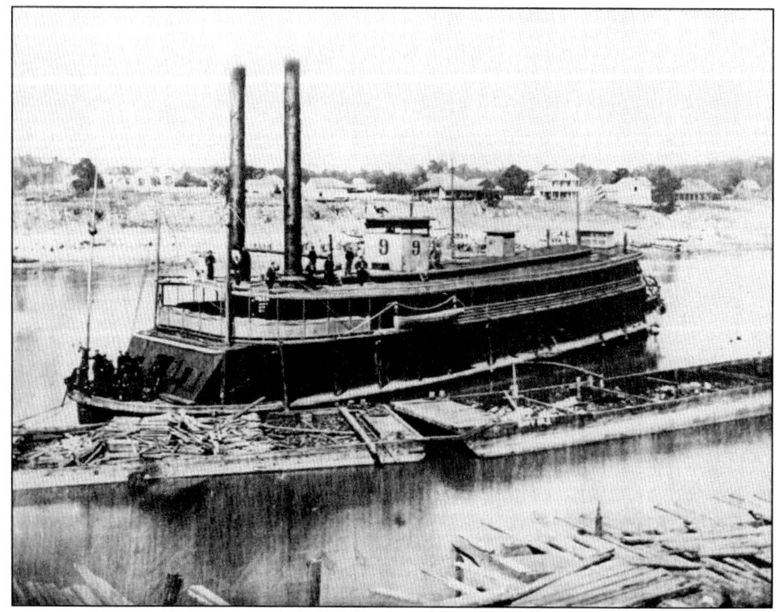

Union steamer *Signal*, shown here assisting with Bailey's Dam, was captured by the Confederates along with the *Covington* at Alexandria, but Banks's army and the rest of the fleet escaped to safety on May 13.

Herbert Bennett, son of Ezra and Sarah Bennett of Bayou Boeuf and a private in the Confederate States Army, was killed at Fort Randolph while stationed at the Red River at Pineville opposite Alexandria. He died during a training accident when a defective cannon exploded in June 1865, a month after Lee's surrender to Grant.

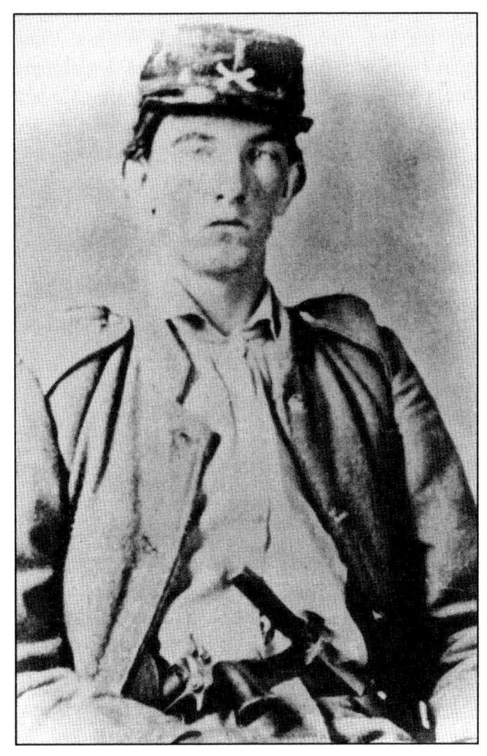

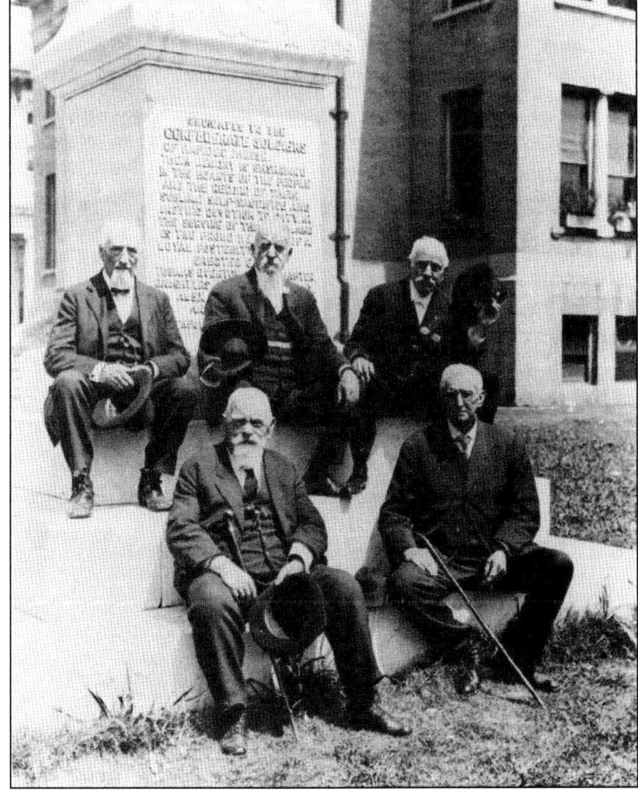

Pictured is a group of Confederate veterans at the Confederate Soldiers' Monument at the City Hall Square in 1921. From left to right are (first row) W.D. Hynson and Judge Wilmer Blackman; (second row) Isaac Miller, R.G. Maddox, and Jonas Rosenthal.

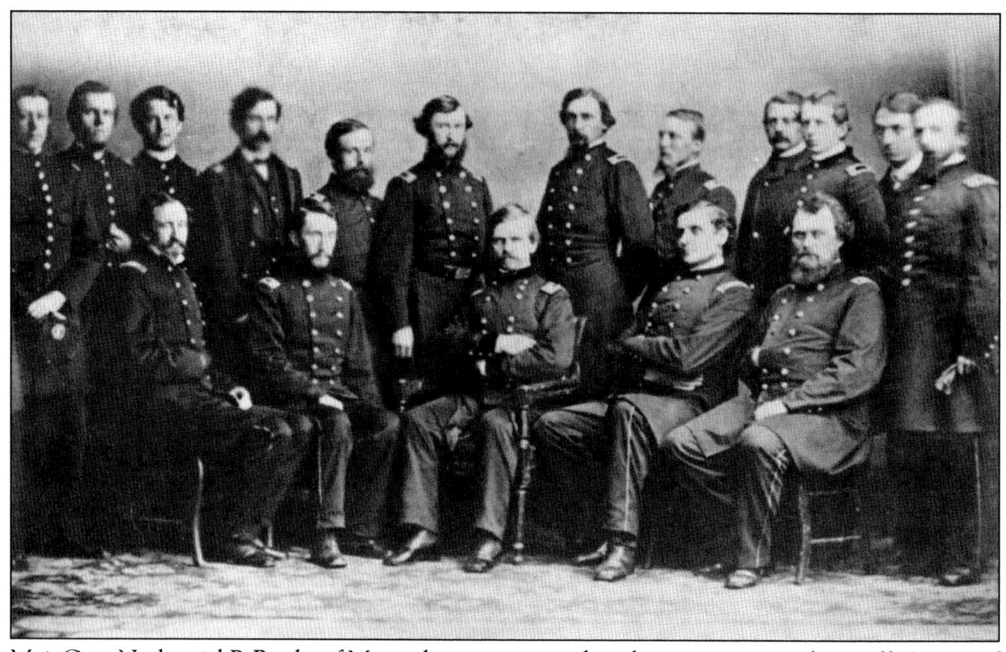

Maj. Gen. Nathaniel P. Banks of Massachusetts is seated in the center among his staff. A man of no military experience and even less ability, Banks was a career politician and an ally of Abraham Lincoln. General Halleck, the Army chief of staff, complained that it was "little better than murder" to place men under his command.

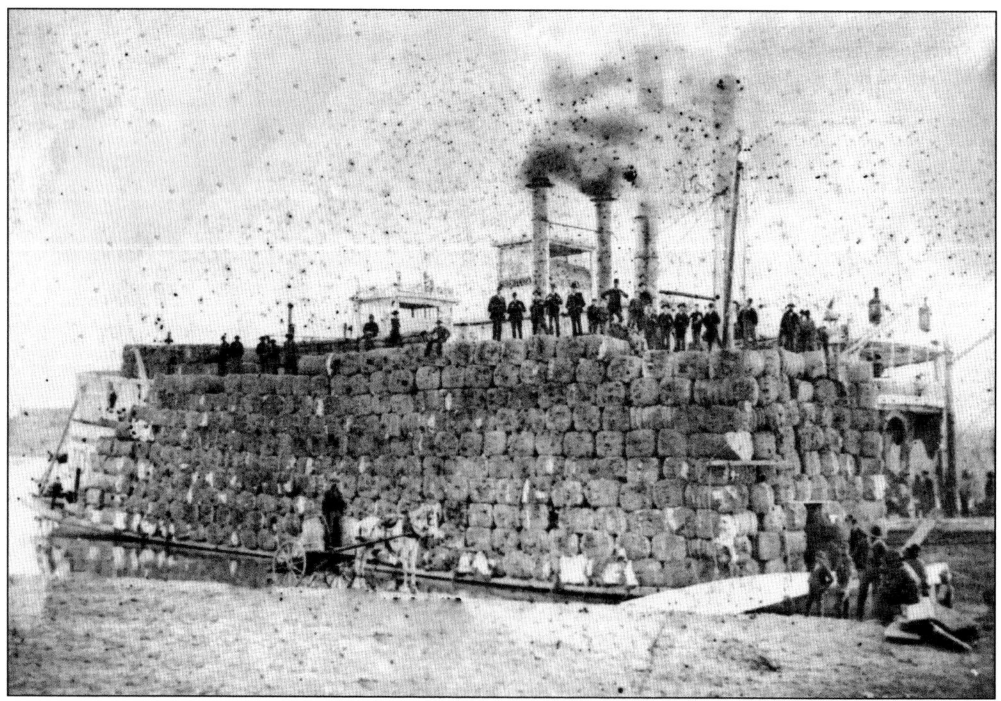

A Red River steamboat is shown here loaded with cotton bound for New Orleans. With no capital to encourage manufacturing and few natural resources, cotton remained the mainstay of central Louisiana's agrarian economy until the coming of the railroads.

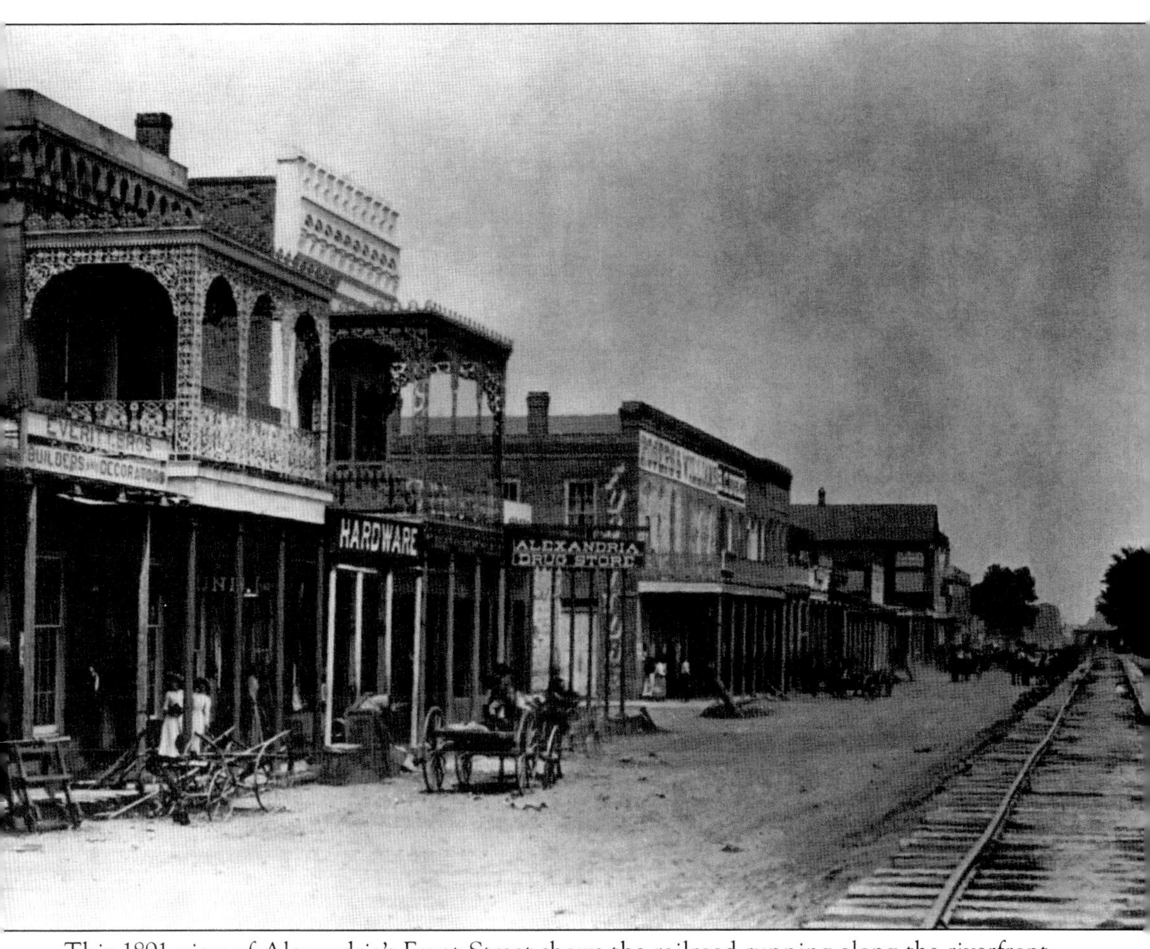

This 1891 view of Alexandria's Front Street shows the railroad running along the riverfront. In 1882, the Texas & Pacific Railway opened a line linking Shreveport to New Orleans with a terminal in Alexandria. Other lines would follow in 1887 and 1890, making Alexandria a central hub of rail transport for the state. Front Street was eventually destroyed to make way for improved levee construction after the 1927 flood season.

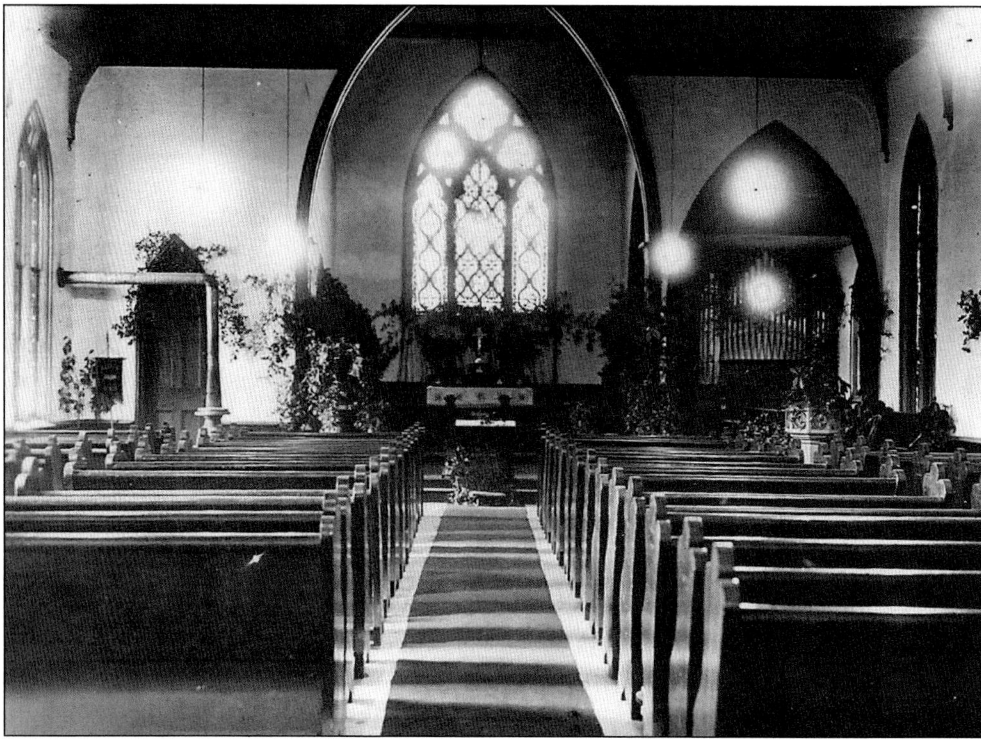

Pictured here is an interior view of the second Episcopal Church of St. James, which was built in the 1870s. The first church was destroyed by Union arsonists in 1864.

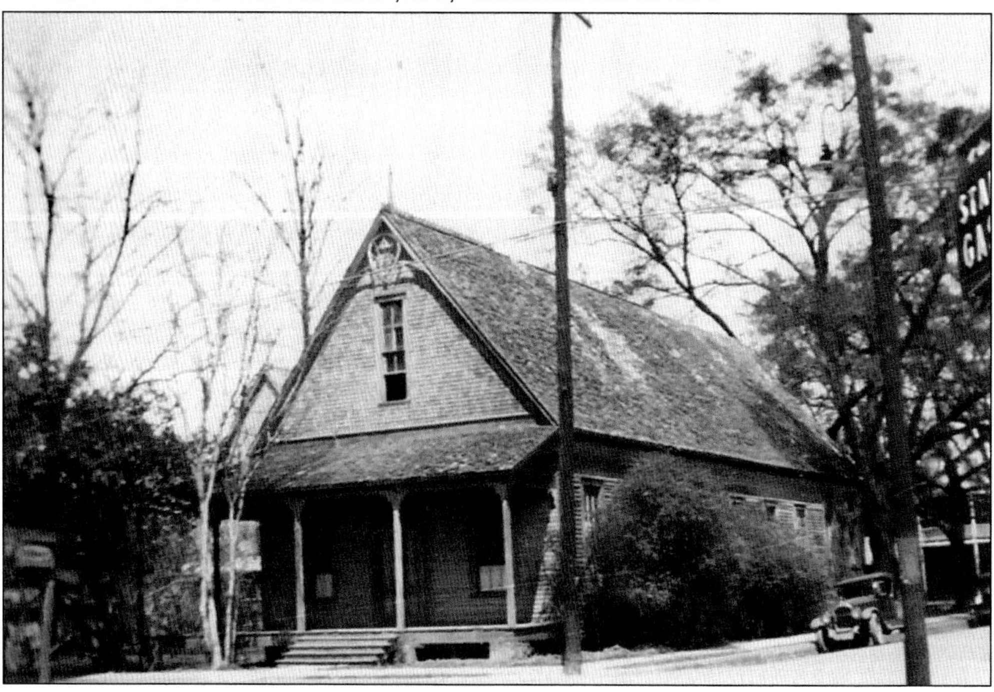

This is the Episcopal Church of St. James parsonage or parish house. The structure was part of the parish facility built after the Civil War.

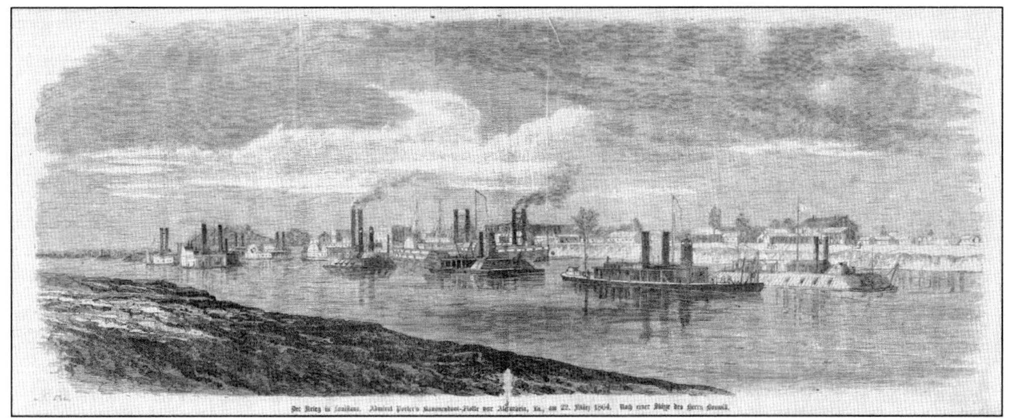

A contemporary engraving depicts the struggle to control the Red River, with the Union Fleet at Alexandria in May 1864.

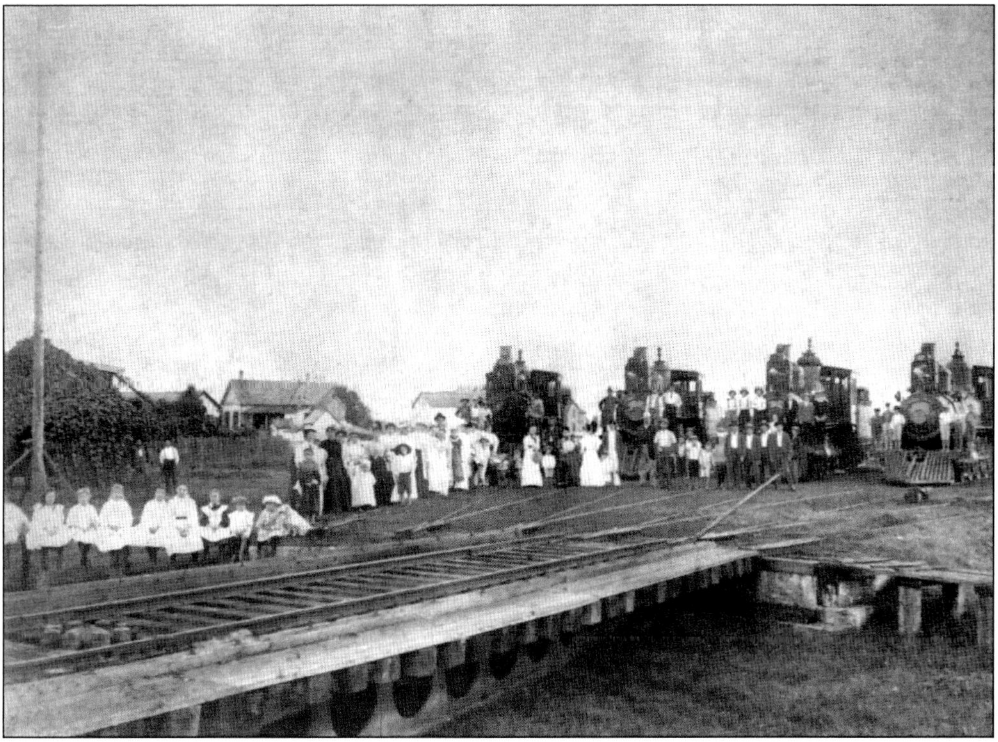

This railroad roundhouse on Second Street was completed in 1898. The railroads brought the timber boom that helped lift central Louisiana out of an economic malaise brought on by the war and Reconstruction.

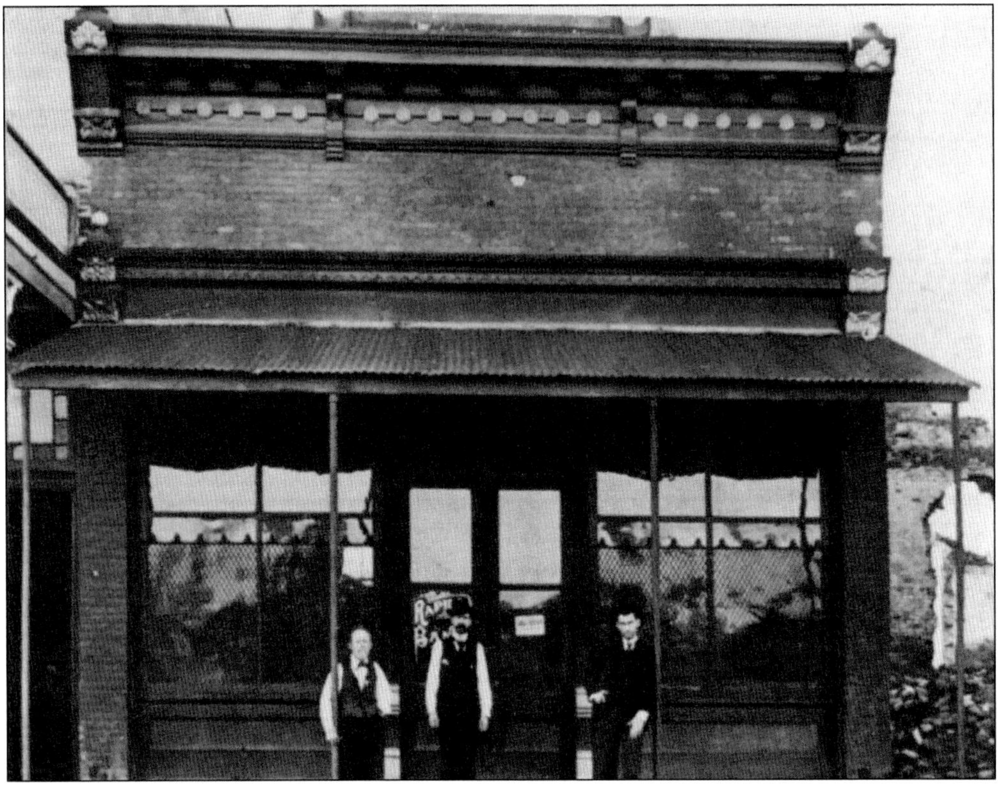

Pictured is the first Rapides Bank building. Chartered by Confederate veteran George Washington Bolton (center, with the hat on) in 1888, the Rapides Bank and Trust Company was one of the first financial institutions in the city.

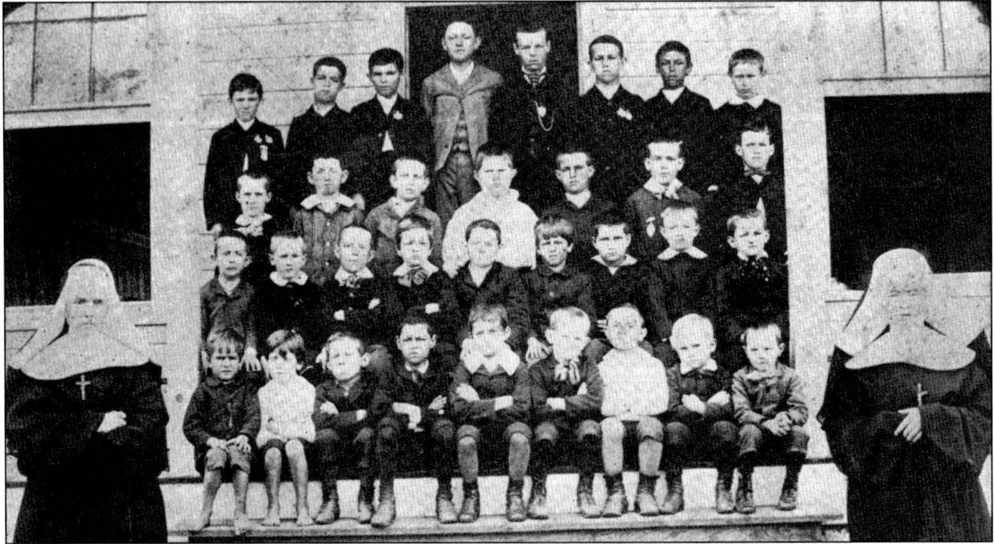

Posing for the camera in 1887 are the first Sisters of Divine Providence with their students at St. Francis Xavier Academy. The Sisters of Divine Providence, a Catholic religious congregation of women dedicated to teaching, came from San Antonio at the invitation of Bishop Antoine Durier to establish a school in Alexandria.

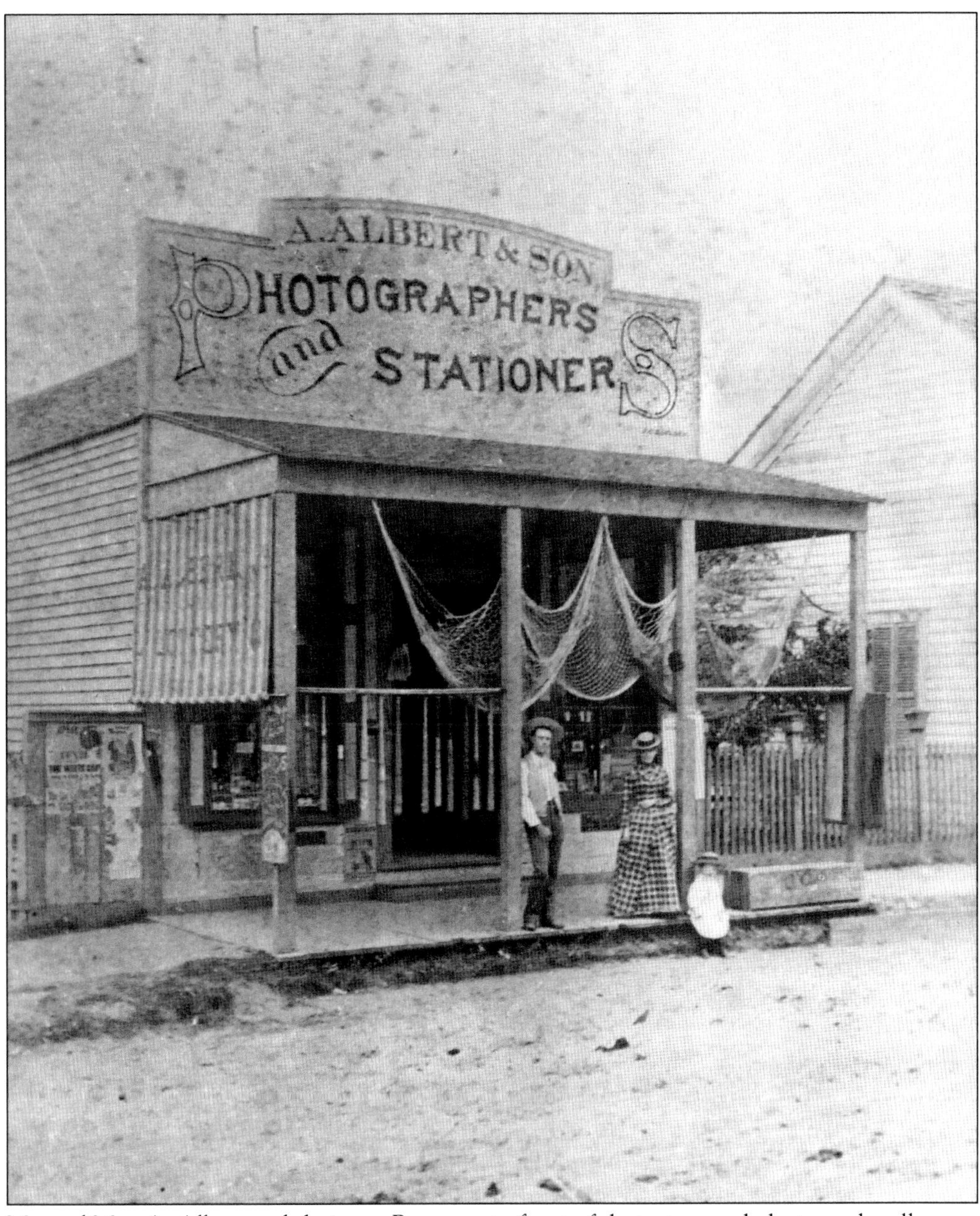

Mr. and Mrs. A. Albert and their son Roy pose in front of their store and photograph gallery on Second Street in Alexandria in 1886.

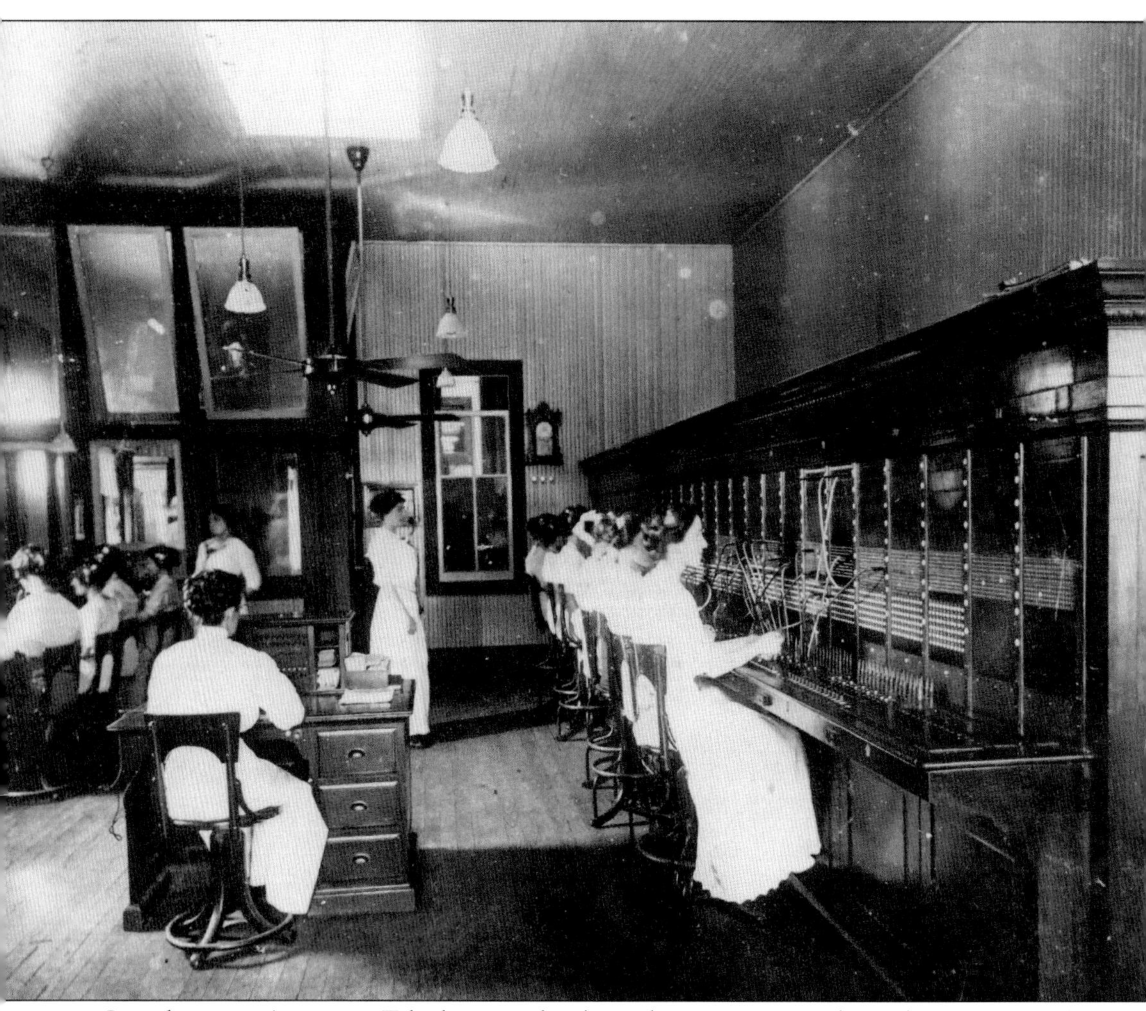

Seen here are American Telephone and Telegraph operators in Alexandria in 1923. The Alexandria Telephone Company was in operation by June 1895, urging its customers, "Don't shout; just talk."

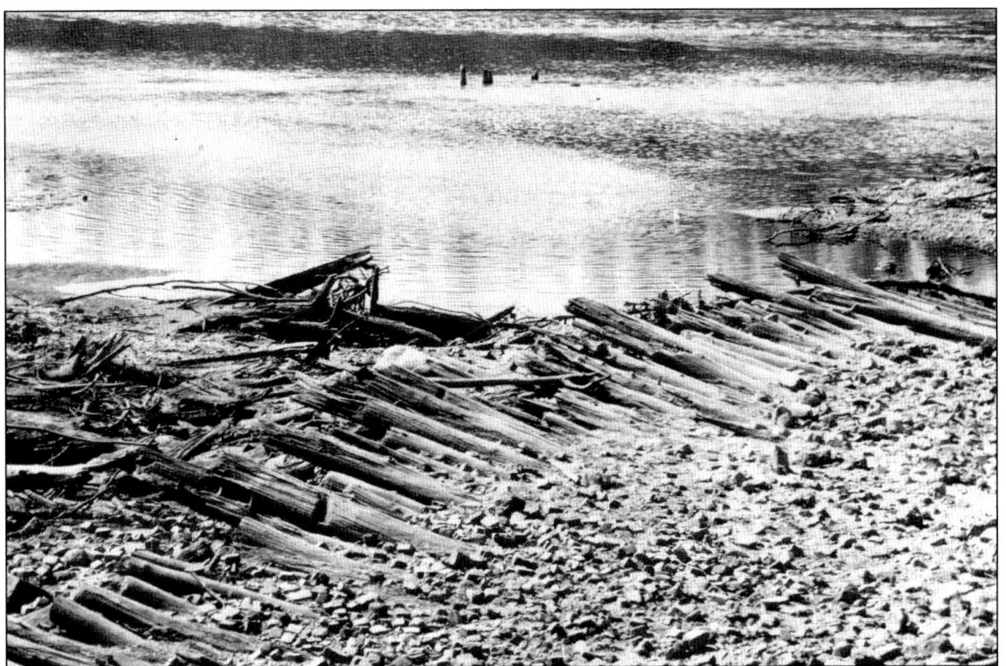

Bailey's Dam has been in the Red River channel since its construction in May 1864. The remains of the dam were visible for years at times of low-water levels. The Red River Waterway Project raised the water table in the river, covering the remains of the dam.

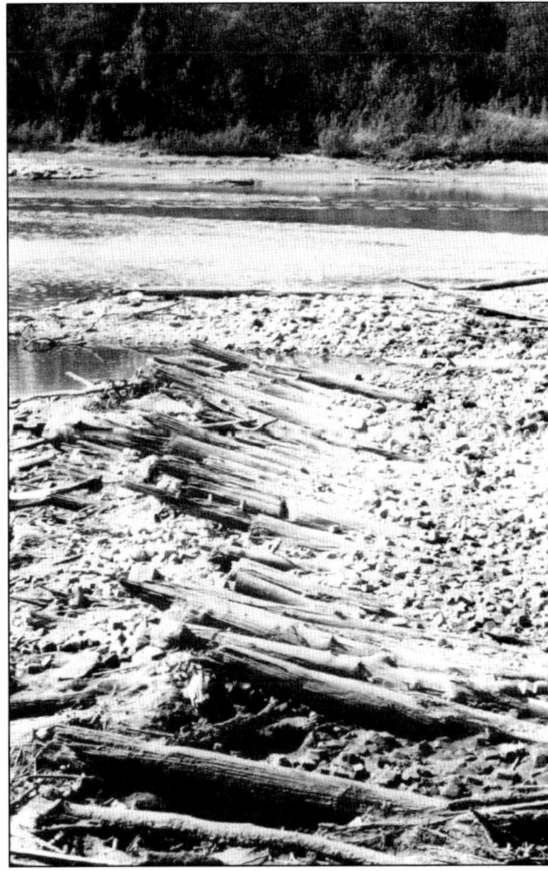

The remains of Bailey's Dam in the Red River at Alexandria remained as a tangible reminder of the Civil War in central Louisiana for years.

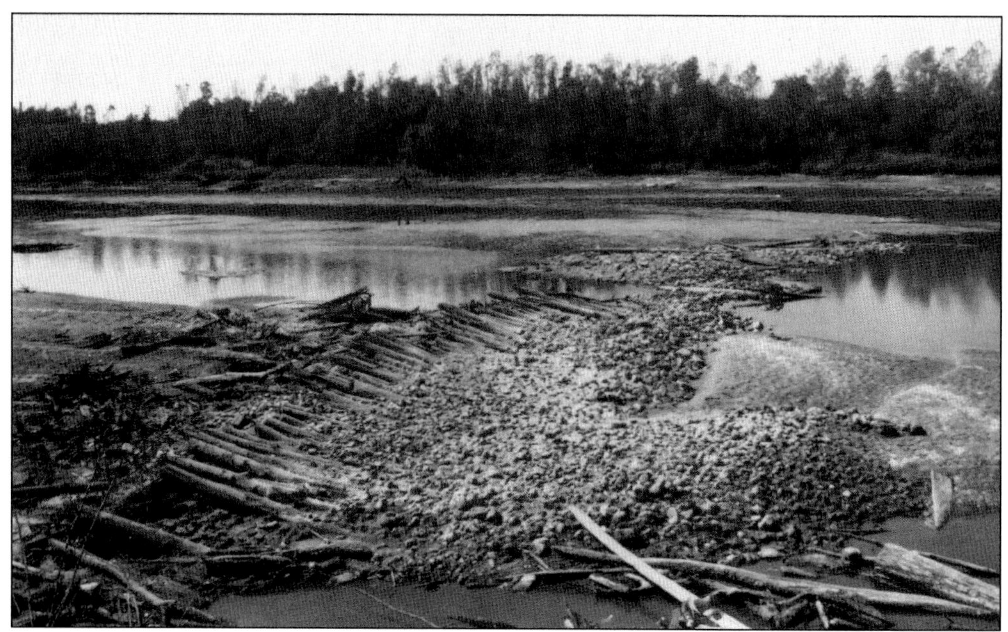

This is a 20th-century view of the remains of Bailey's Dam, which is now covered forever by the waters of the Red River.

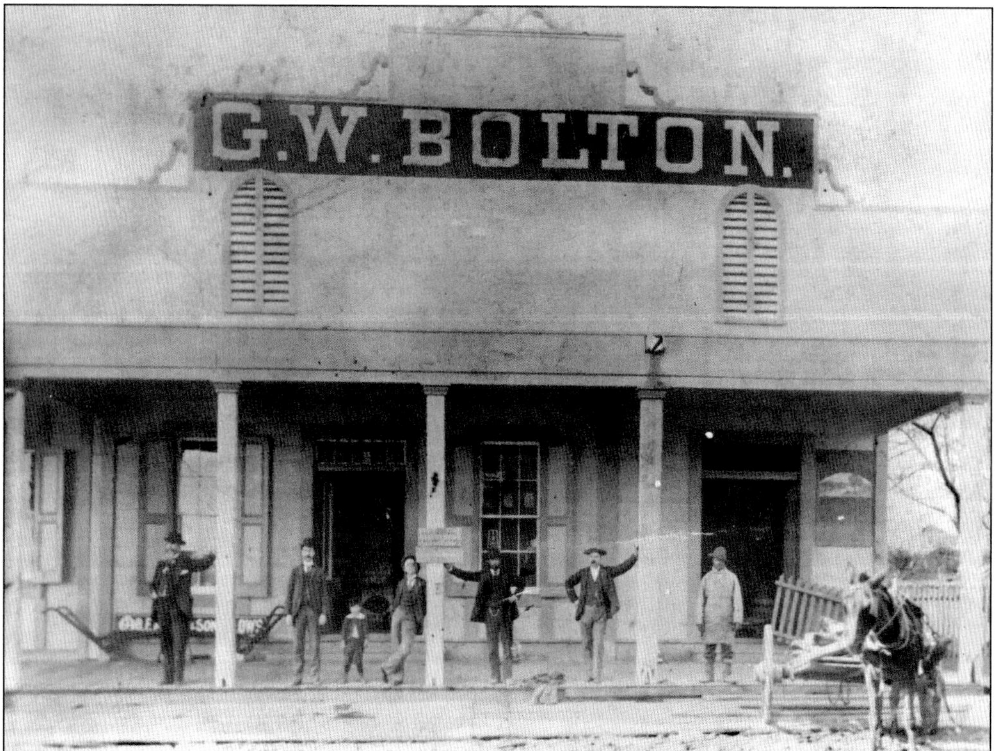

Here is George Washington Bolton's storefront. A native of Union Parish, Bolton settled in Pineville after the Civil War and made his living through trade. In 1888, he chartered the Rapides Bank and Trust Company and served as its first president.

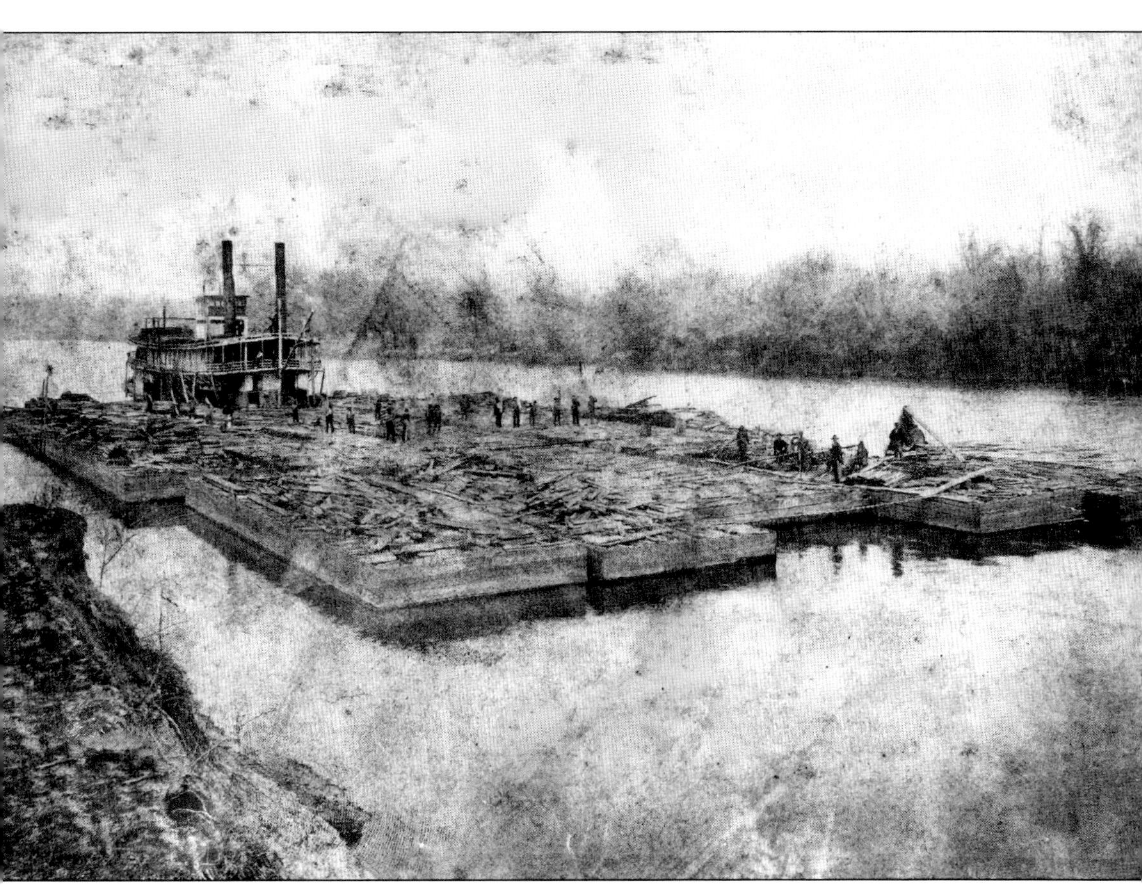

A Red River steamer pushes lumber downriver. With the coming of the railroads in the 1880s, lumber production soared, creating a new industry in central Louisiana.

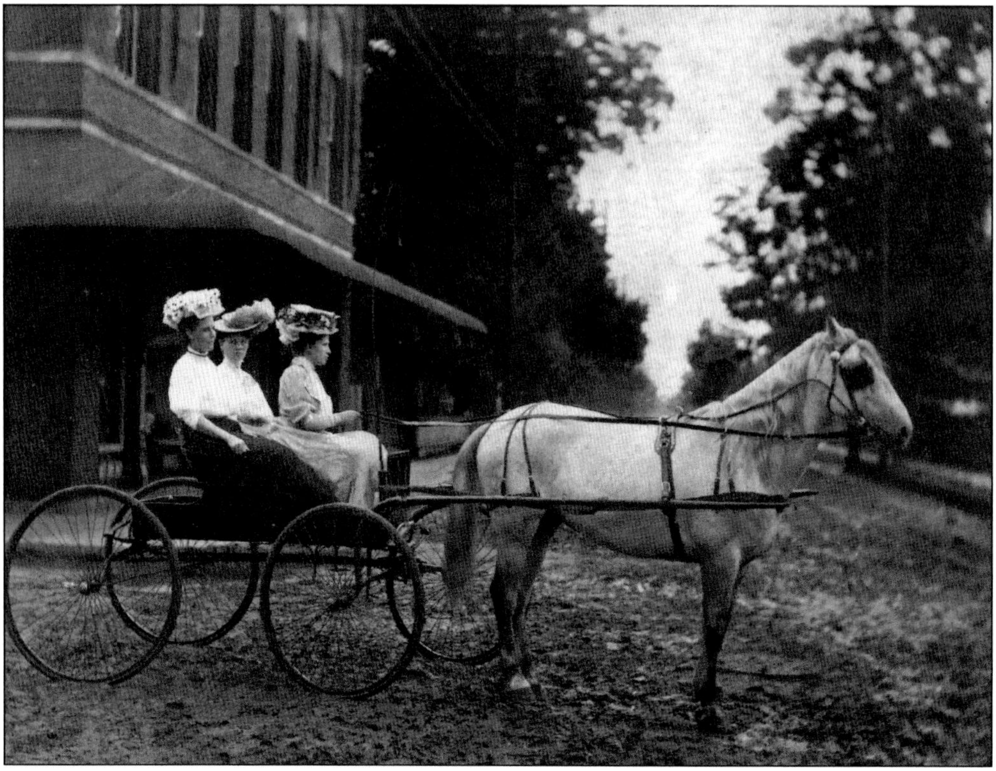

Cora Hixson, Edith Hixson, and Annie Hixson are shown in a horse-drawn buggy at Fourth and DeSoto Streets in Alexandria in 1909. At that time, the town had only three and a half miles of brick and gravel-paved streets.

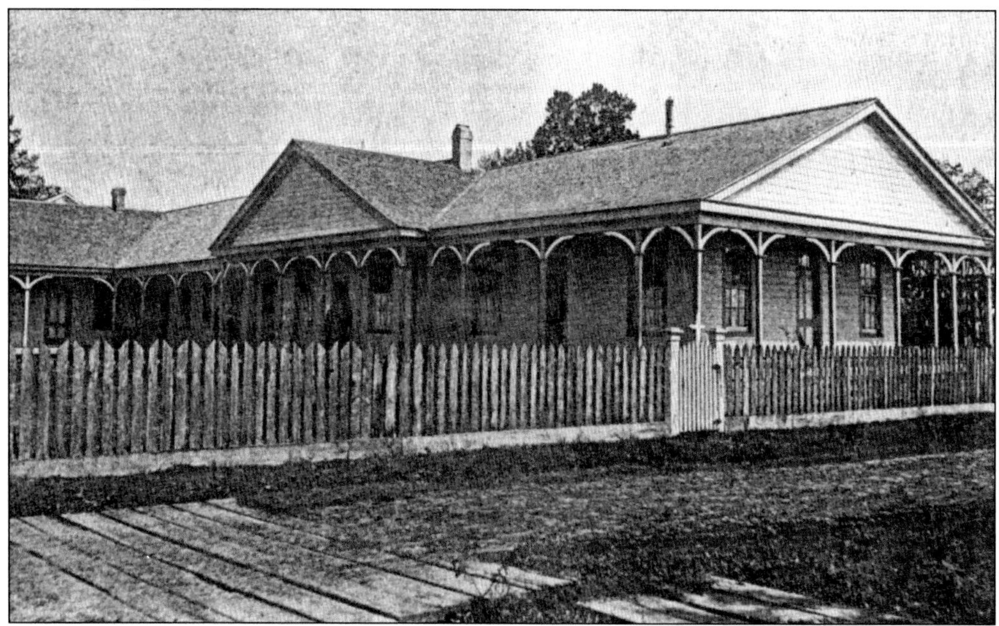

This is the St. Francis Xavier Academy building in 1887 at its original location on Front Street between Xavier and Bellier Streets.

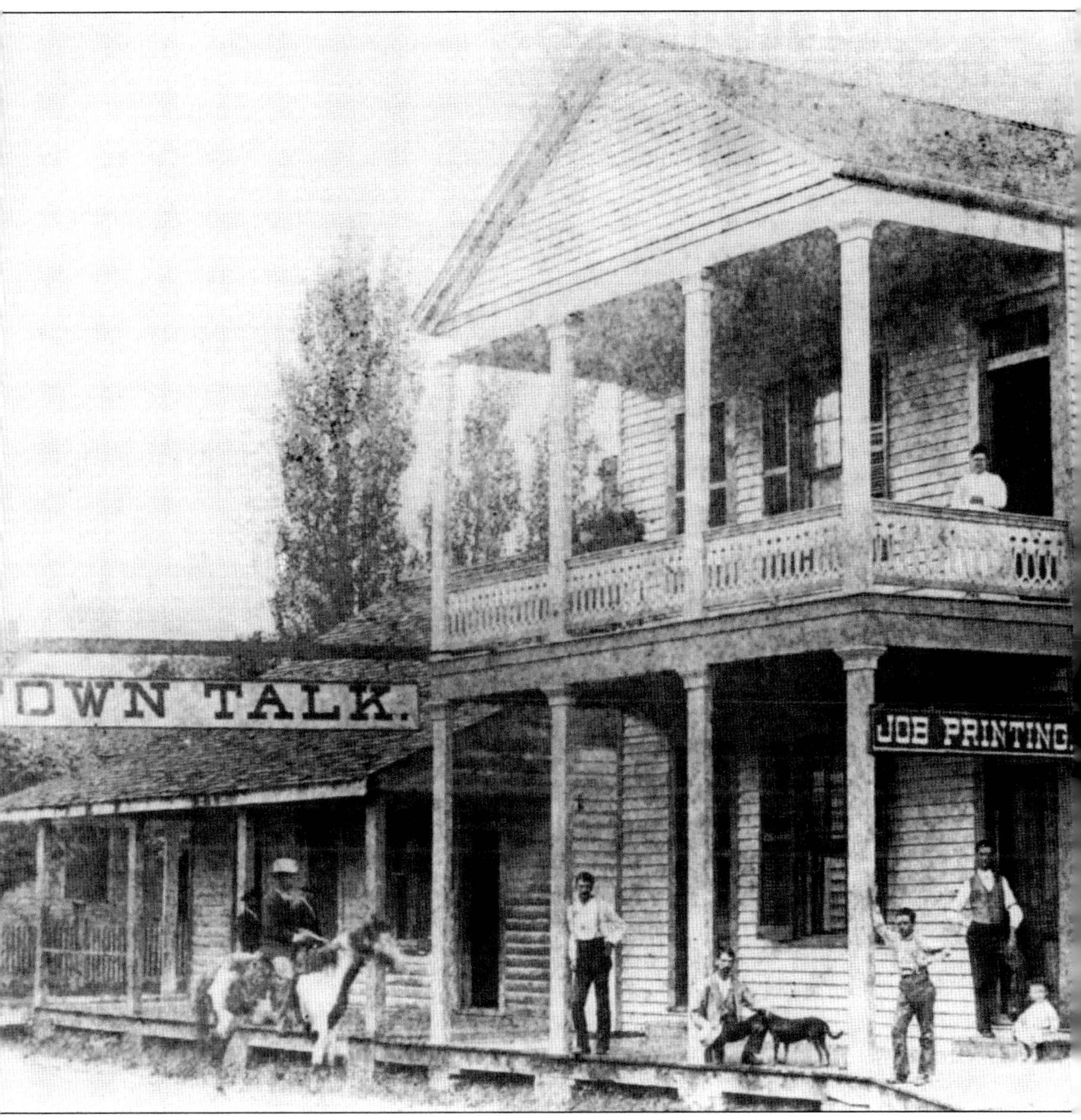

Seen here is the Alexandria Town Talk office in 1889. Living quarters for the McCormicks were on the second floor. Mrs. E.H. McCormick is pictured on the gallery, and H.M. Huie is on horseback on the left. Edgar McCormick is shown with his dog Trip. Hunter Jarreau and R.C. Jarreau are seen at right with a young Roy Albert.

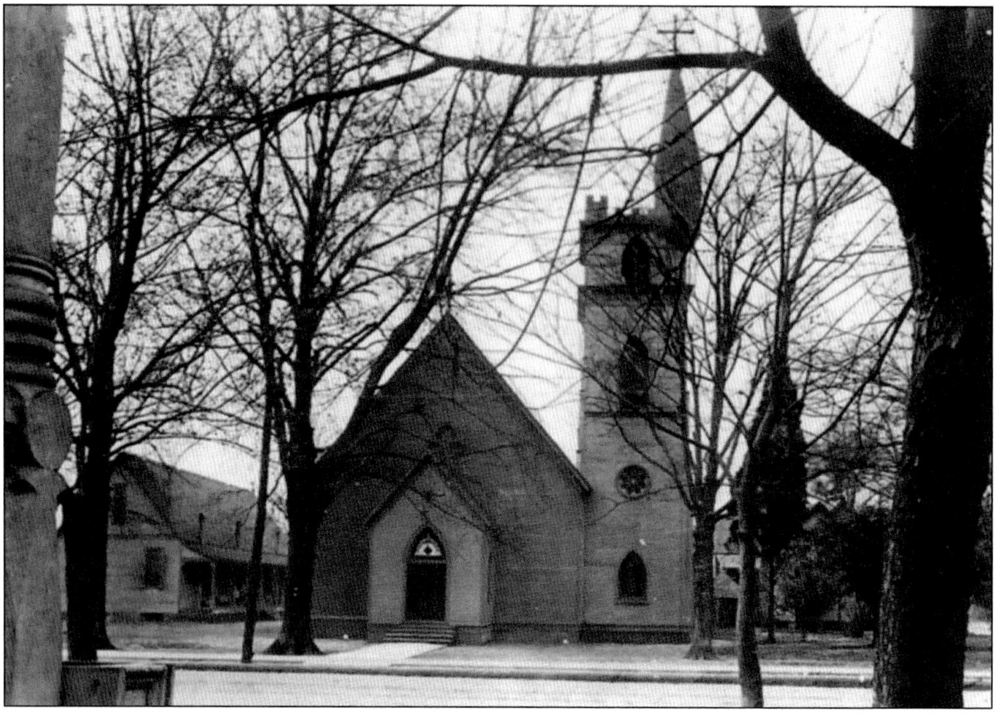

This is an exterior view of the second Episcopal Church of St. James on Second and Fulton Streets. The structure was later replaced in the 1920s by an elegant brick church of English Gothic design on Bolton Avenue.

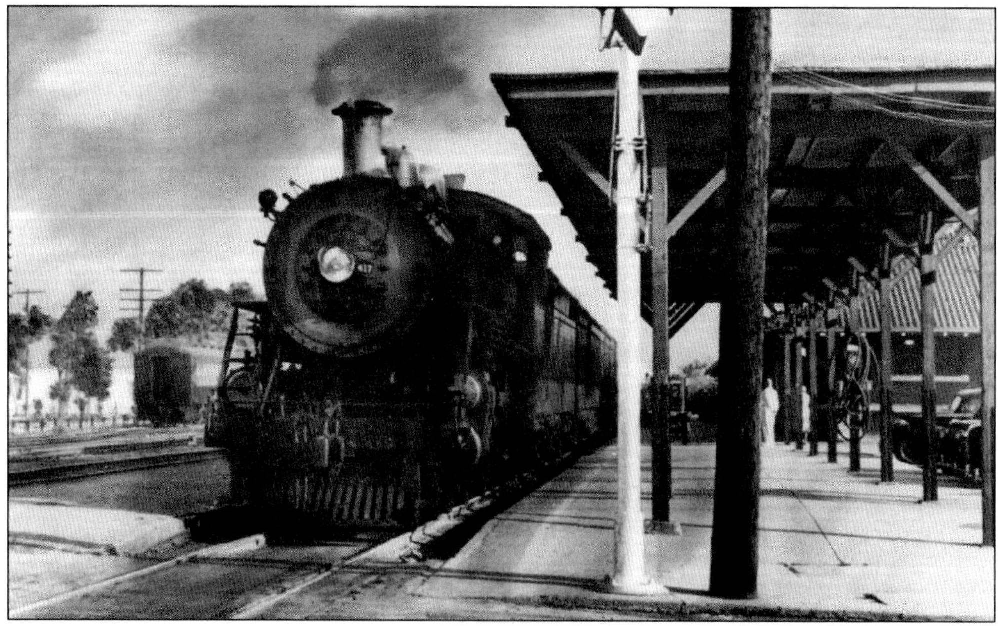

Texas & Pacific (T&P) Railway train No. 24 pulls into Union Station in Alexandria. The coming of the T&P Railway transformed central Louisiana and helped finally end the economic depression that lingered after the war and Reconstruction. Passenger and freight services were provided on the T&P line, which came to Alexandria in 1882.

Four

A New Century

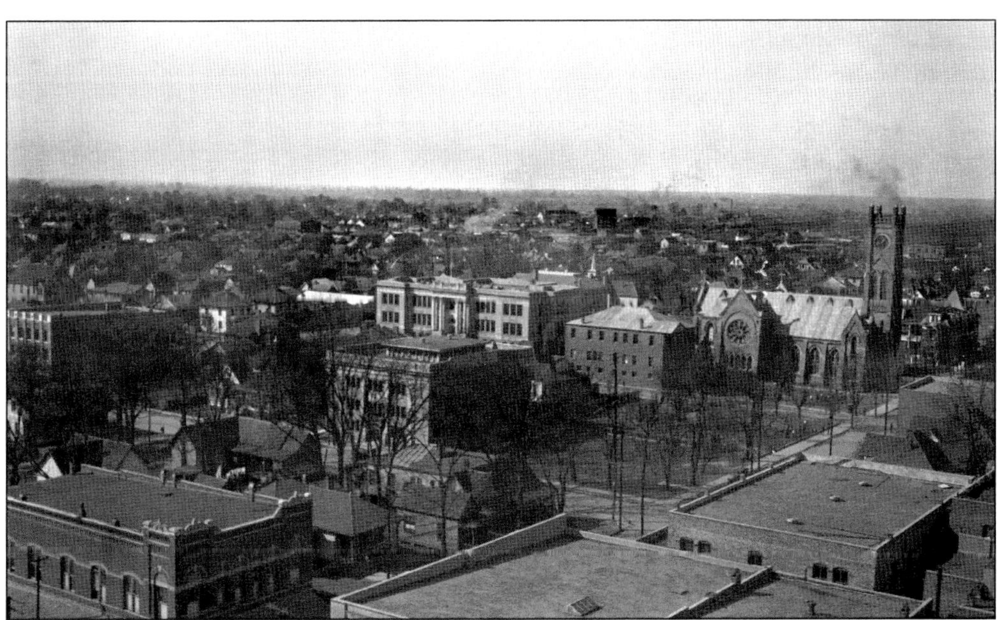

A view of downtown Alexandria shows the old Central Grammar School, Emmanuel Baptist Church, and St. Francis Xavier Cathedral around 1920. The Central Grammar School building (to the left of the cathedral) was originally constructed as the first Bolton High School. This building was later torn down for the construction of the present school board complex.

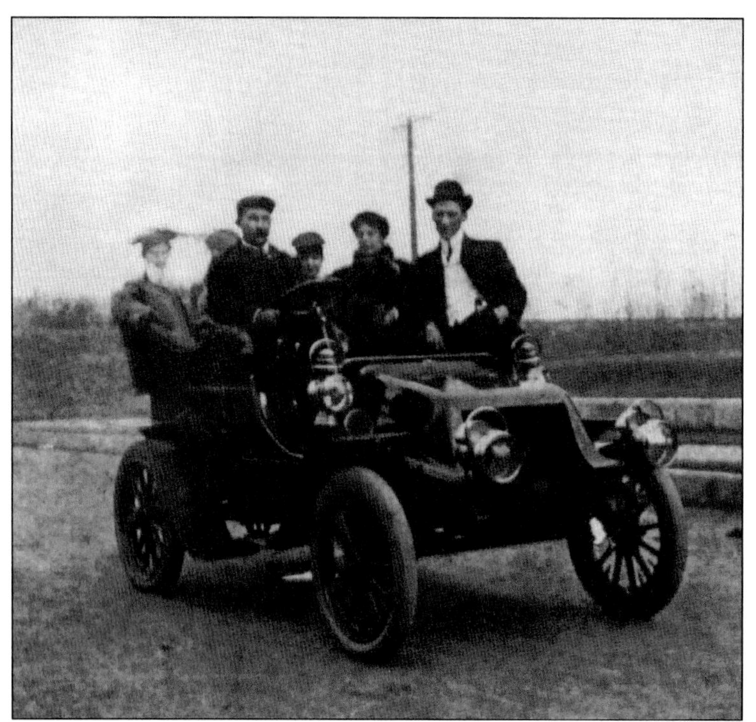

Joseph Bentley is at the wheel of the first automobile in Alexandria, seen here around 1907. M.G. Jarreau is in the front seat, and Irene Boyce and D.H. Staples sit in the back.

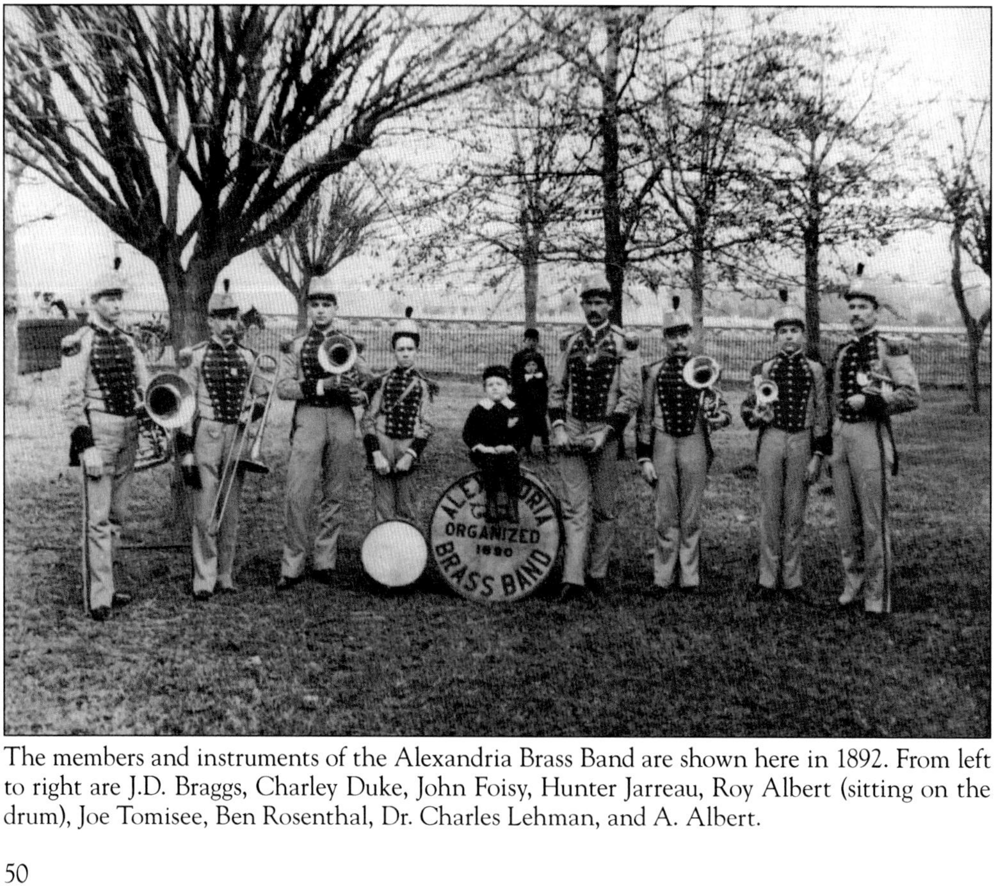

The members and instruments of the Alexandria Brass Band are shown here in 1892. From left to right are J.D. Braggs, Charley Duke, John Foisy, Hunter Jarreau, Roy Albert (sitting on the drum), Joe Tomisee, Ben Rosenthal, Dr. Charles Lehman, and A. Albert.

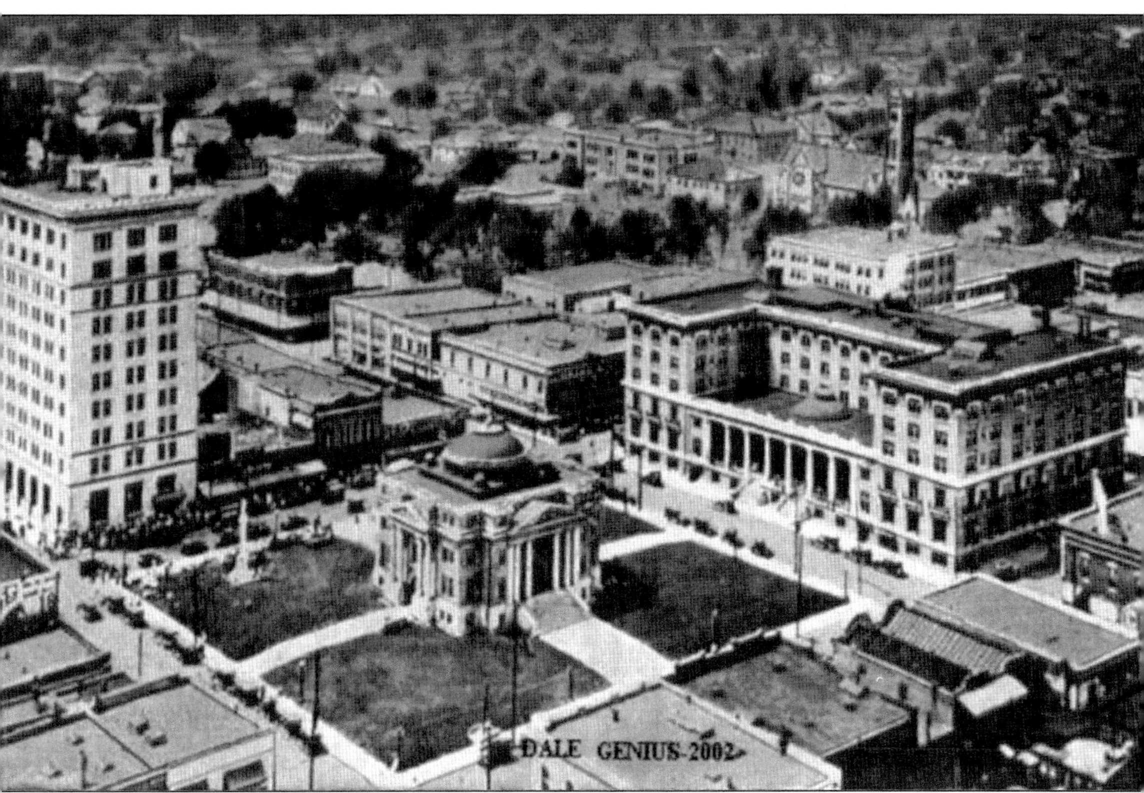

This postcard features the Bentley Hotel, the "Biltmore on the bayou," built by lumber baron Joseph Bentley in 1908. Reportedly dissatisfied with the service he received at the Rapides Hotel, Bentley constructed the palatial 175-room hotel with 125 private baths to rival anything north of New Orleans.

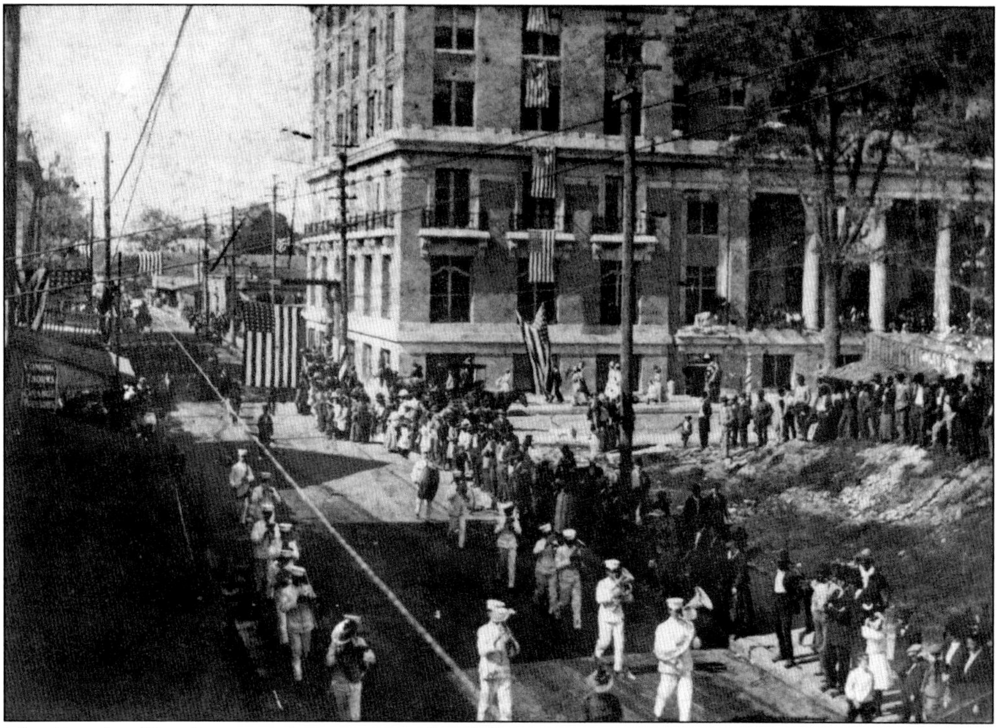

The Bentley Hotel is seen during a parade of the Louisiana National Guard around 1912. The Guard held its annual summer camp and maneuvers on the Pineville side of the Red River at the old Louisiana Seminary of Learning site. The same ground would be developed into training camps for the American Expeditionary Force during World War I. Later, the grounds were home to the Veteran Affairs Hospital.

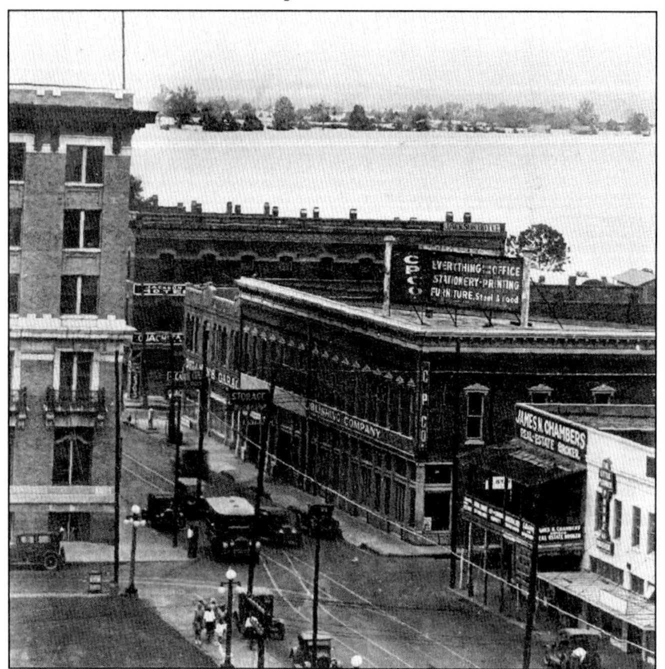

This downtown view of the Bentley and Jackson Hotels shows high water in the Red River. Flooding continued to be a serious problem before the construction of a modern levee system by the Army Corps of Engineers was adopted, due to the efforts of Sen. John Overton, an Alexandria attorney and legislator.

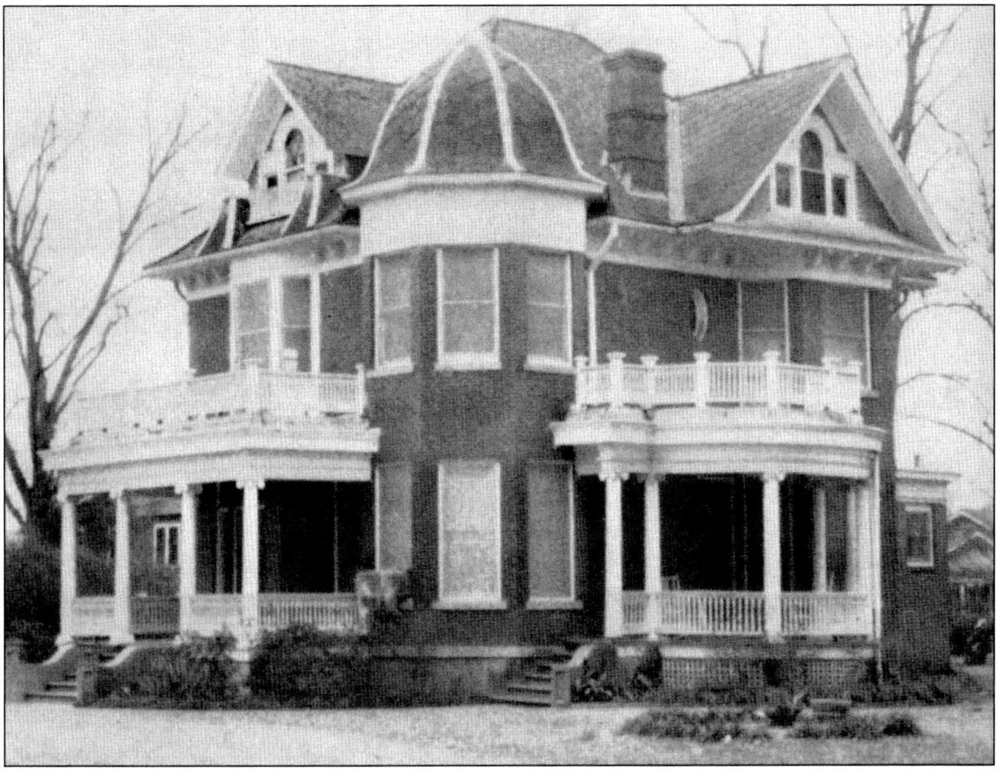

One of the area's premier examples of the Queen Anne style, the Cook House on Florence Avenue, remains a local landmark and is in the National Register of Historic Places.

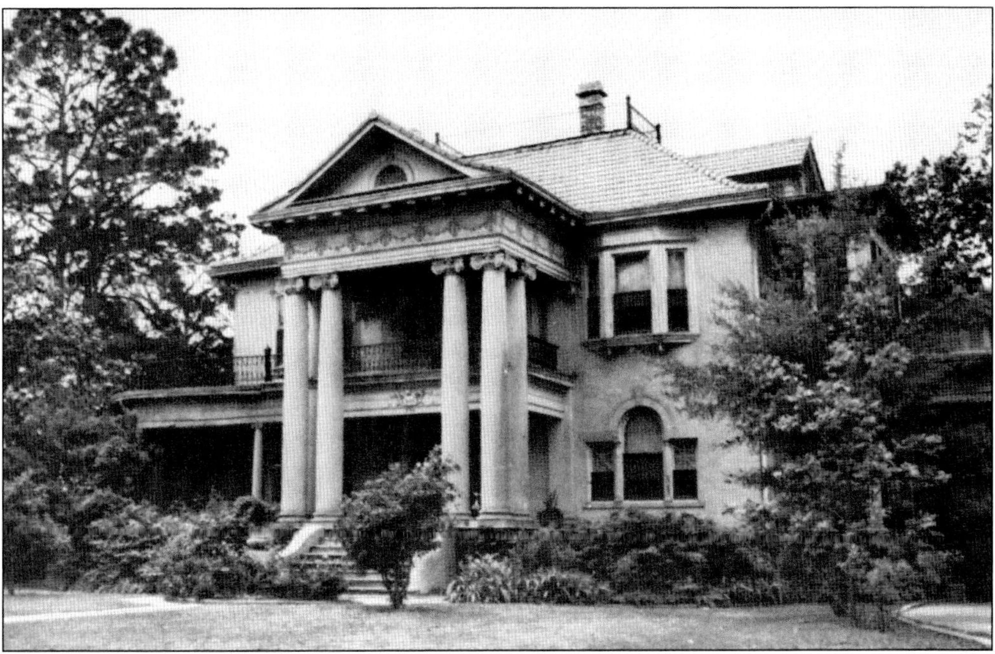

Seen here is the Albert House, one of the grand old homes on Bolton Avenue, as it appeared in the late 1960s shortly before its demolition.

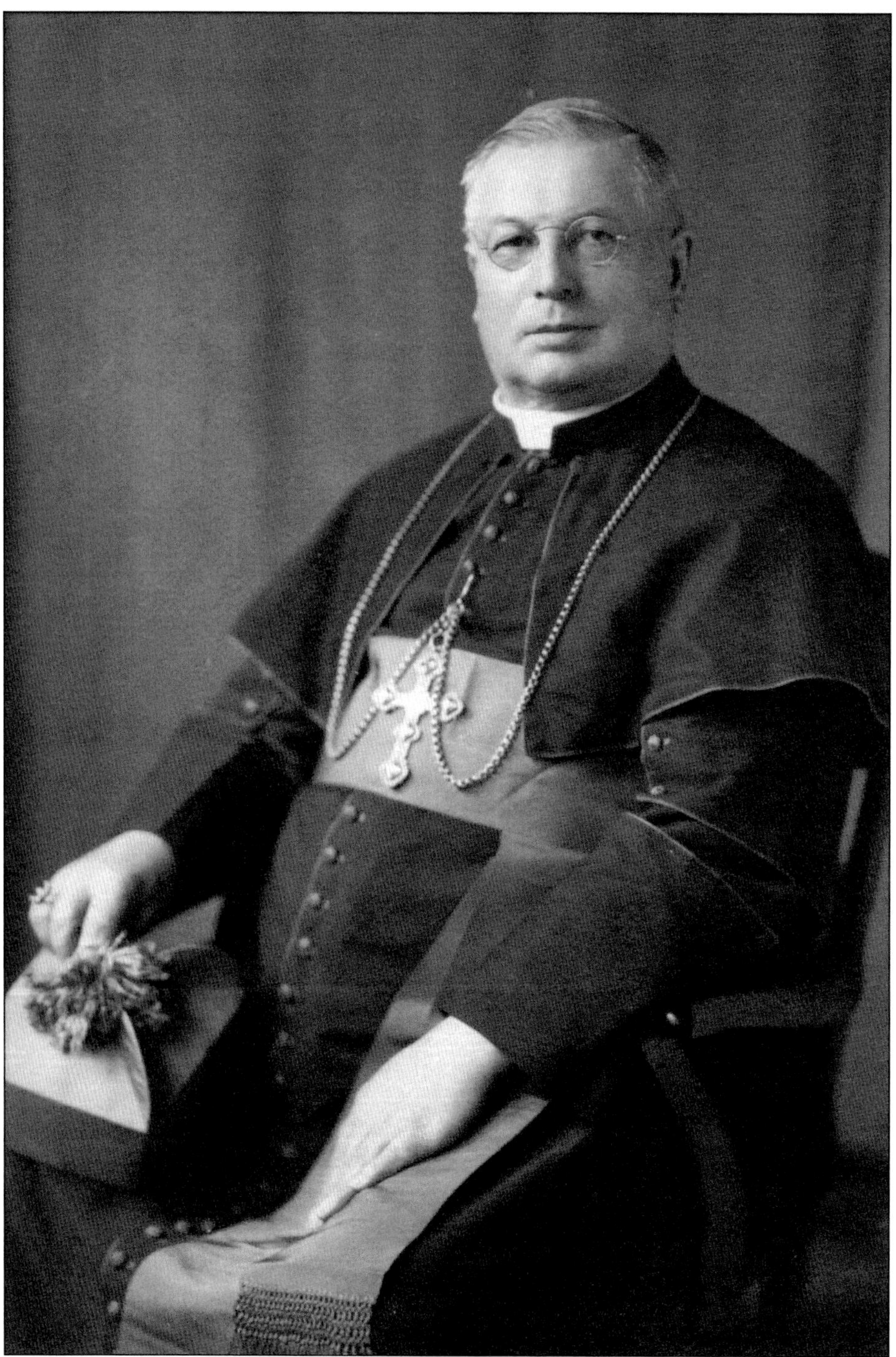

Bishop Cornelius Van de Ven served as the fourth Roman Catholic bishop of the Diocese of Natchitoches. Due to his efforts, the See was transferred from Natchitoches to Alexandria by Pope St. Pius X in August 1910, making Bishop Van de Ven the first bishop of Alexandria. He served as bishop from 1906 until his death in 1936. The large metal cross on the top of the cathedral tower was erected in his memory.

Built at a cost of $52,792 in 1909, Alexandria's second city hall, a Neoclassical domed structure designed by George Mann of Little Rock and patterned after the administration building at the Chicago World's Fair, became an iconic part of the city's landscape. Its construction marked the end of one era and the beginning of another; a concrete sign of the unbounded hopes and optimism at the beginning of the 20th century.

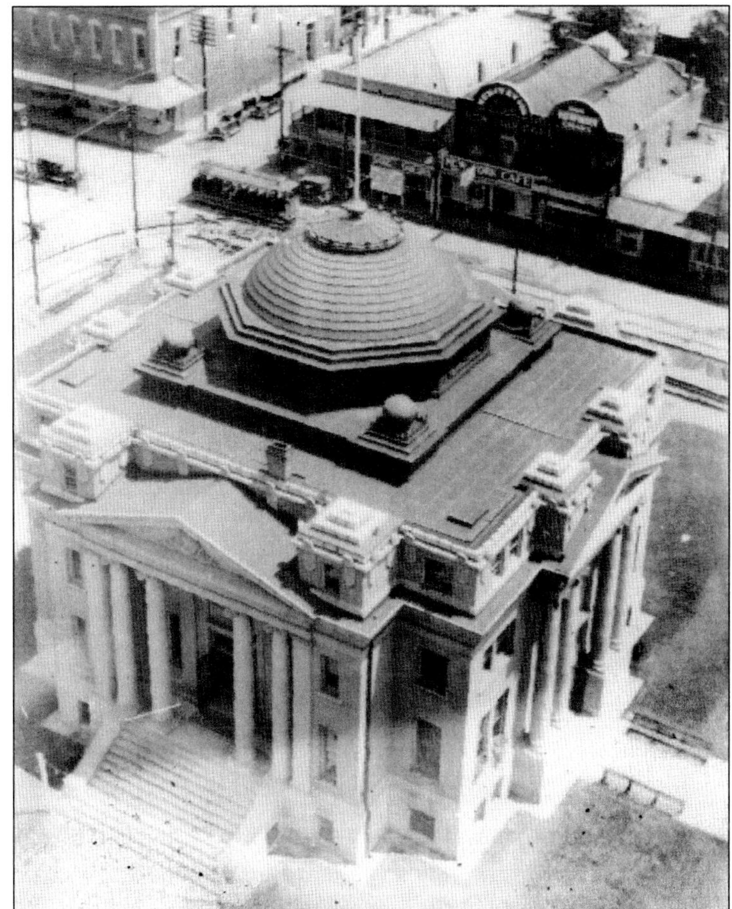

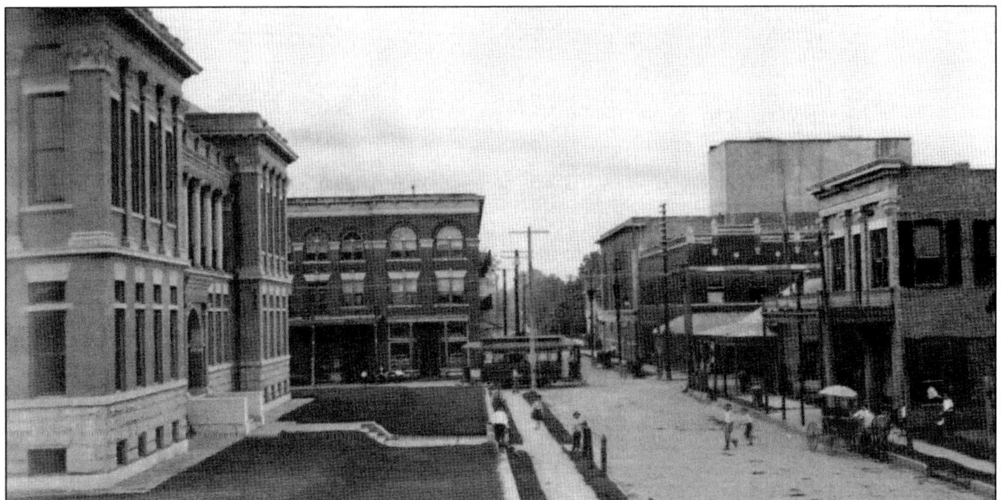

This is a c. 1912 street scene from the banks of the Red River. On the left is part of the Rapides Parish Courthouse. Beyond it is the Rapides Hotel on the corner of Washington and Second Streets. On the right is the gabled front of W.W. Whittington's law office, which was also the law office of Judge Michael Ryan at one time. Beyond it is the Town Talk office.

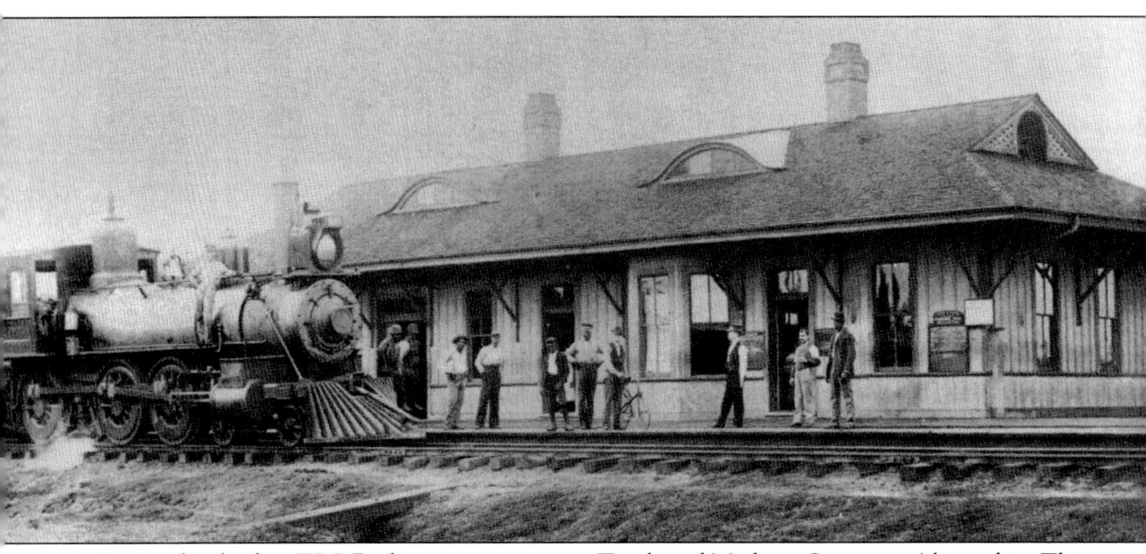

Pictured is the first T&P Railway train station at Tenth and Madison Streets in Alexandria. This wood-framed structure was later replaced by the brick and stone Union Station in the 1910s.

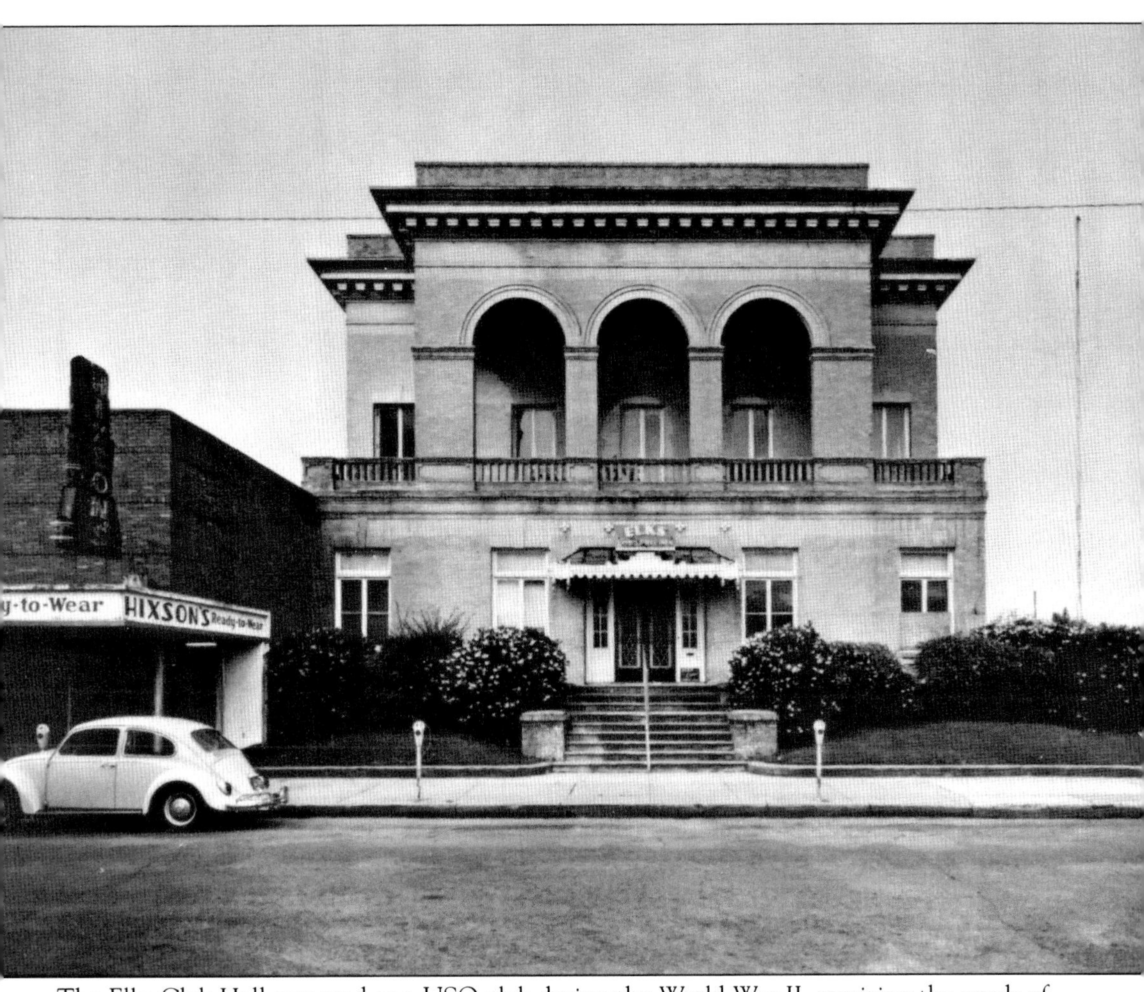

The Elks Club Hall was used as a USO club during the World War II, servicing the needs of thousands of servicemen between 1940 and 1945.

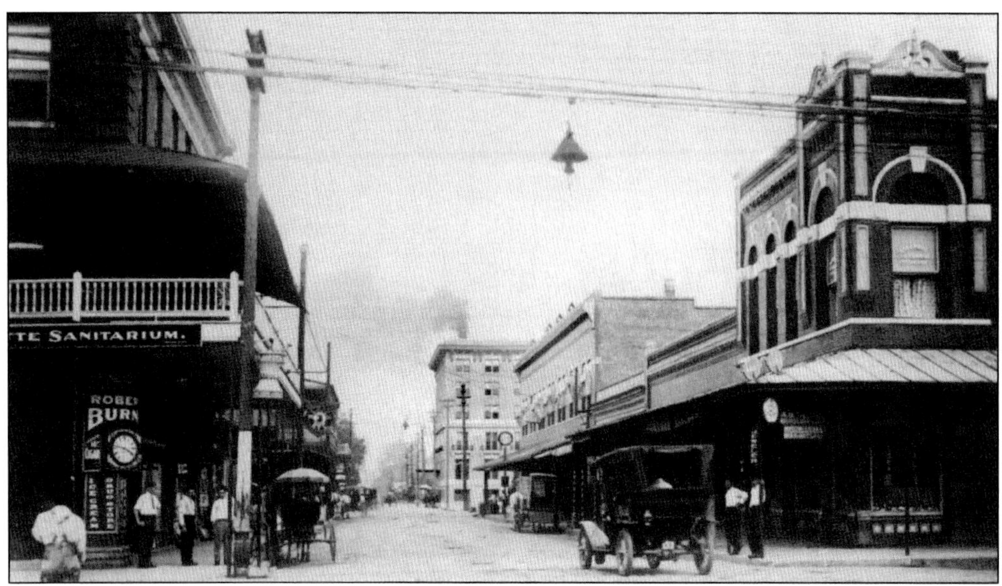

This is the corner of Johnson and Third Streets in Alexandria around 1910. The street scene shows a marked development of the central business district since 1900.

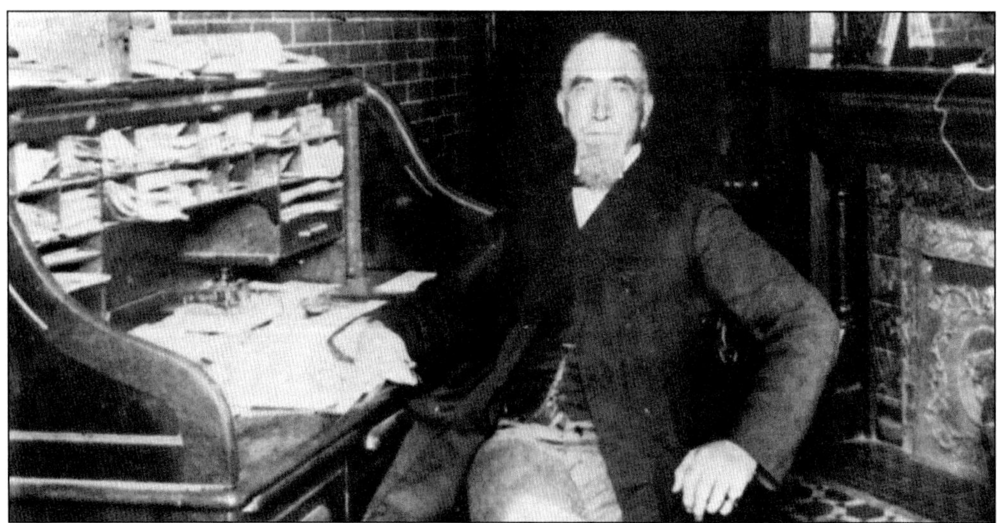

George Washington Bolton was a native of Union Parish and was a Confederate veteran, merchant, and first president of the Rapides Bank and Trust Company. Bolton High School and Bolton Avenue are both named for him.

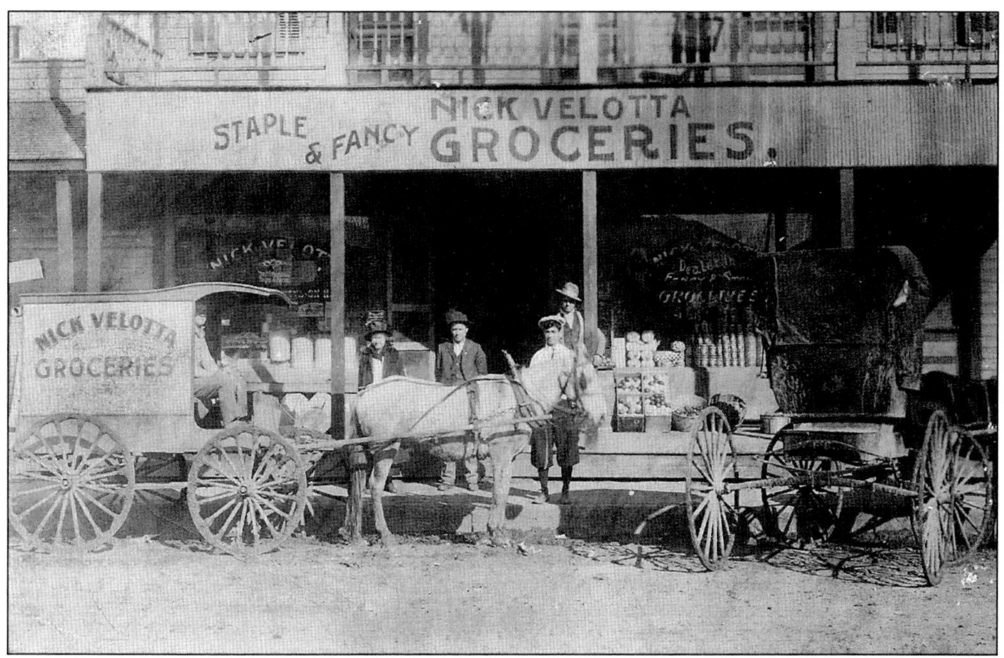

This is a c. 1900 image of Nick Velotta Grocery on Rapides Avenue. Italian and Sicilian immigrants have remained a vibrant part of Alexandria's cultural economic scene since the start of the 20th century.

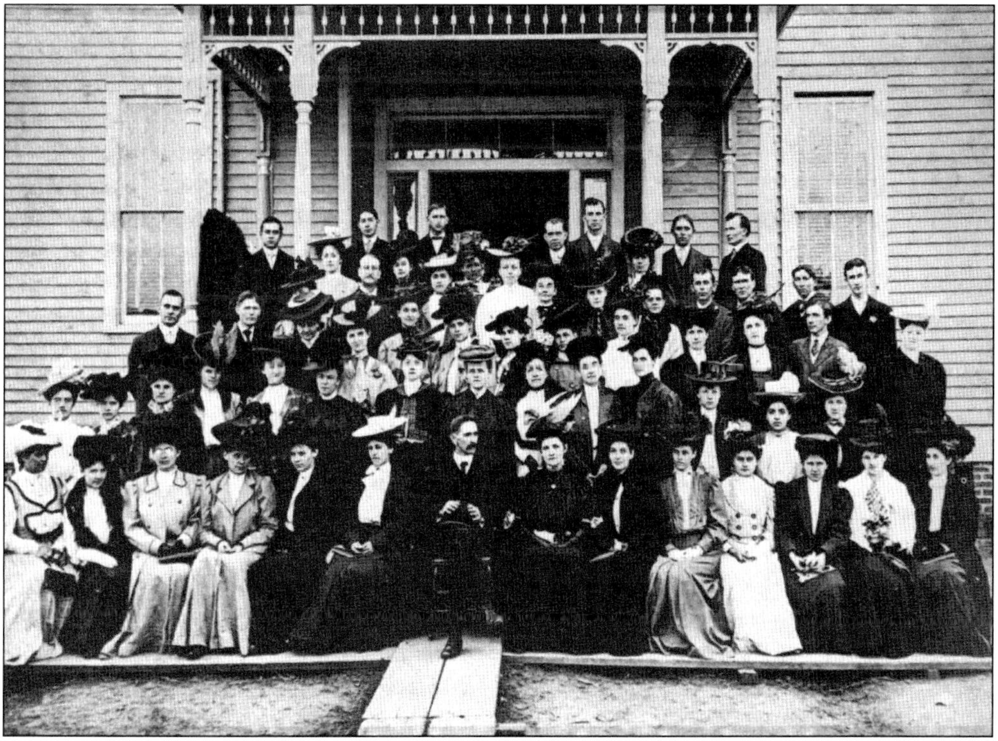

Rapides Parish teachers are pictured with Supt. V.L. Roy (front row, center) around 1908. Roy pioneered the Corn Club, the forerunner of today's 4-H clubs.

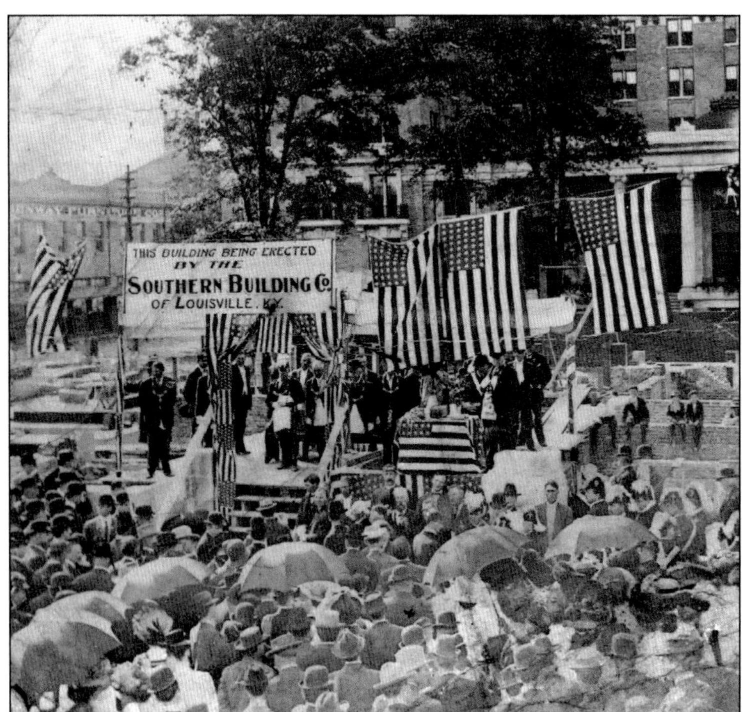

The laying the cornerstone for the new city hall is captured on the afternoon of April 15, 1909. L.E. Thomas, the most worshipful grand master of Louisiana, performed the Masonic ritual for the laying of the stone. John Overton gave the day's oration, proclaiming, "The city of Alexandria has often been called the central queen of Louisiana. . . . The new city hall is the crown for the queen's brow."

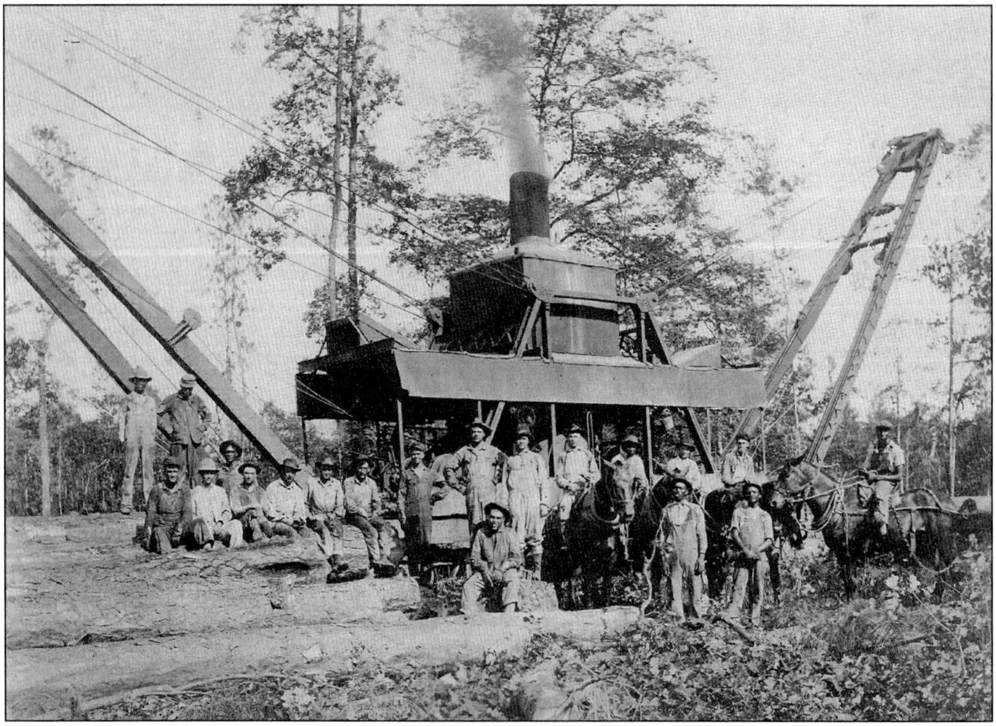

Lumber operations at the turn of the 20th century provided a major economic boost and helped lift the local economy out of the malaise left from the war and Reconstruction.

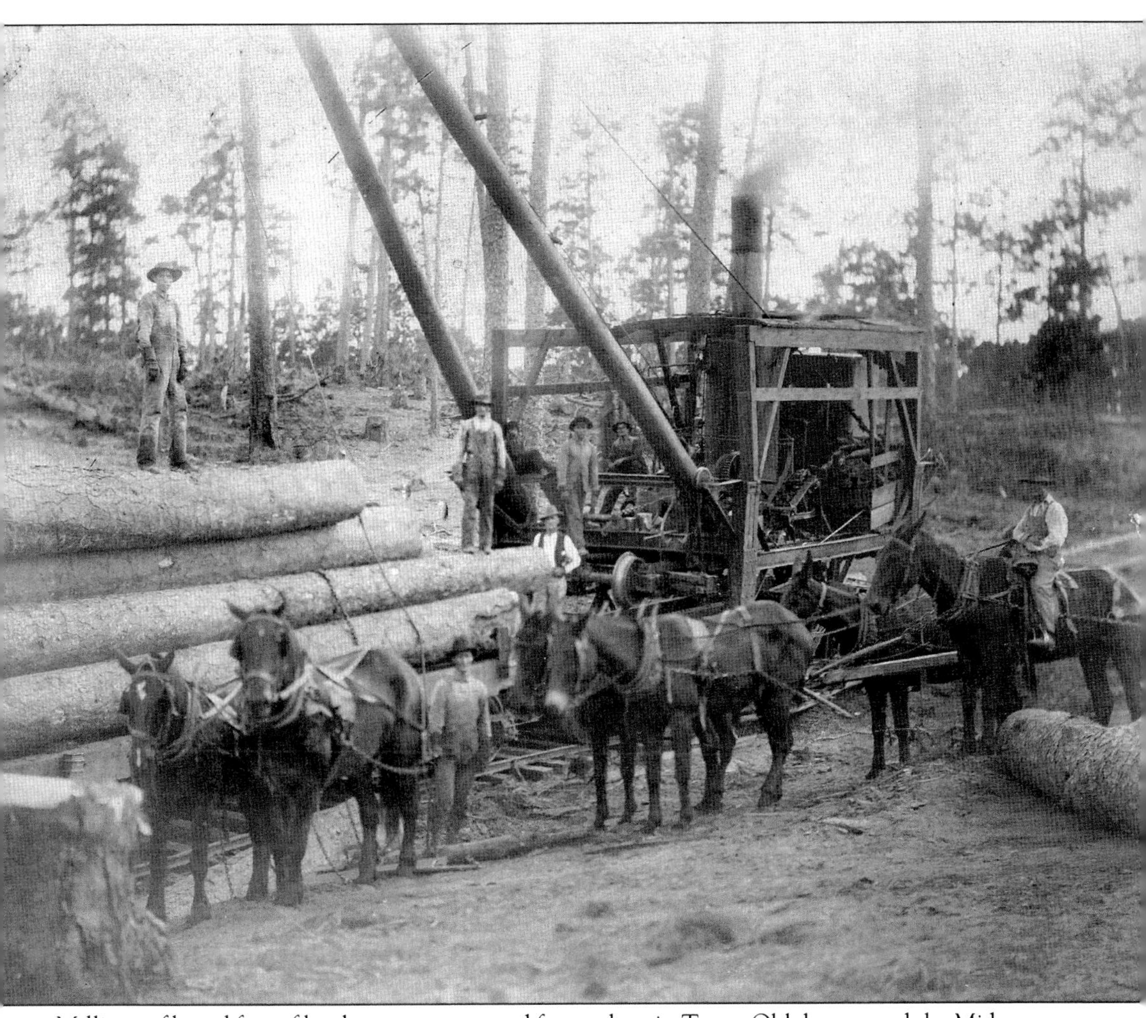

Millions of board feet of lumber were processed for markets in Texas, Oklahoma, and the Midwest. Vast tracts of land were left bare, as huge stands of long-leaf pine, oak, ash, hickory, walnut, and cypress trees were cleared and milled in mill towns that sprang up around Alexandria: Woodworth, Long Leaf, Forest Hill, Pollock, and Tioga.

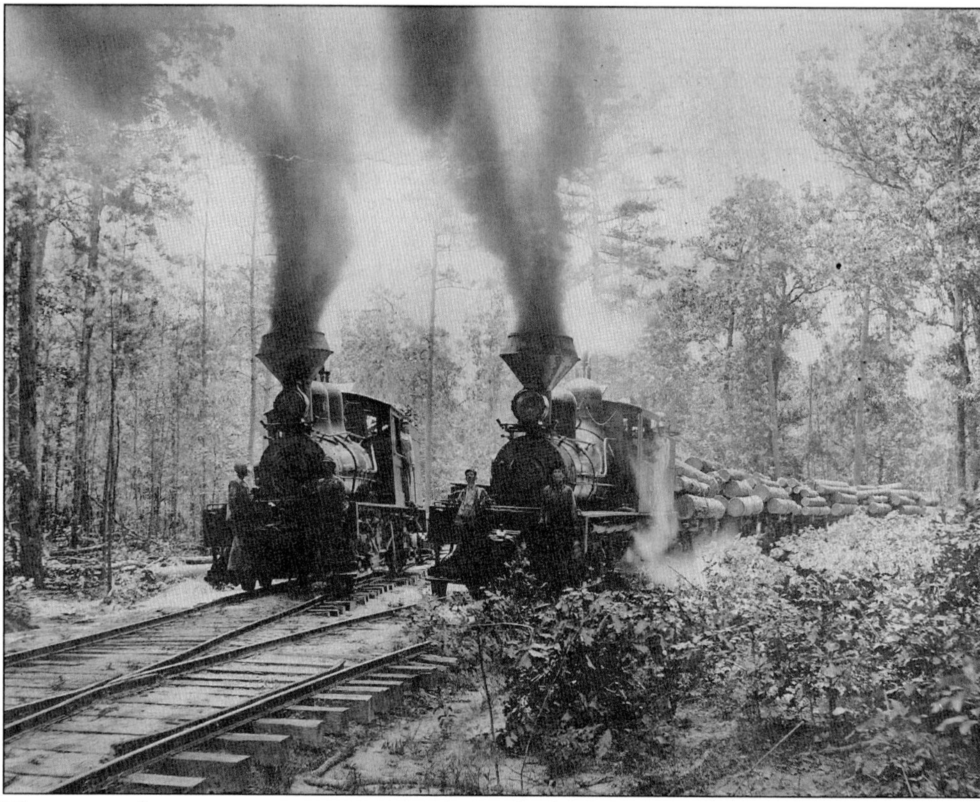

These are timber trains on narrow-gauge rail spurs hauling trees to mill towns around Alexandria. When the work was done and the forests cleared, only tracks remained.

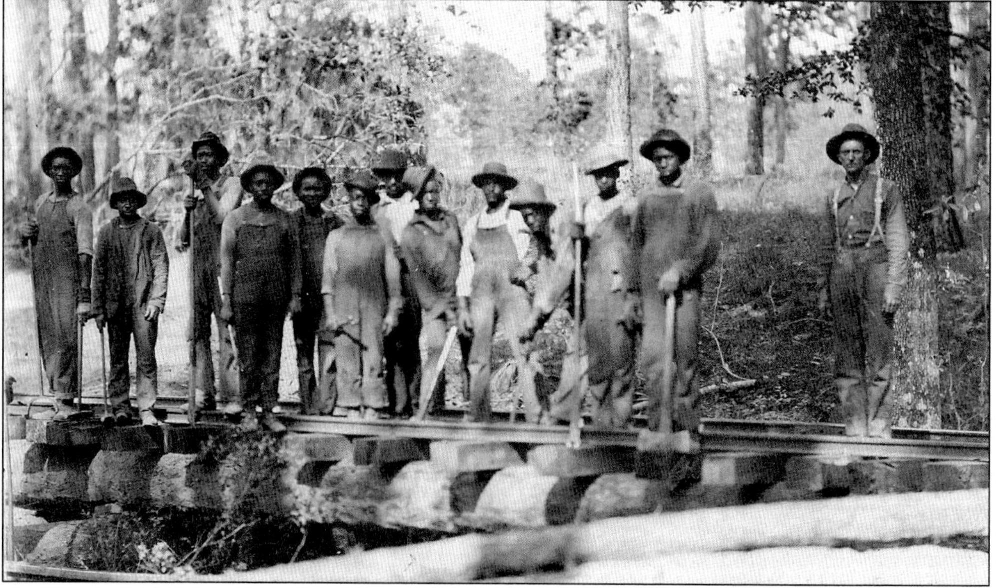

Louisiana loggers are pictured here at the turn of the 20th century. The timber boom made some men rich: Julius Levin, J. Stamps Crowell, Henry Hardtner, Joseph Bentley, and Joseph Pollack made fortunes. Most men found work for a few years, but when the trees disappeared, so did the work.

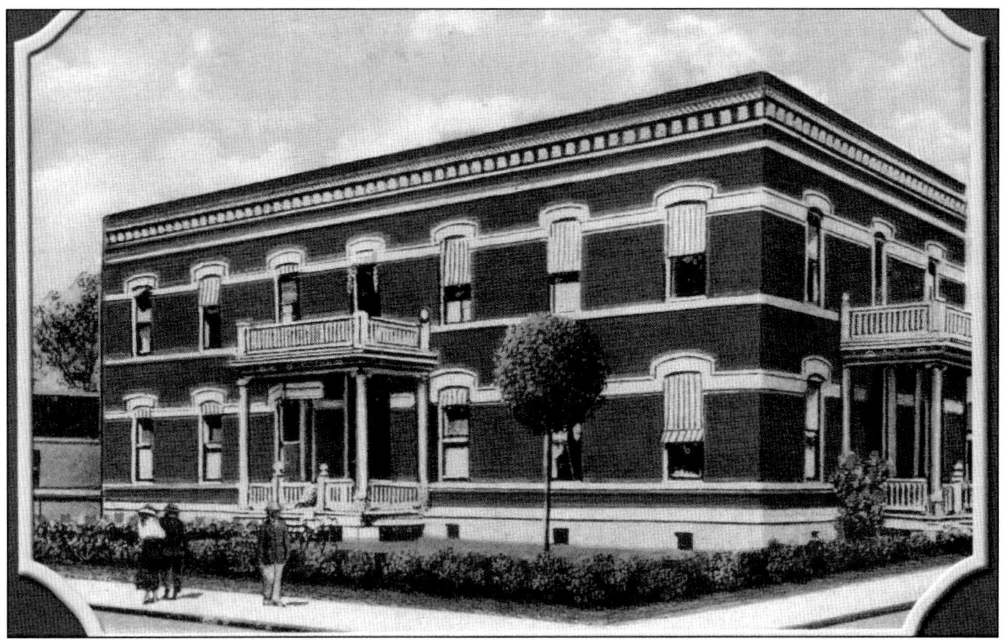

The Alexandria Sanitarium, the first medical center in Alexandria, was established by local physicians at the turn of the 20th century with 20 beds. The building shown here was the second erected at Third and Scott Streets. The two-story, 35-bed brick hospital also served as a training school for nurses. Later incorporated as the Baptist Hospital, today Rapides Regional Medical Center continues the same tradition of quality medical care.

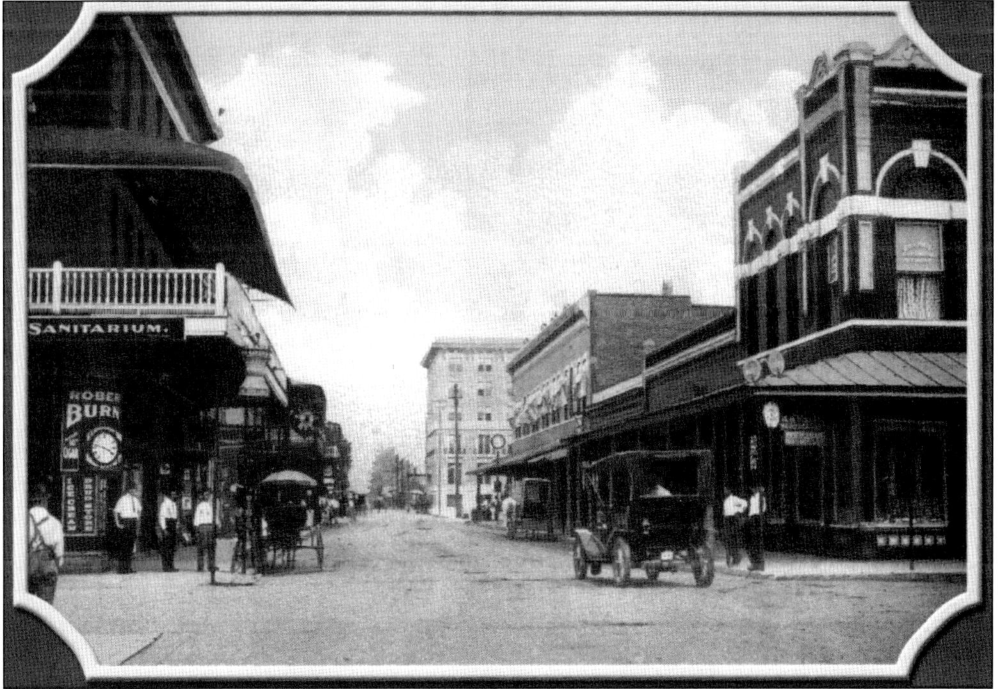

A c. 1910 postcard view created from a photograph of Alexandria's Third Street shows the progress of civic life and social comforts, including brick paved streets and telephone connections.

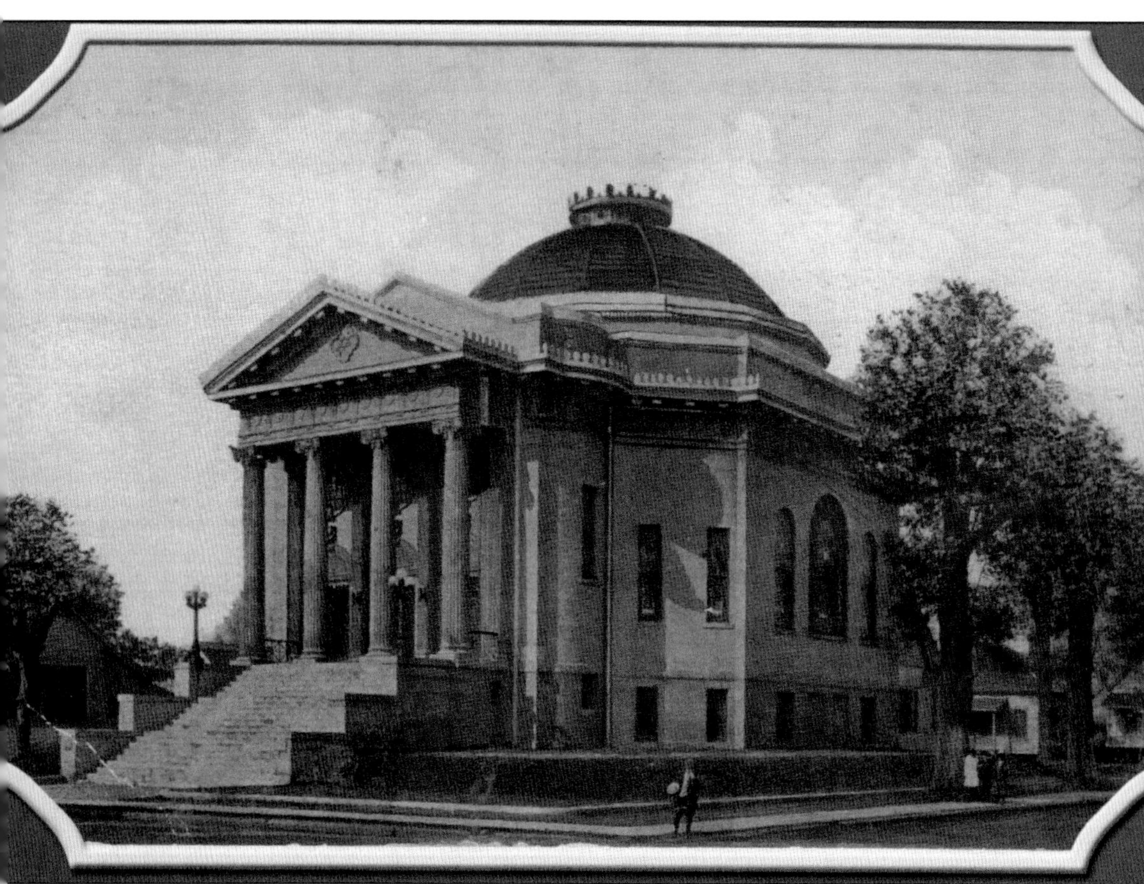

The beautiful domed and pillared Jewish temple for the Gelimuth Chassodim congregation was erected on the corner of Fisk and Fourth Streets in 1908 at a cost of $30,000. Located across from St. Francis Xavier Academy, the temple's large flight of steps was a natural staging point for school group pictures.

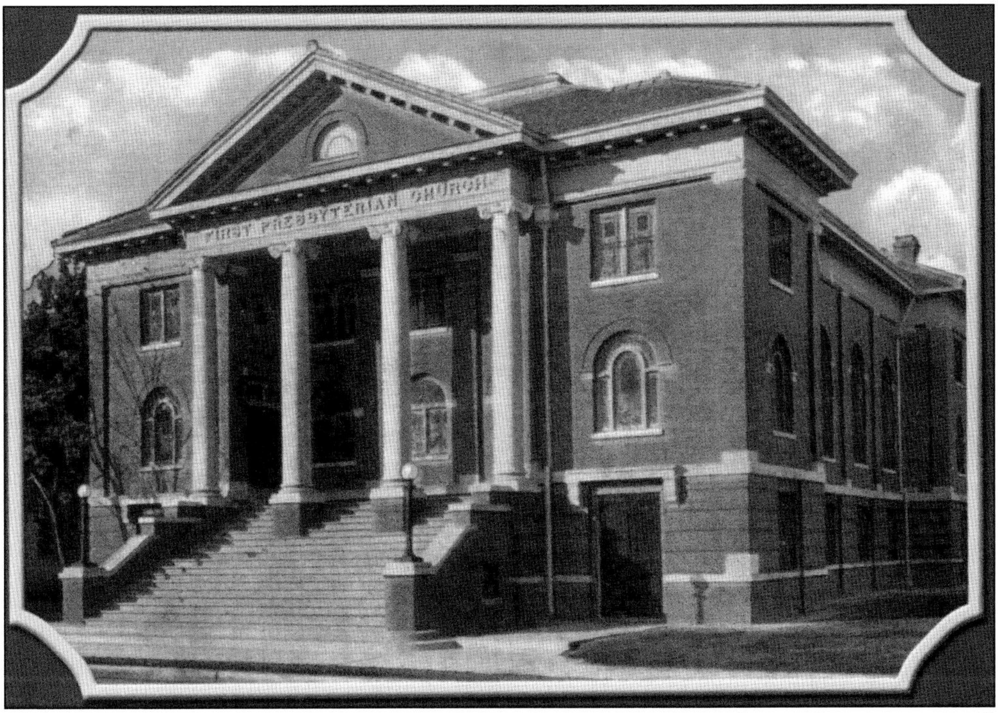

The c. 1900 Presbyterian church in downtown Alexandria is shown here. This structure still stands and is used as a storage facility by the Rapides Parish School Board.

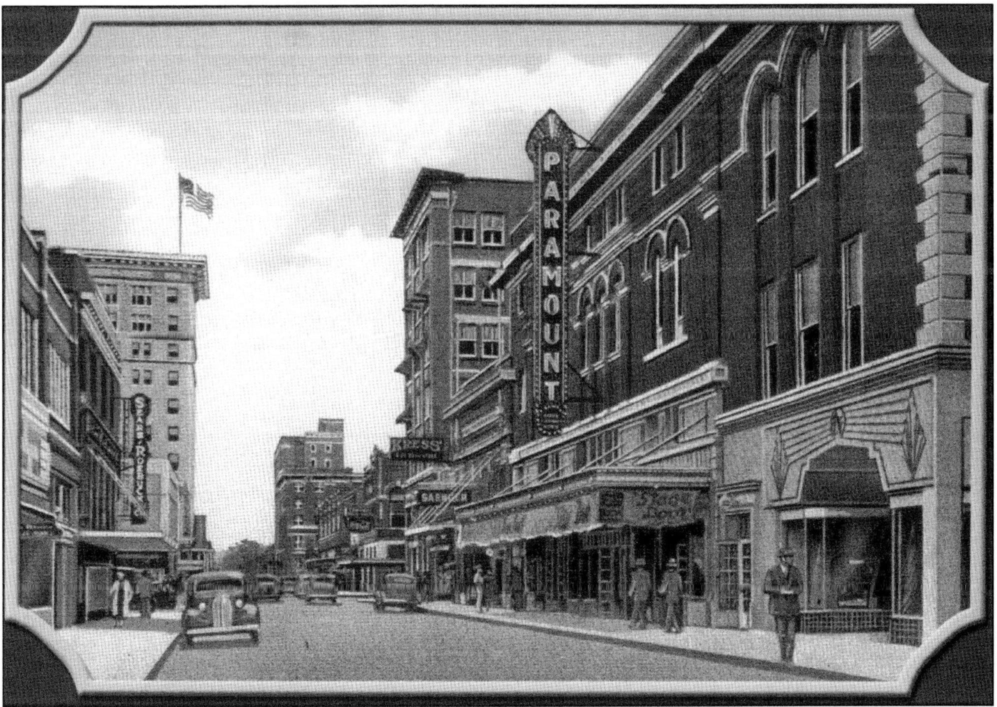

The Paramount Theater was designed to be Alexandria's premier movie house. Neglected for years, the structure was slated for renovation when the roof collapsed in the 1980s.

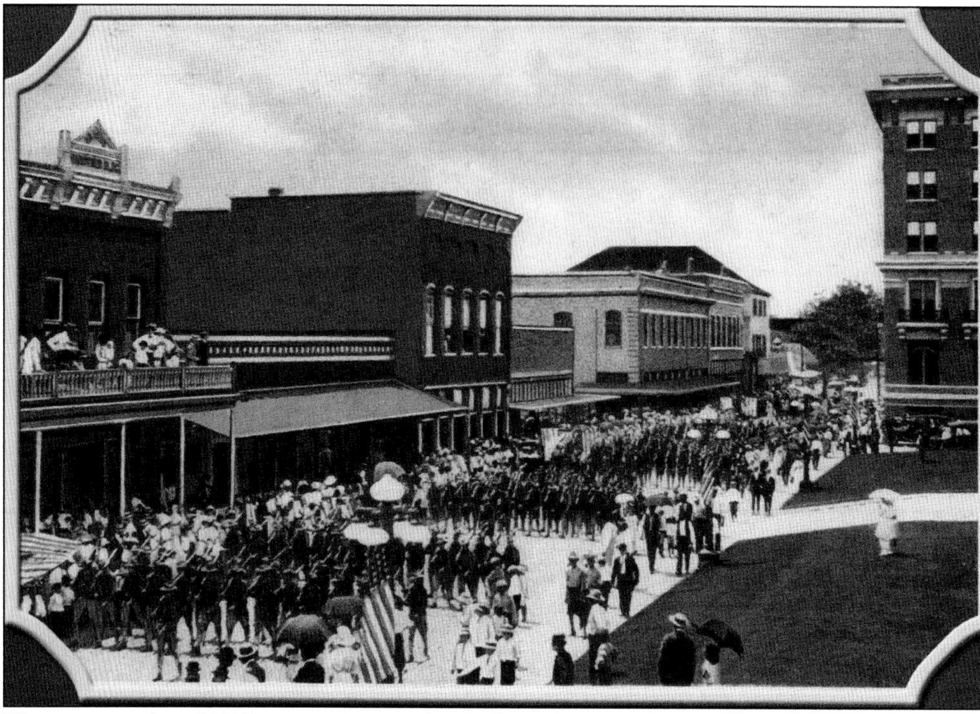

This image is of a c. 1900 Louisiana National Guard Parade on Fourth Street in downtown Alexandria. The annual summer encampment was one of the highlights of the year's social calendar.

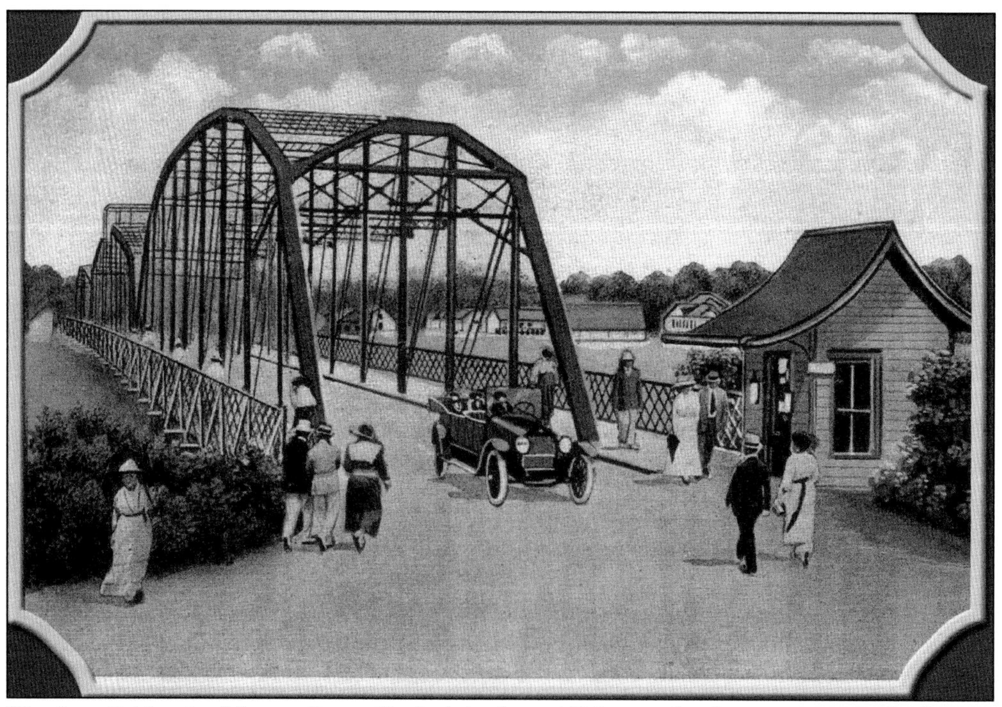

The Iron Bridge (or Murray Street Bridge), built in 1900, was the first to span the Red River linking Alexandria and Pineville.

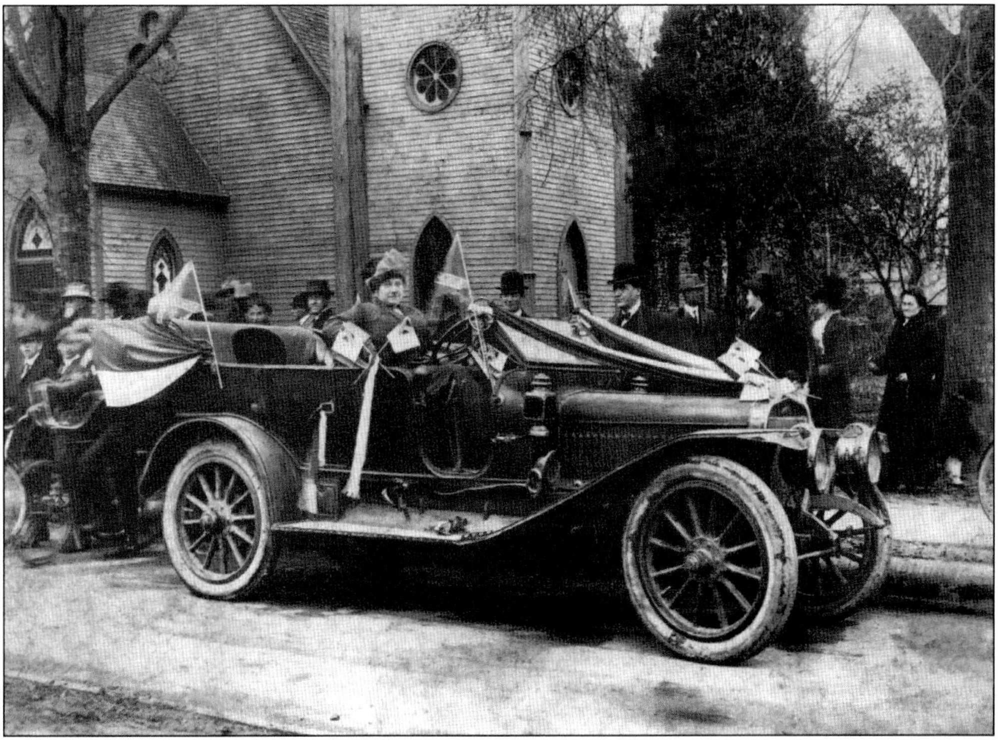

Emily Whittington is at the wheel of an early automobile. The vehicle sits in front of the old St. James Episcopal Church in Alexandria in 1920.

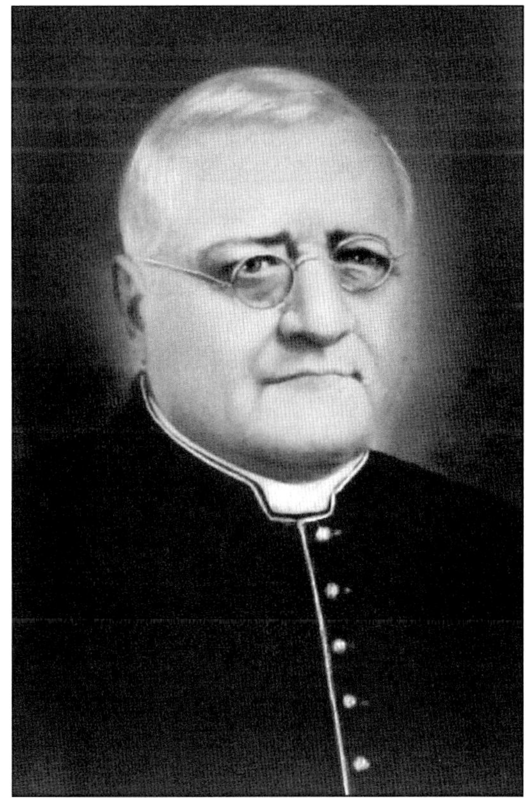

Msgr. Leonard Menard, a native of Brittany in France, served as the pastor of St. Francis Xavier Church in Alexandria for 39 years (1883 to 1912) and was responsible for the construction of the present brick church. He was honored with the rank and title of right reverend monsignor by Pope Benedict XV and celebrated his Golden Sacerdotal Jubilee at the cathedral he had built in 1927. Monsignor Menard died on January 16, 1930, and is buried at the priests' cemetery at Maryhill. Menard Memorial High School was named in his honor.

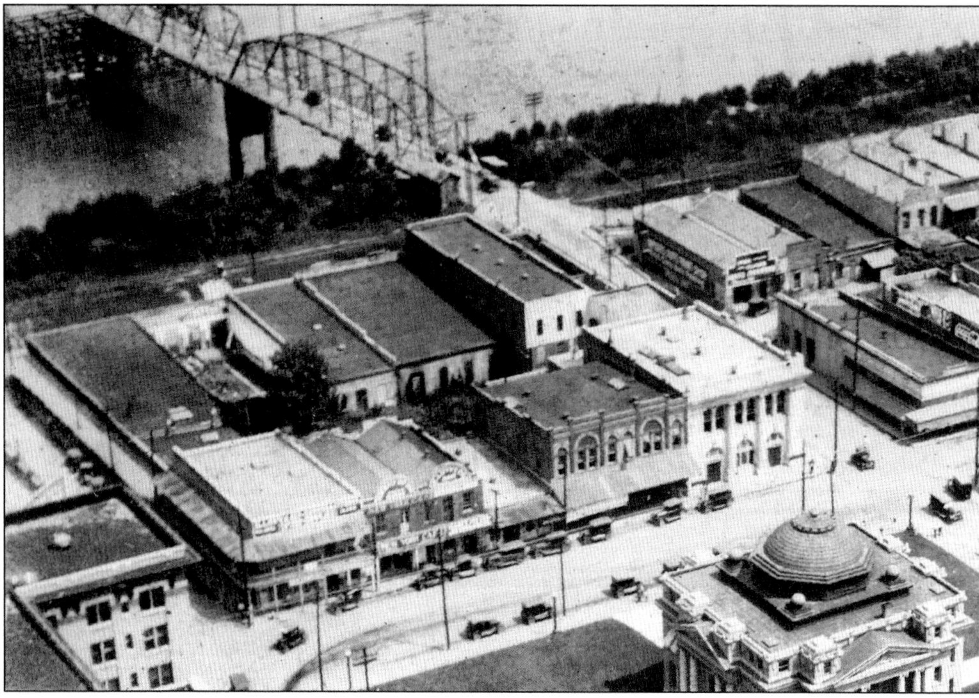

This is an aerial view of the city hall and the Murray Street Bridge in downtown Alexandria. The first principle connection between Alexandria and Pineville, the Murray Street Bridge was later replaced by the Jackson Street Bridge and the Pineville Expressway.

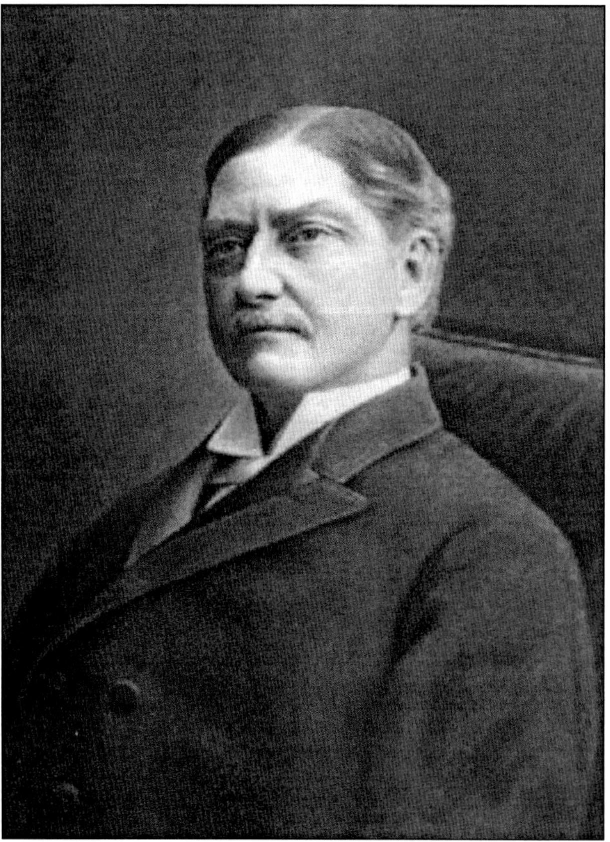

Newton Blanchard, a Rapides Parish attorney and congressman, obtained funds for improving the Red River levee system after the flood of 1892. Blanchard later went on to serve as governor of the state.

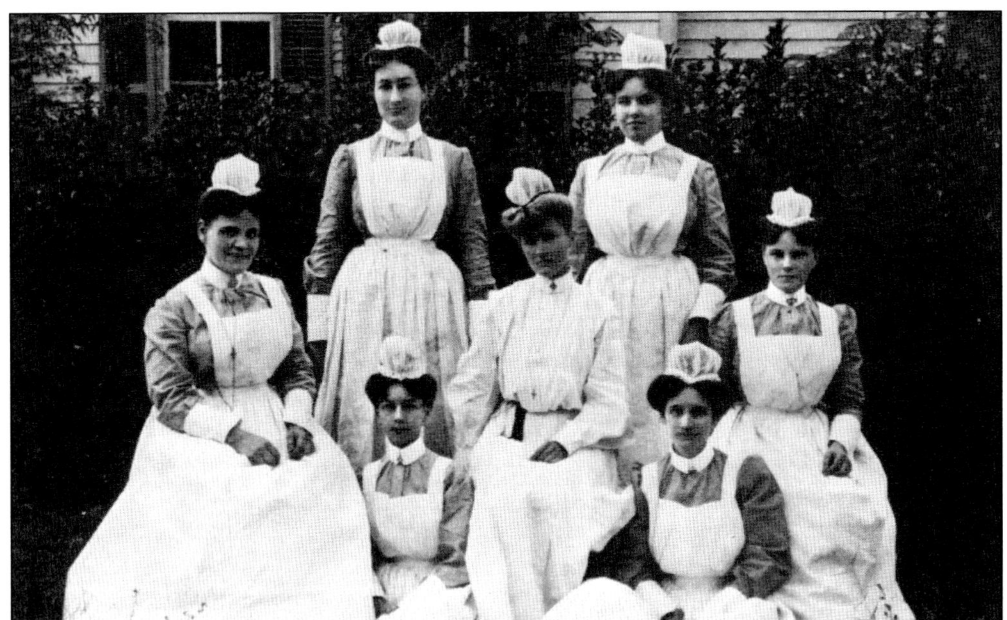

Pictured are the first and second graduating classes of nurses at the Alexandria Sanitarium. The directress, Tuboff Debogary, sits in the center. The first class consisted of Margaret Gueringer, May Taylor, and Ollie Camilla (with neck chains). The second class consisted of Cecile Gueringer, Ludie Jackson, and Virgie Morris.

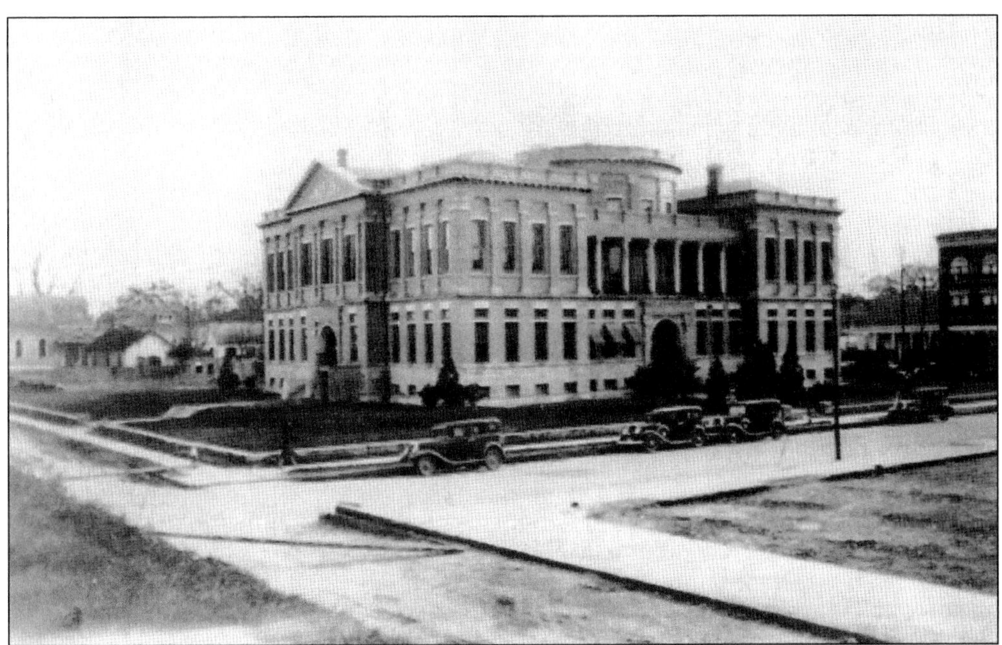

Pictured here is the Rapides Parish Courthouse in the 1920s. It was replaced by a new Art Deco–style courthouse on Murray Street.

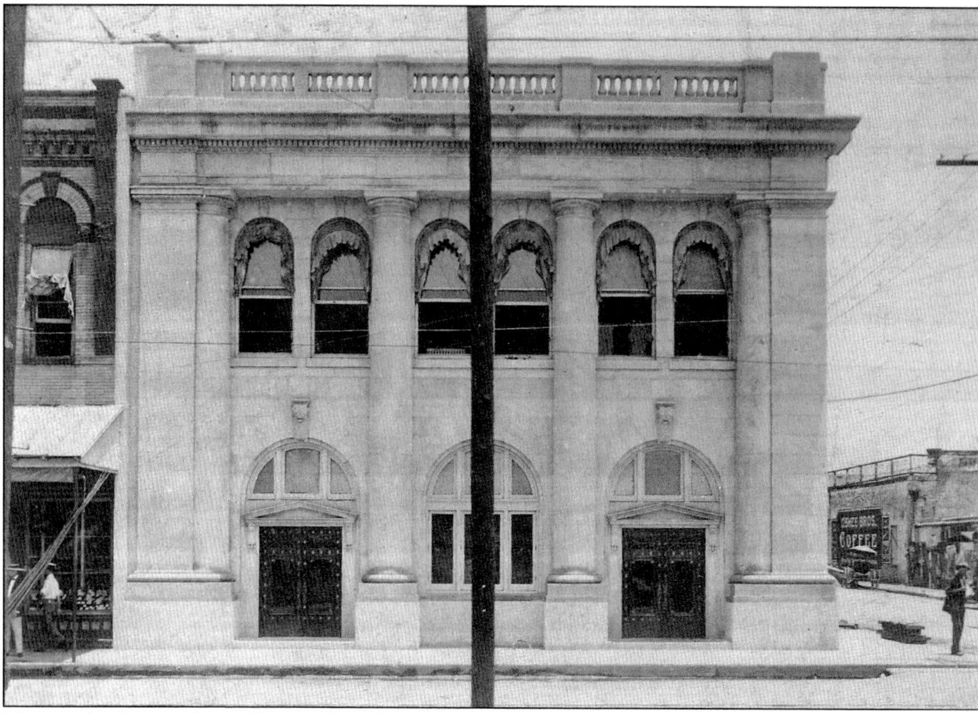

This is the Second Rapides Bank and Trust Company building. The core of the historic structure now houses the Alexandria Museum of Art.

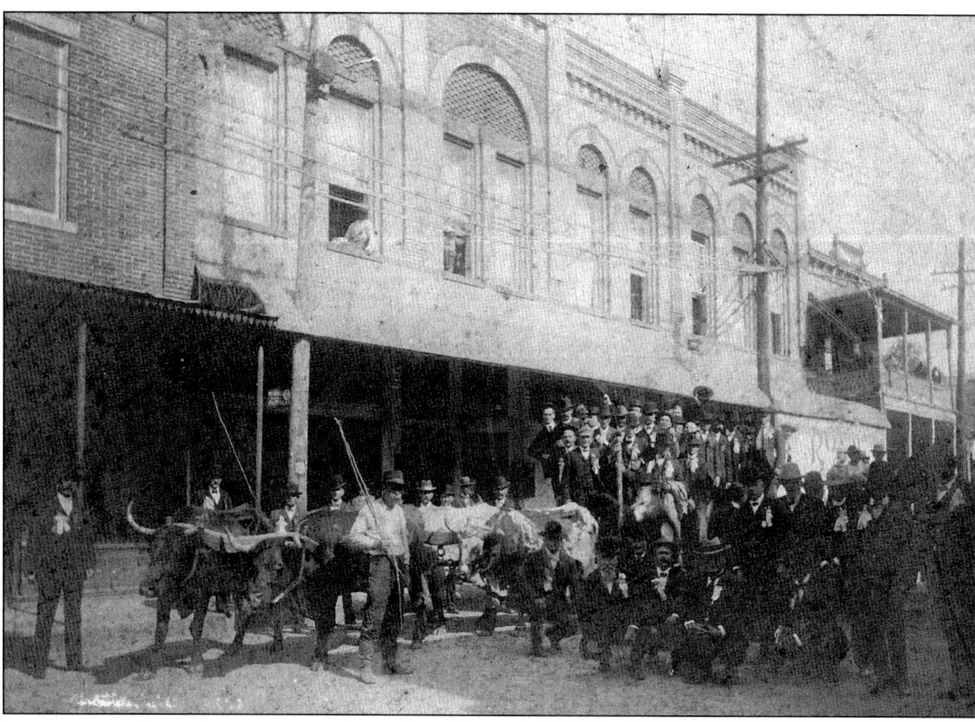

Downtown Alexandria is seen in the early 1900s. The city's population doubled in the first decade of the 20th century.

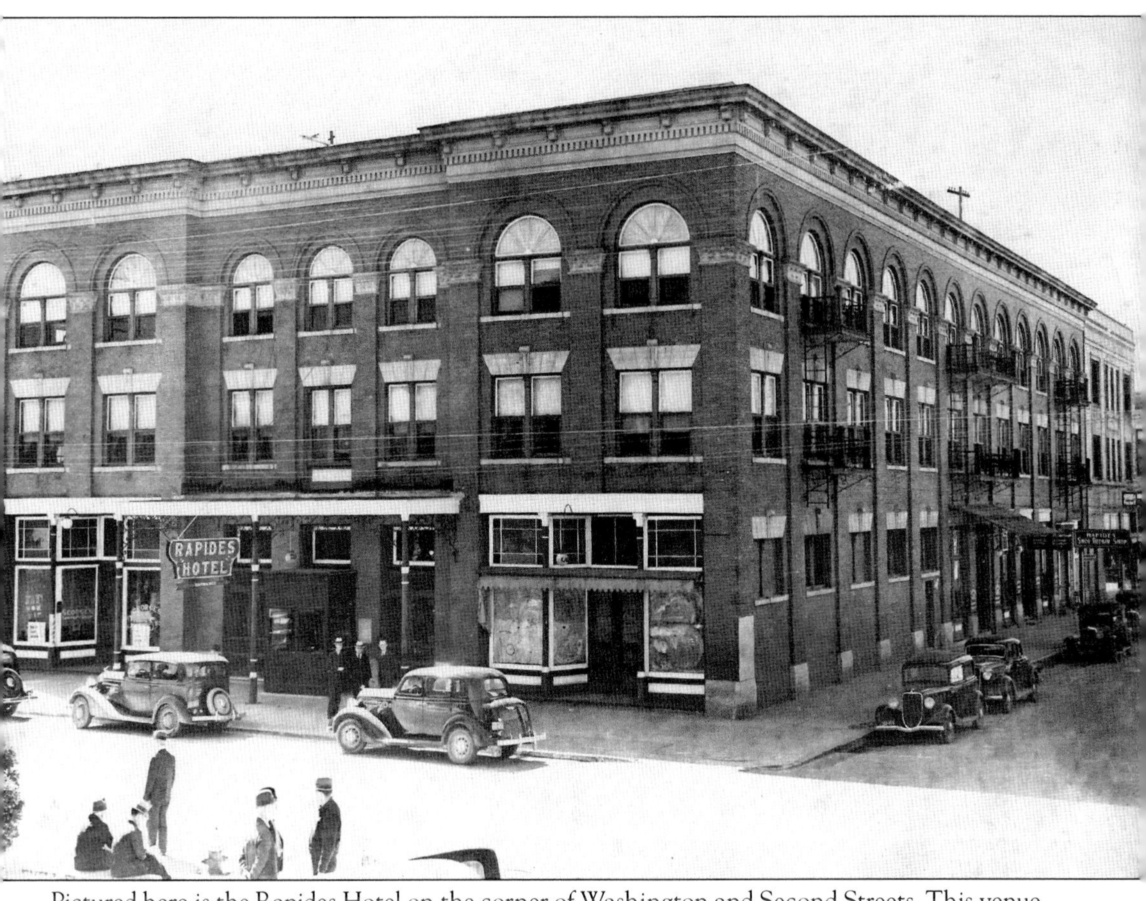

Pictured here is the Rapides Hotel on the corner of Washington and Second Streets. This venue was one of the prime meeting places before the construction of the Hotel Bentley.

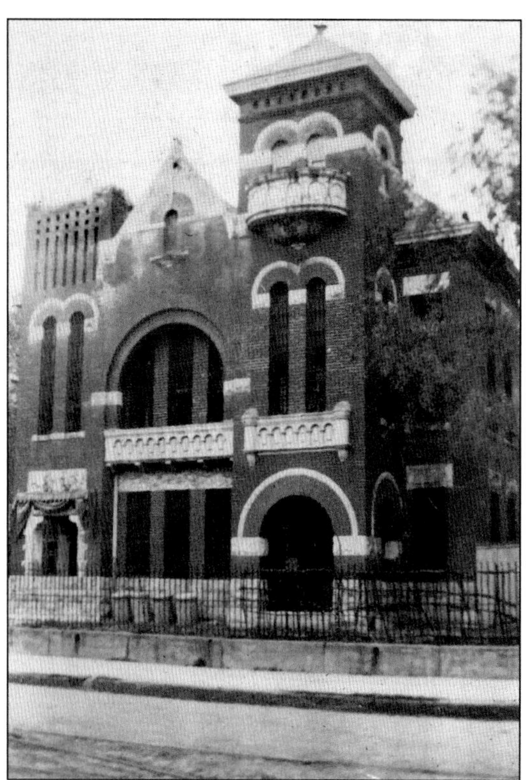

The city jail is seen on the corner of Second and Lee Streets around 1910. This quaint structure was torn down, and the jail facilities were moved to the new courthouse in the 1930s.

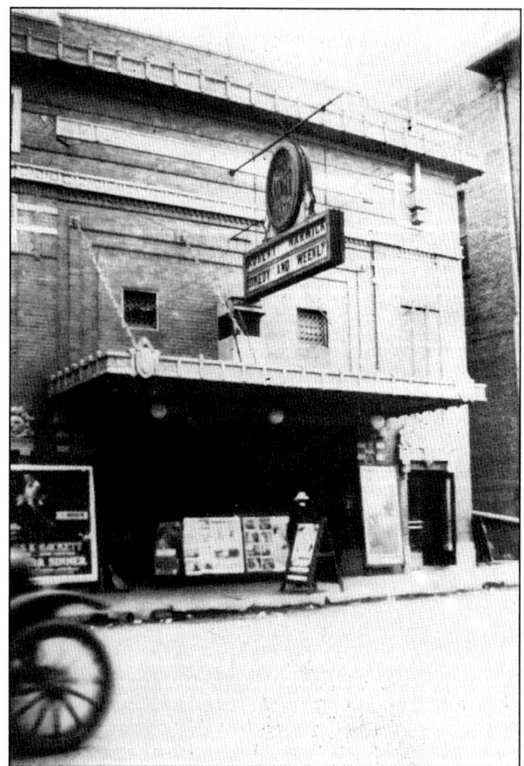

The c. 1900 Saenger Theater in downtown Alexandria is one of the many entertainment centers that did not survive the test of time.

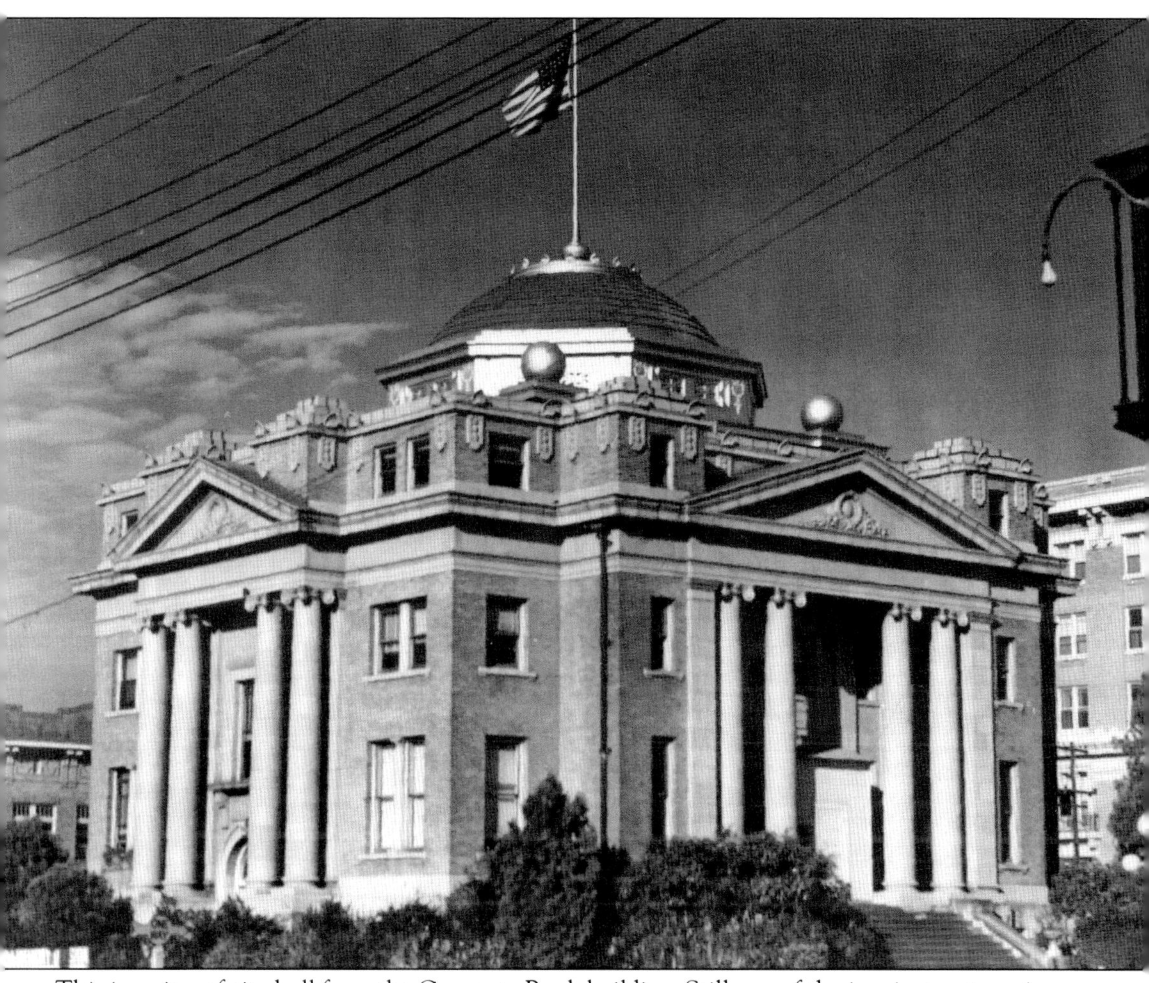

This is a view of city hall from the Guarenty Bank building. Still one of the iconic structures in downtown Alexandria, the Guarenty Bank building now houses Capital One bank offices.

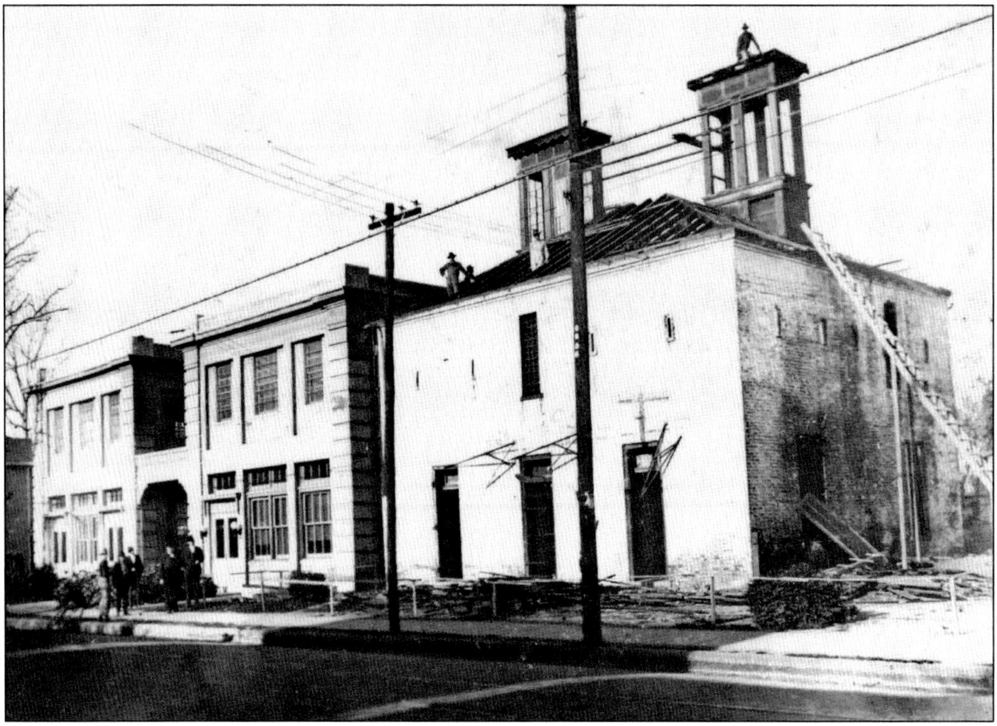

The old Rapides Parish Courthouse, built after the Civil War, served as a jail and firehouse after the construction of a larger courthouse in 1908. It is seen in the process of being razed in the 1920s after the construction of the new firehouse on the left.

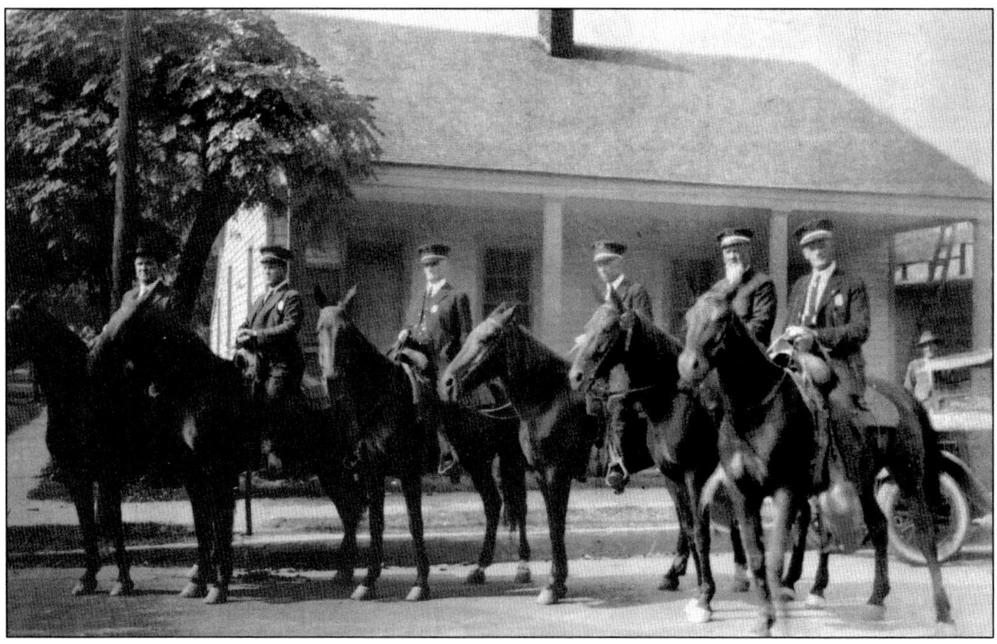

Pictured here is the Alexandria police and fire marshal on parade in the 1930s. Alexandria's police and fire departments underwent dramatic changes after the 1897 murder of town constable Welch Baillio by Joseph Timberlake, which highlighted the needs for these professional services.

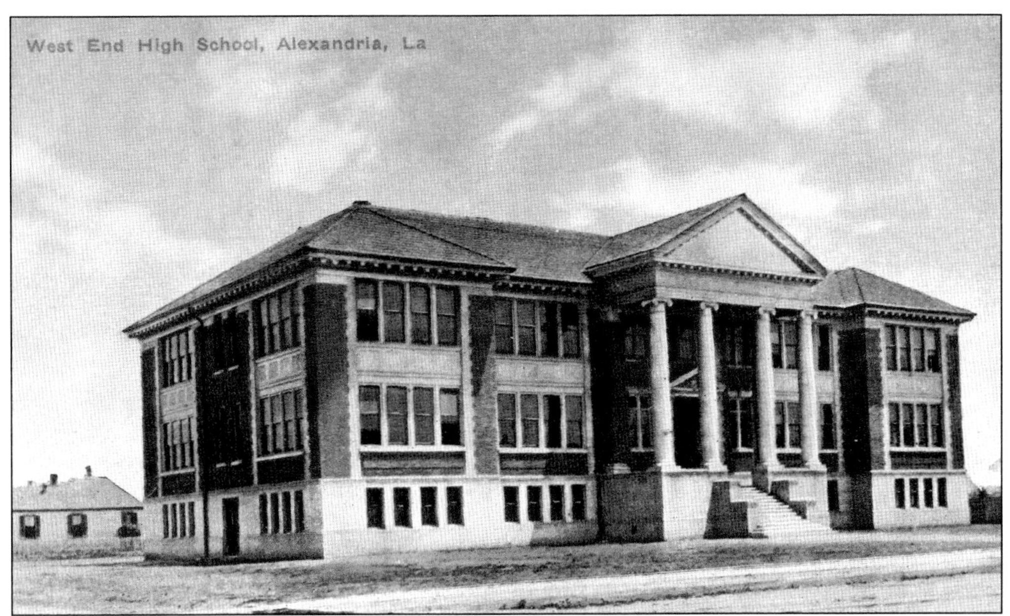

This is a c. 1900 image of the West End High School. The building was eventually torn down after the consolidation that led to the construction of the new Bolton High School in 1926.

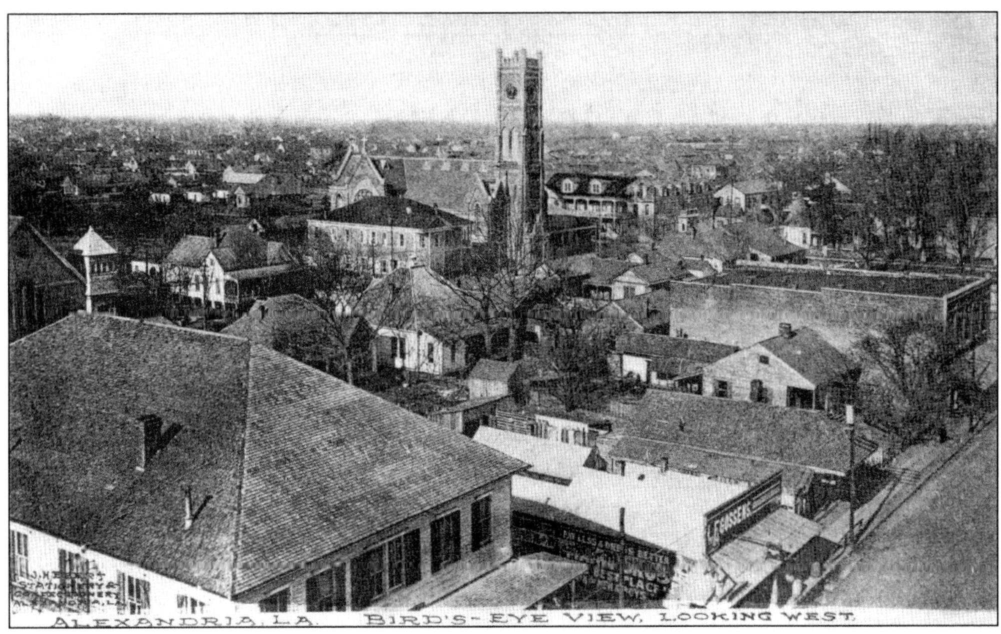

This view of St. Francis Xavier Cathedral was taken after the completion of the bell tower in 1906. The two-story frame building to the left of the church is the old St. Francis Xavier Commercial College, staffed by the Brothers of the Sacred Heart. To the right of the church is St. Francis Xavier Academy, staffed by the Sisters of Divine Providence.

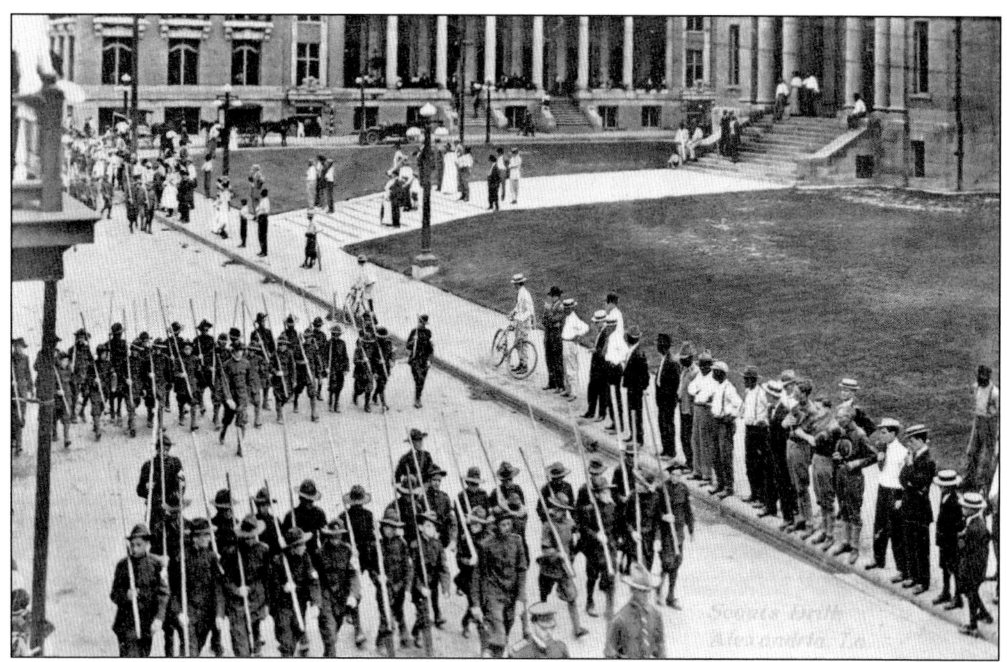

Boy Scouts are on parade in Alexandria. Calvary Baptist Church Troop 12, chartered in 1921, is the oldest operating troop in the area.

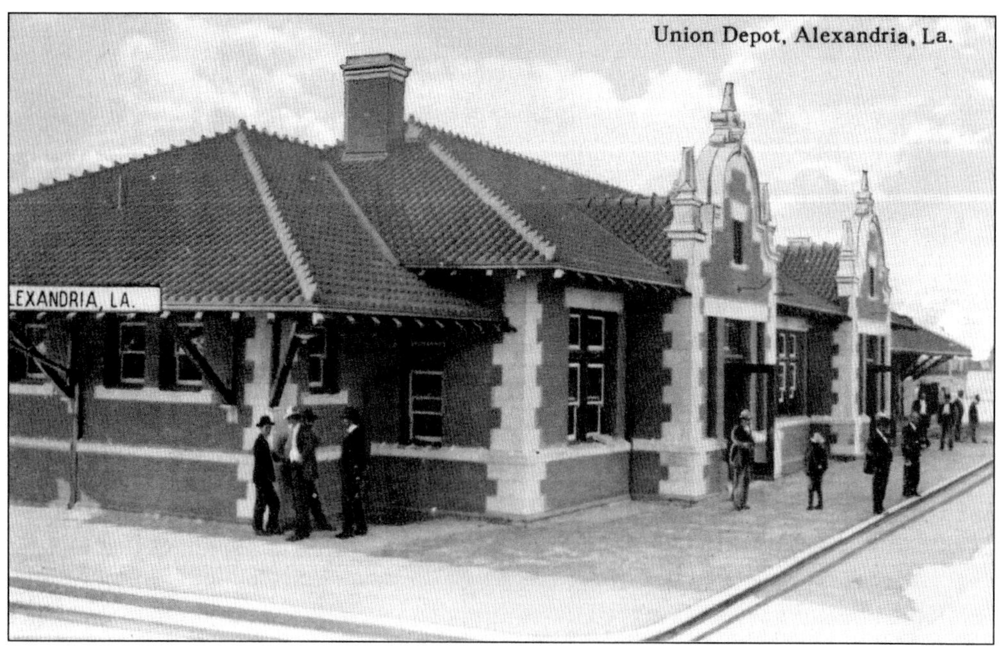

Here is Union Station, the T&P Railway depot, in Alexandria. This Jacobean Revival building was a local landmark, even after it was abandoned. Its demolition in the early 1990s was a source of great controversy and led to a heightened awareness of the need for historic preservation.

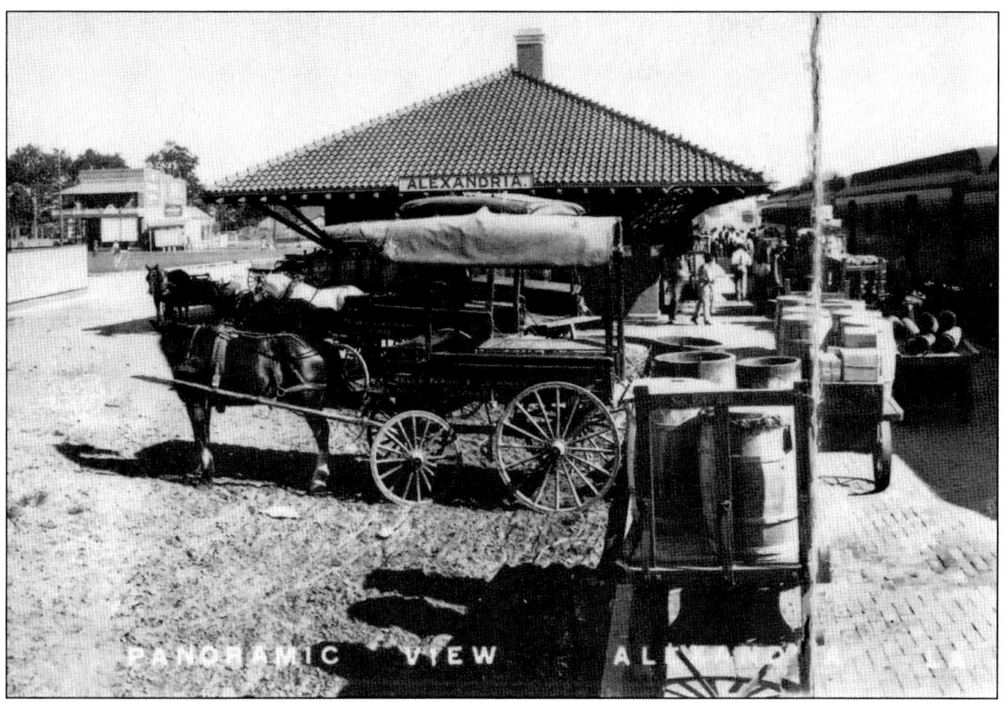

The express wagons in this 1930s photograph wait at Union Station in Alexandria. Passenger service was discontinued in the late 1960s.

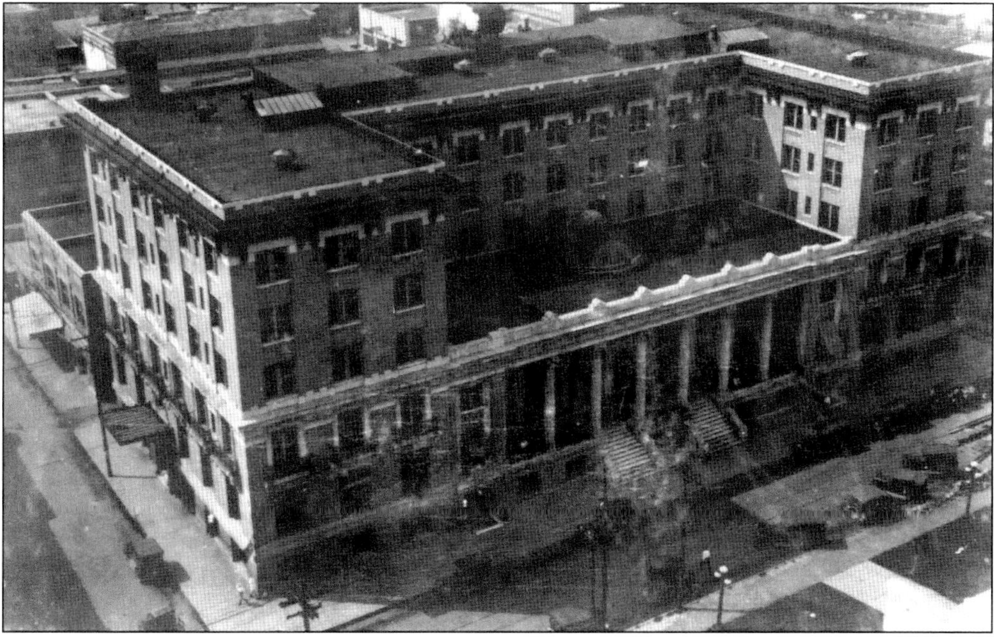

The Hotel Bentley was expanded during the 1940s. Gen. George Marshall and his staff stayed here during Army maneuvers in 1940 and 1941, which included men such as Patton and Eisenhower.

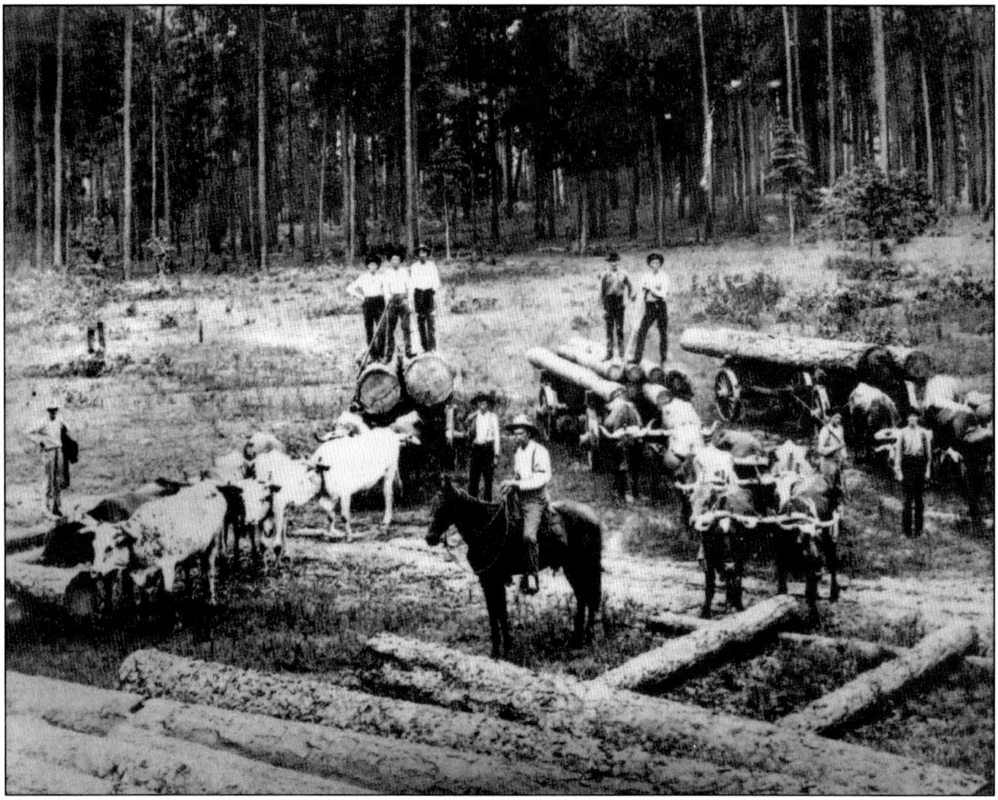

Lumber mule teams are seen in a c. 1900 photograph. Today, small mill towns remain as the only signs of that timber boom.

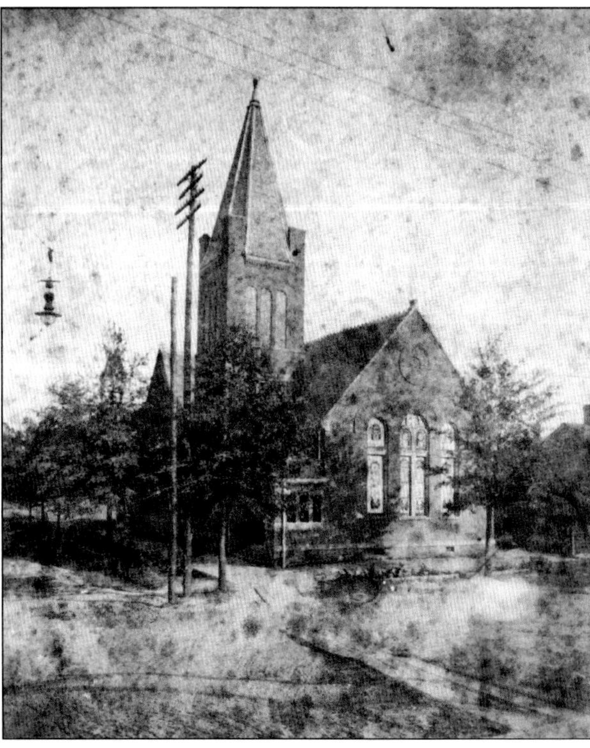

Pictured is the Shiloh Baptist Church. It remains as a surviving historic structure in downtown Alexandria. Efforts have been made to secure this landmark and save it from destruction.

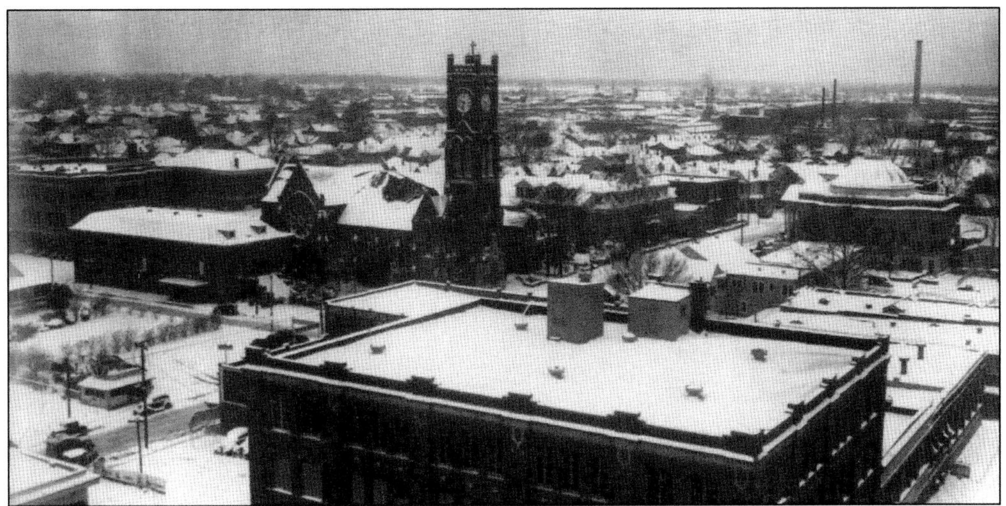

Snowfall blanketing downtown Alexandria, St. Francis Xavier Cathedral, and the domed Jewish temple are visible landmarks in an unfamiliar scene.

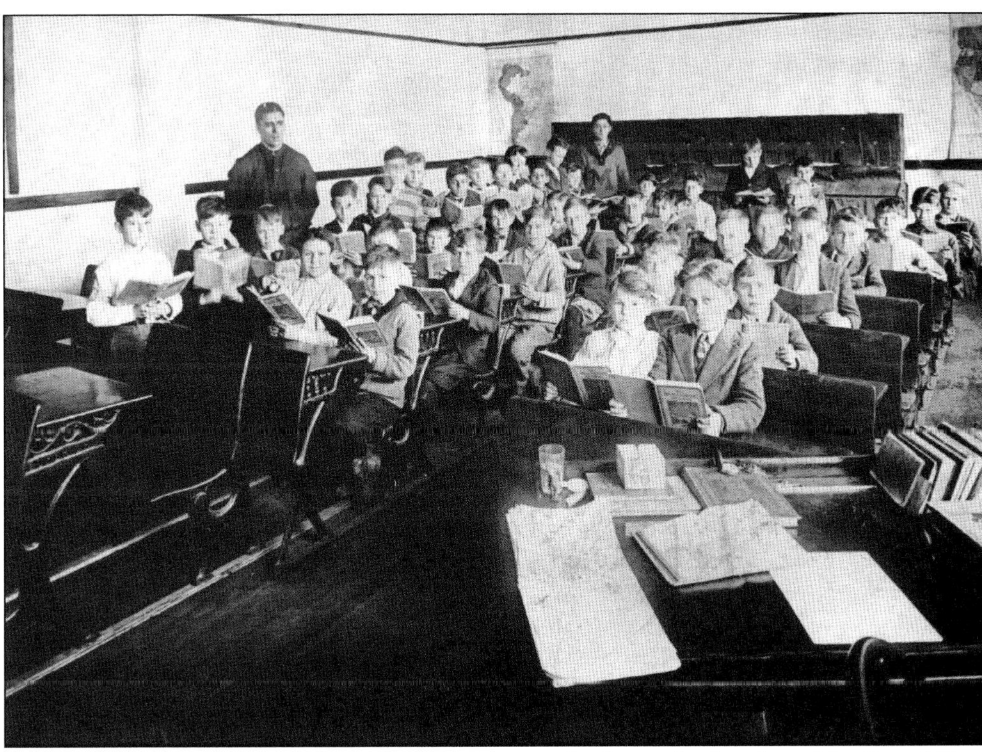

Pictured here is a St. Francis Xavier Academy's first-grade class with a Brother of the Sacred Heart in 1923. The Brothers of the Sacred Heart served as educators at St. Francis Xavier Commercial College, St. Francis Xavier Academy, Menard Memorial High School, and at Holy Savior Menard Memorial High School before declining numbers forced their withdrawal in the late 1960s.

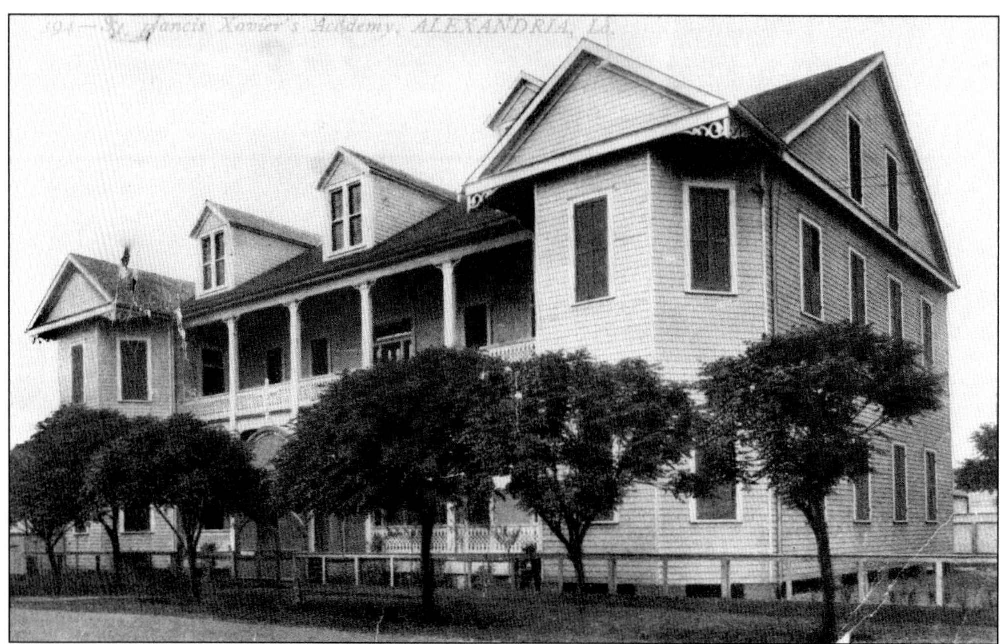

This is St. Francis Xavier Academy in 1899. A Victorian brick addition was later built on the Fourth Street side of the complex in 1906.

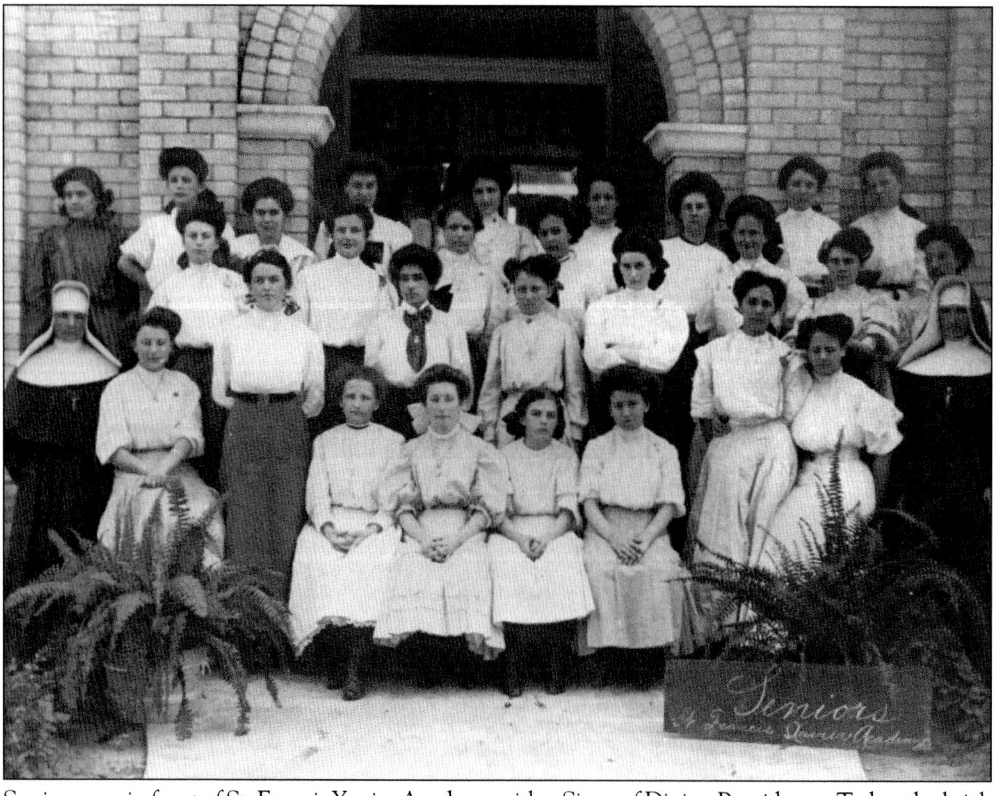

Seniors pose in front of St. Francis Xavier Academy with a Sister of Divine Providence. Today, the brick facade of the academy remains as one of downtown Alexandria's iconic Victorian structures.

The clock mechanism for the cathedral tower clock is seen here. The four clock faces are each nine feet in diameter. The massive clock works were installed in August 1908 and weigh 1,200 pounds. Three bells in the tower toll the hour and each quarter hour. The largest bell, dedicated to the Sacred Heart of Jesus, weighs 2,000 pounds.

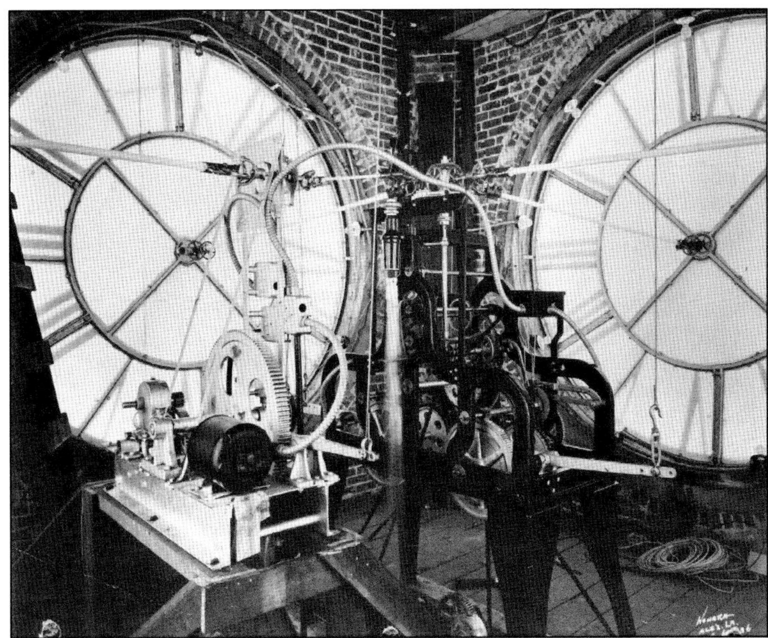

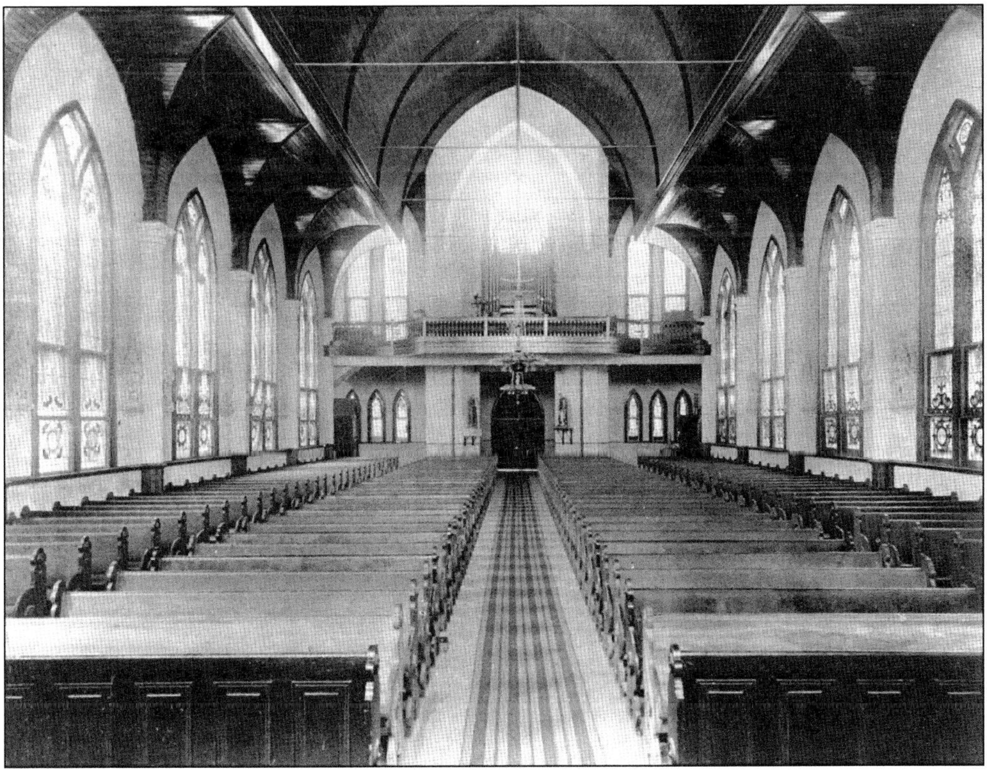

Here is an interior view of the cathedral church at its dedication in November 1899. Designed by Nicholas Clayton of Galveston, Texas, the Neo-Gothic church was erected at the corner of Fourth and Beauregard Streets. Over 1.8 million bricks were used in its construction at a cost of over $40,000.

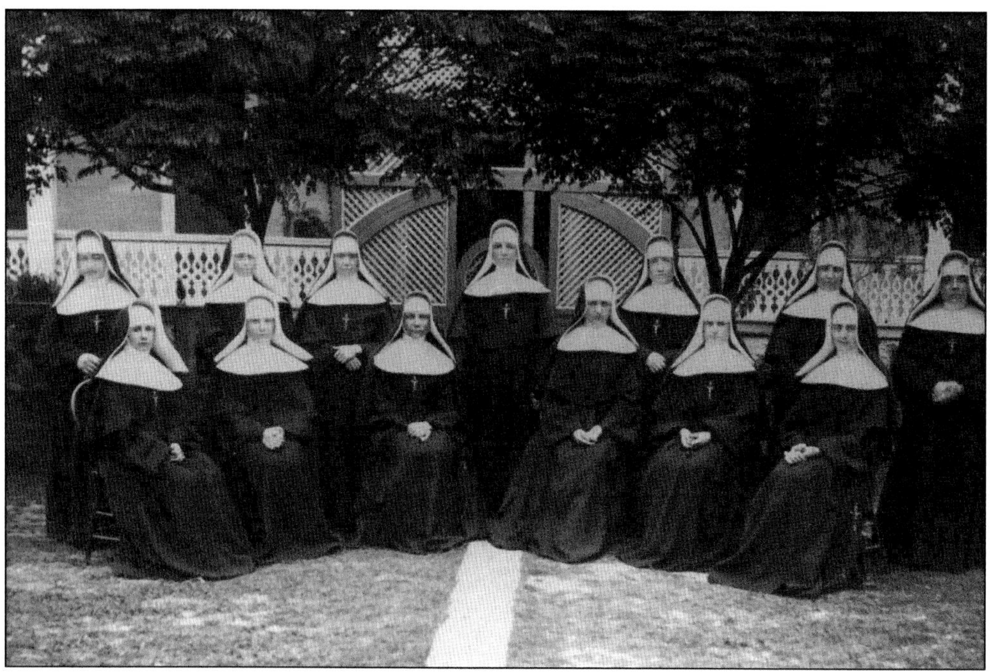

The Sisters of Divine Providence of St. Francis Xavier Academy pose for the camera. Invited by Bishop Antoine Durier to staff schools in north Louisiana, this congregation of religious Sisters has given over 125 years of dedicated service to generations of Alexandria's Catholic children.

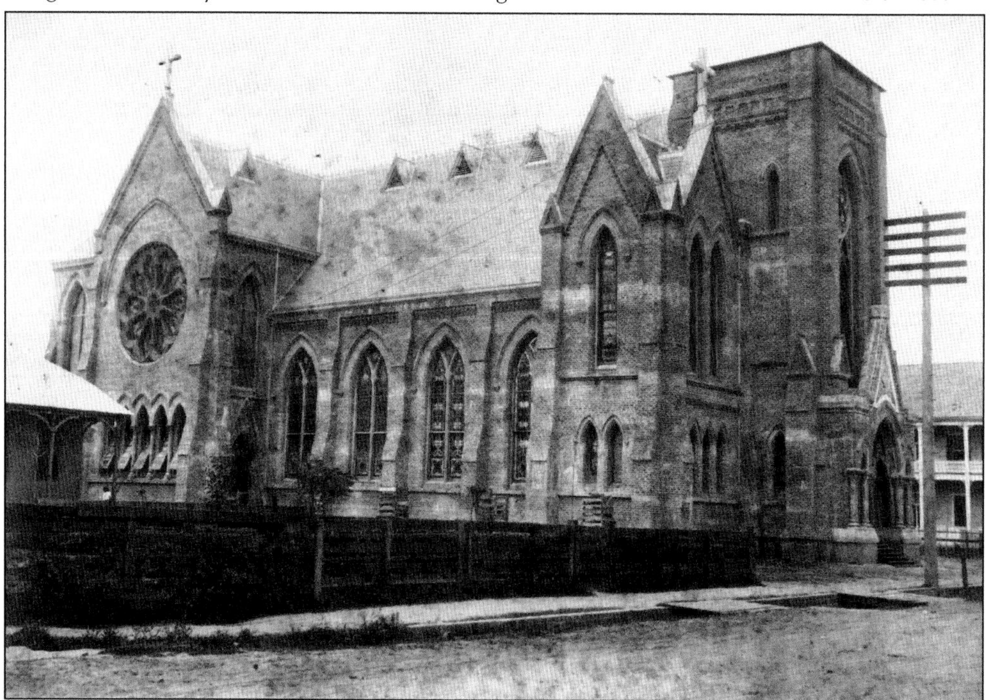

This image of St. Francis Xavier Church was captured before the completion of its bell tower in 1908. St. Francis Xavier Cathedral remained the only Catholic church in Alexandria until the establishment of St. James Memorial Catholic Church in 1910.

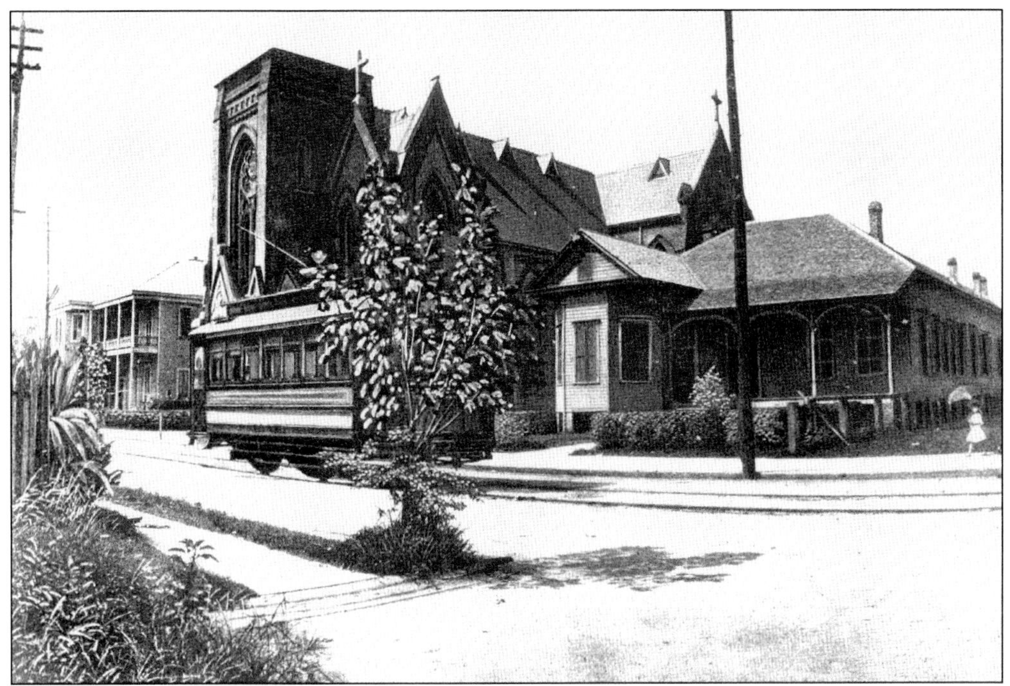

This 1906 postcard features the Catholic church before the completion of its bell tower. The priests' house, or rectory, is to the right of the church.

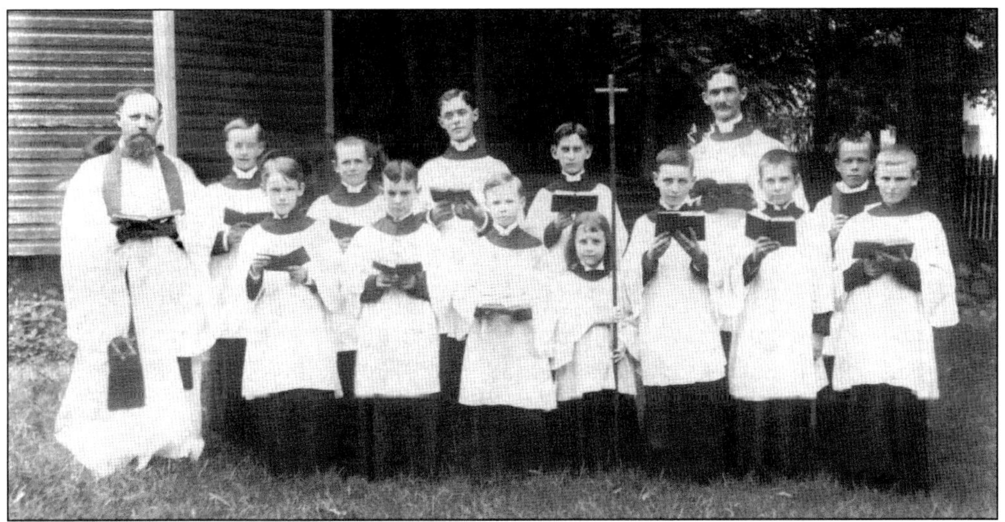

Reverend Duncan (far left) and Rollo Jarreau (back right) pose with the children's choir at St. James Episcopal Church on Second Street around 1900.

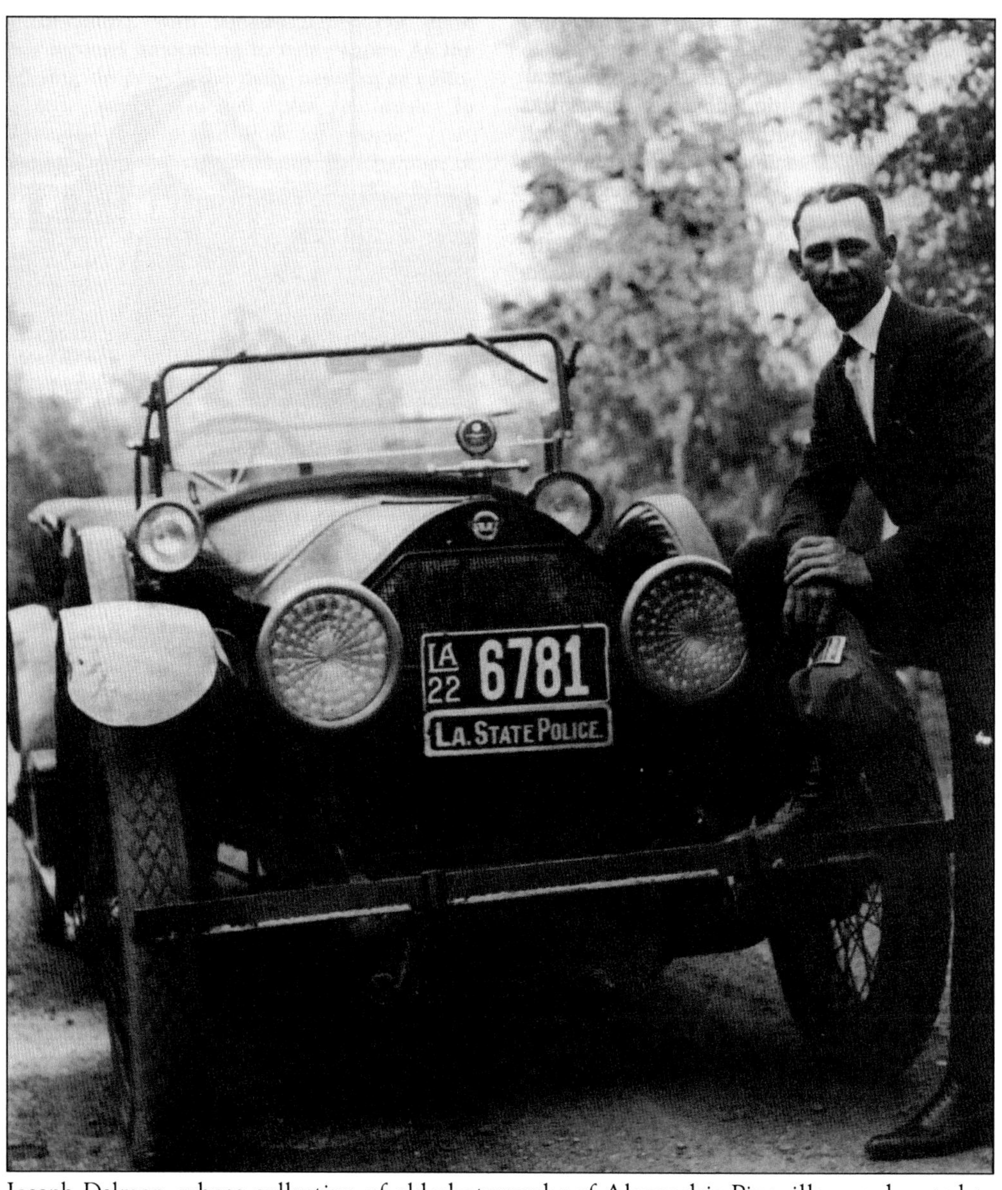

Joseph Delmon, whose collection of old photographs of Alexandria-Pineville was donated to Northwestern State University, is pictured with his 1920 model Stuz Bulldog in 1922.

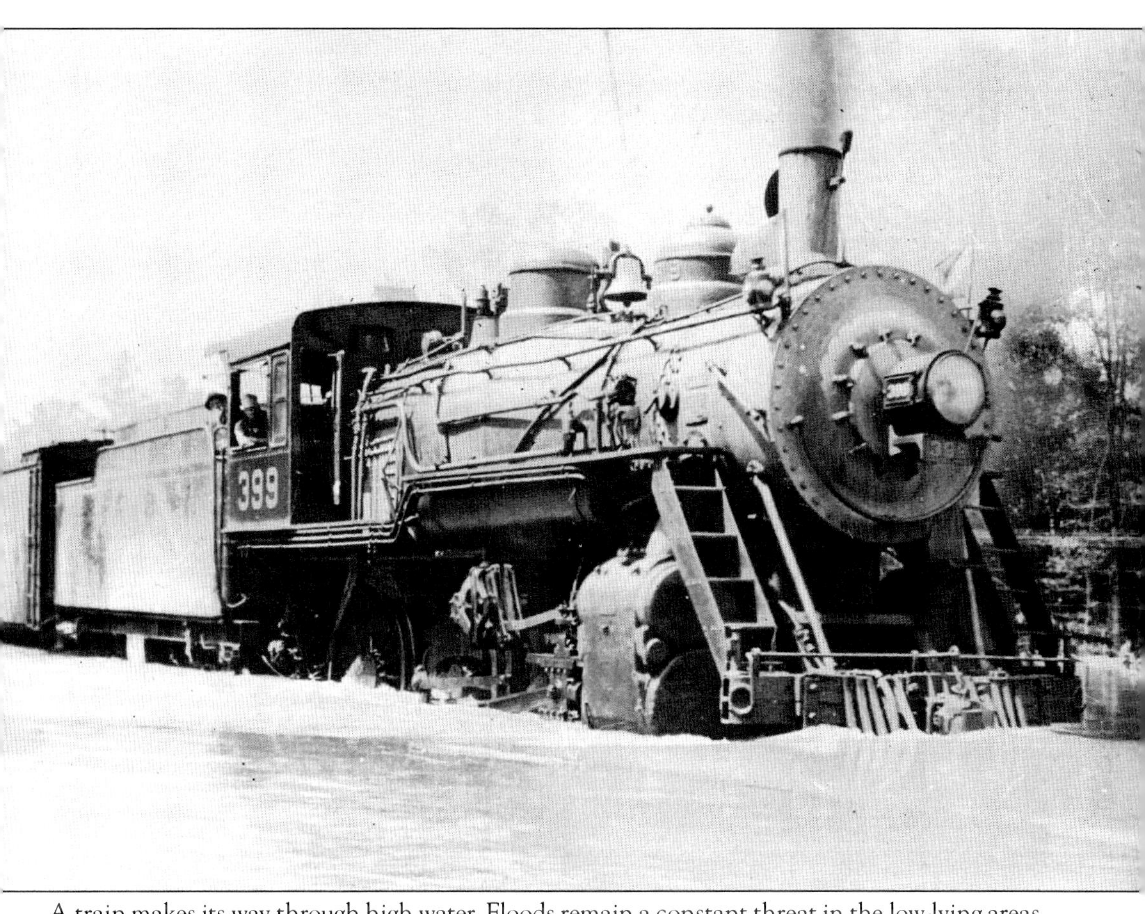

A train makes its way through high water. Floods remain a constant threat in the low-lying areas in and around Alexandria.

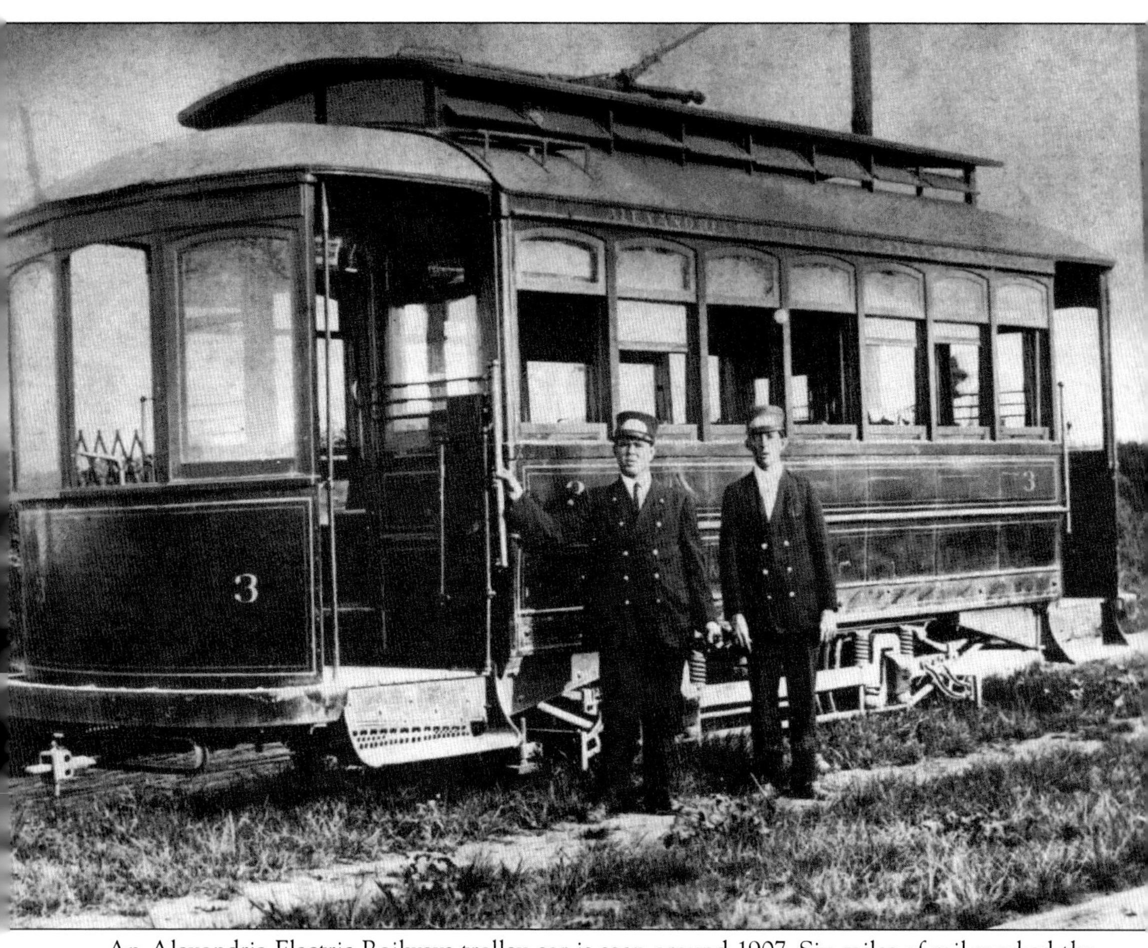

An Alexandria Electric Railways trolley car is seen around 1907. Six miles of rail marked the trolley line through Alexandria during the heyday of the electric line.

Five

Growing Pains

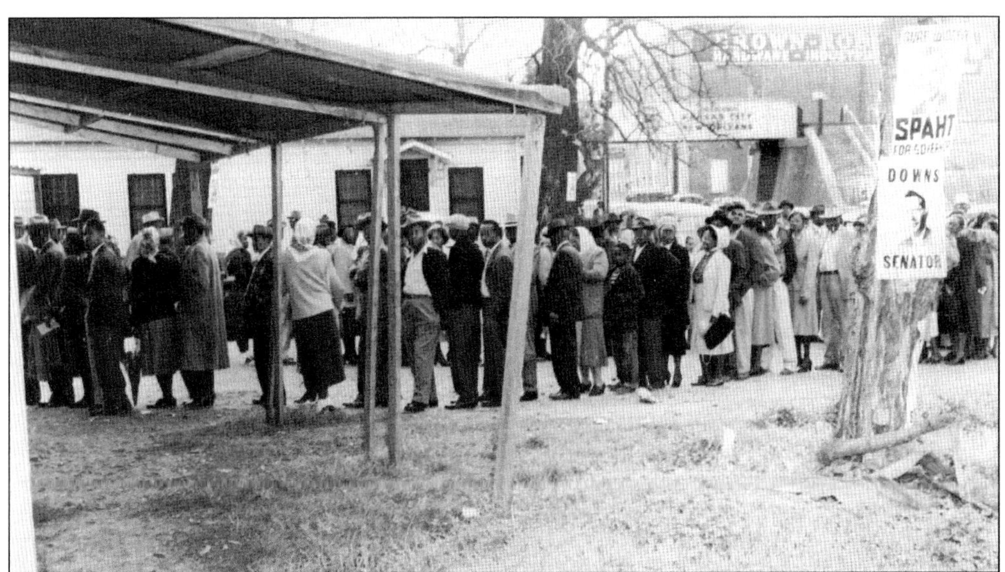

In 1953, African American residents wait with endless patience to cast their votes. For many, this was their first taste of enfranchisement since Reconstruction ended in 1877. In 1944, seventeen African Americans had registered to vote in Rapides Parish, the first to do so in 20 years.

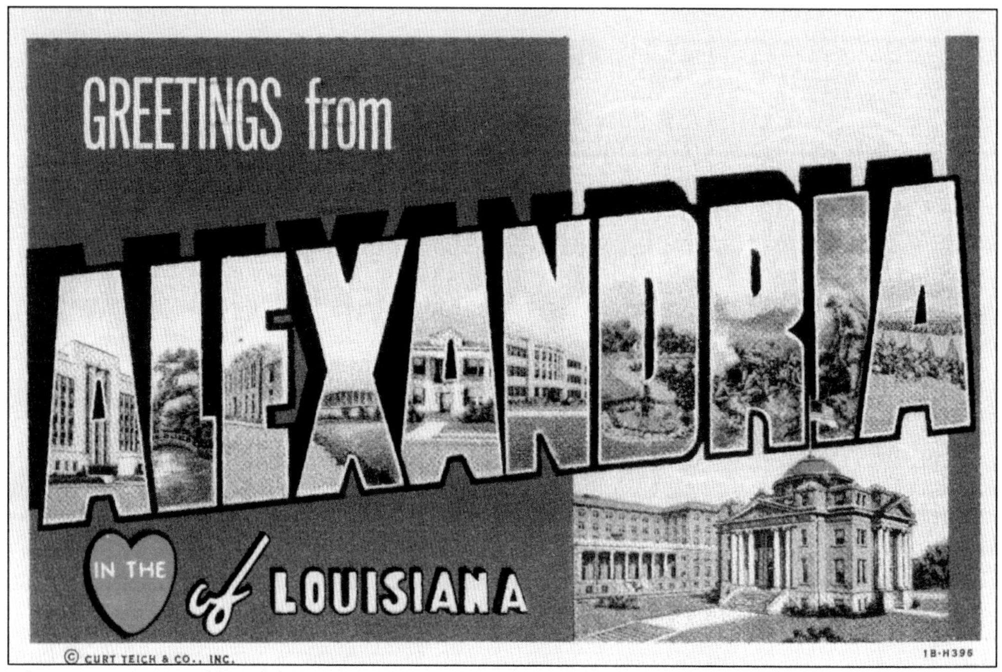

This 1940s postcard heralding Alexandria as the "Heart of Louisiana" shows the domed city hall, an iconic landmark for the town.

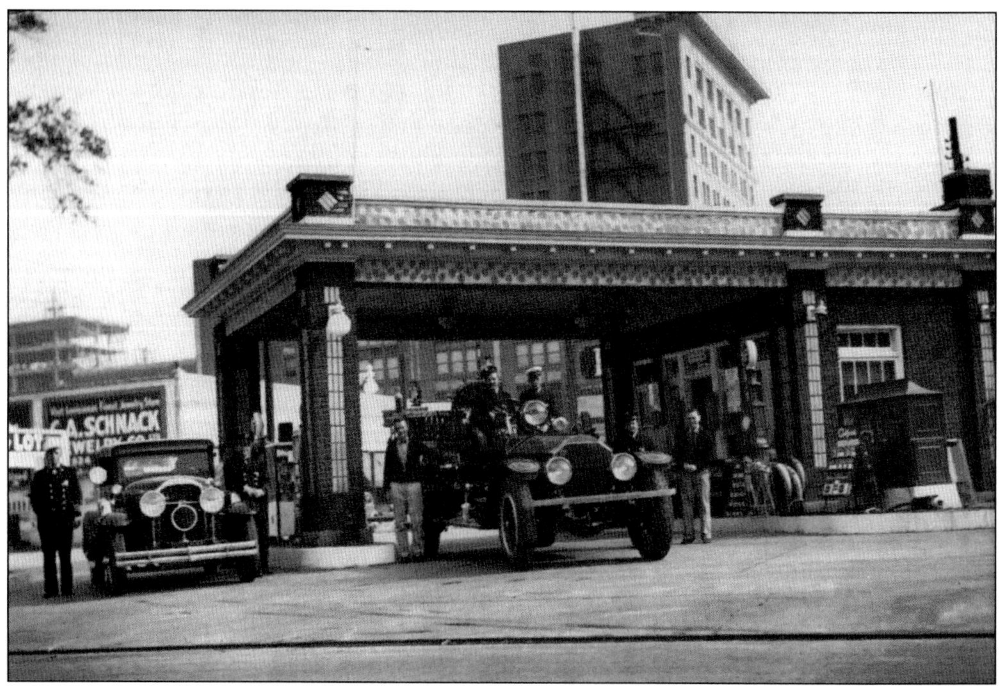

Leon Bergeron's Gulf filling station is seen on the corner of Fifth and Murray Streets in 1937. The fire department is filling up their latest truck.

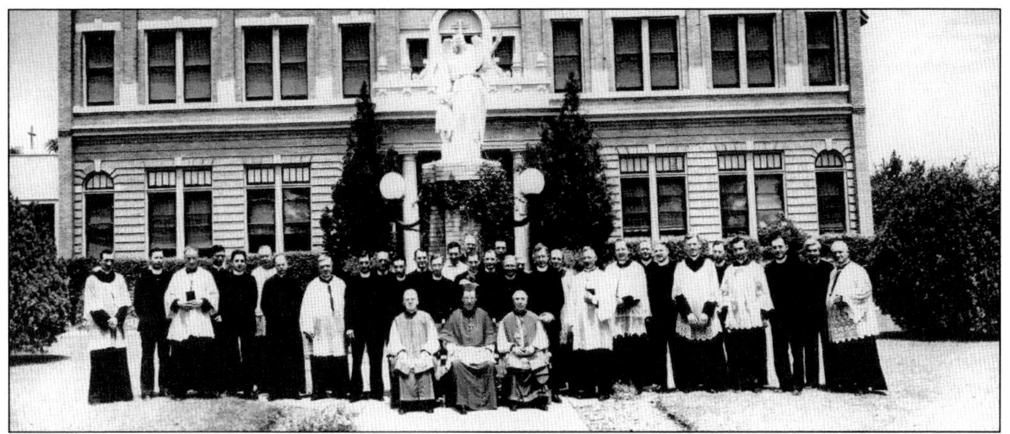

Pictured here are Bishop Daniel Desmond and priests of the Diocese of Alexandria commemorating Bishop Desmond's Silver Sacerdotal Jubilee. Bishop Desmond of Massachusetts was the first native-born American to lead the diocese (1936 to 1946). He is seen in front of the old Providence Academy on Elliott Street. The academy was an all-girls' high school run by the Sisters of Divine Providence. Providence and Menard Memorial, the boys' school, later merged to form Holy Savior Menard Central High School. The old Providence Academy building was torn down for the construction of the new Our Lady of Prompt Succor Church in 1976.

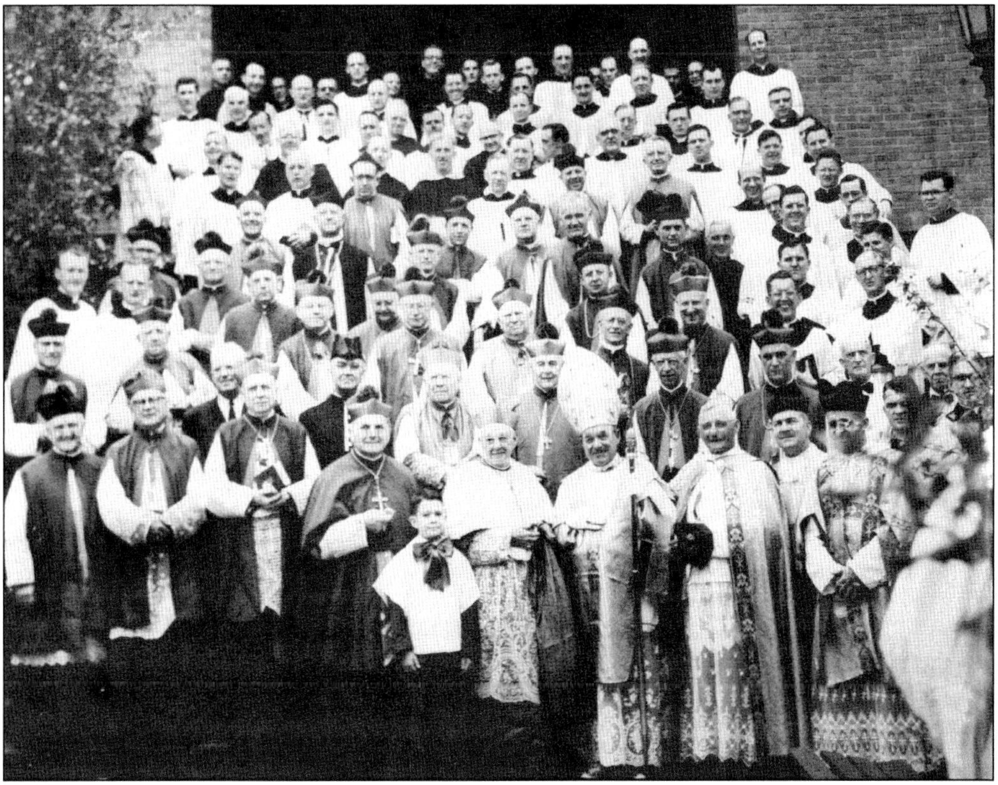

Bishop Greco (front row, seventh from the left) and Samuel Cardinal Stritch (front row, sixth from the left) of Chicago pose in 1953 with bishops and priests of the province on the steps of Victory Hall to commemorate the centennial of the founding of the Diocese of Natchitoches.

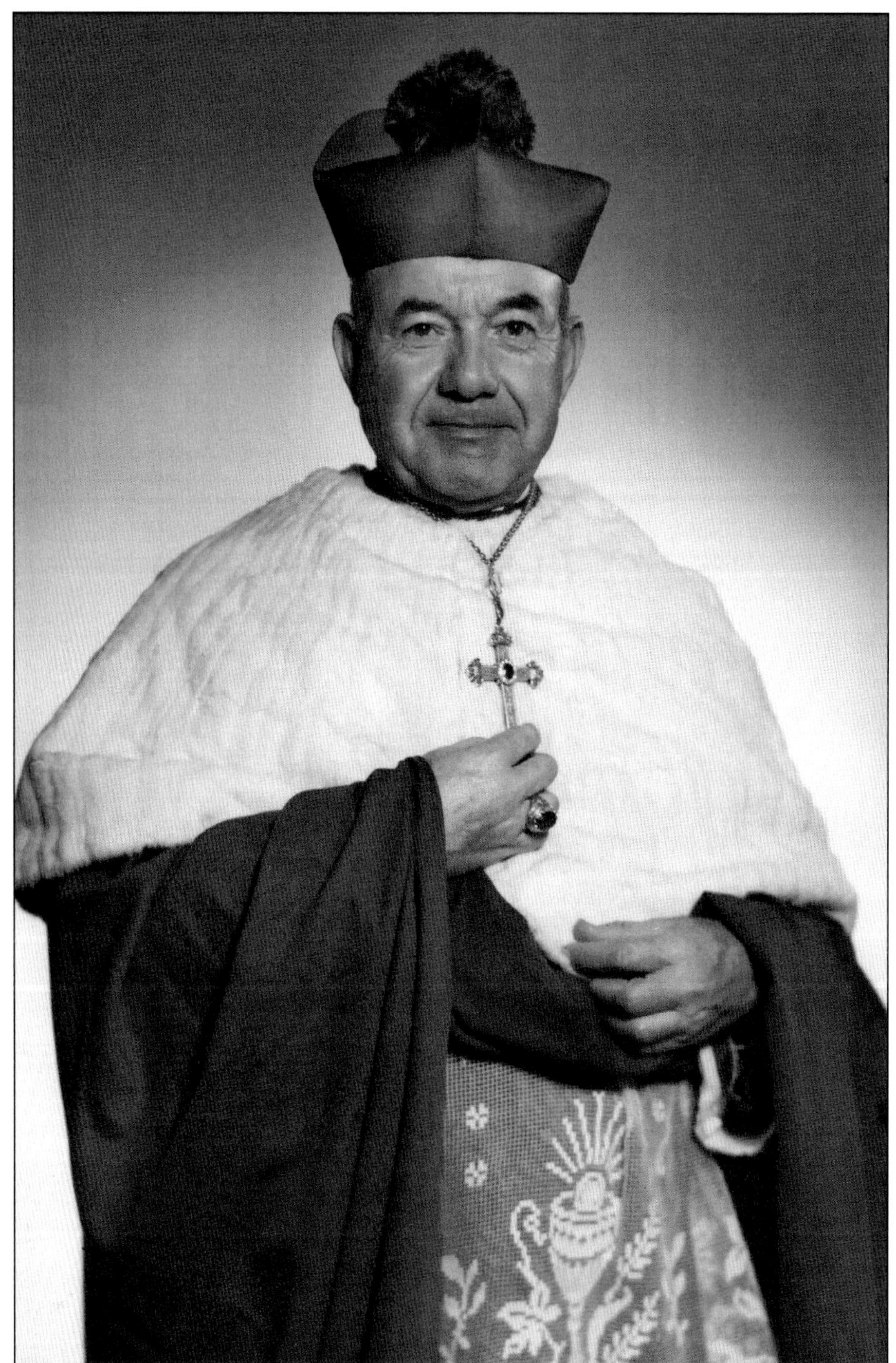

Bishop Charles Pascal Greco served as the sixth bishop of the Diocese of Alexandria, from 1946 until his retirement in 1977. Bishop Greco was responsible for the vast expansion of the diocese and the creation of new parishes in the city. He spearheaded the construction of St. Frances Cabrini Hospital on Masonic Drive and established St. Mary's Training School for mentally handicapped children.

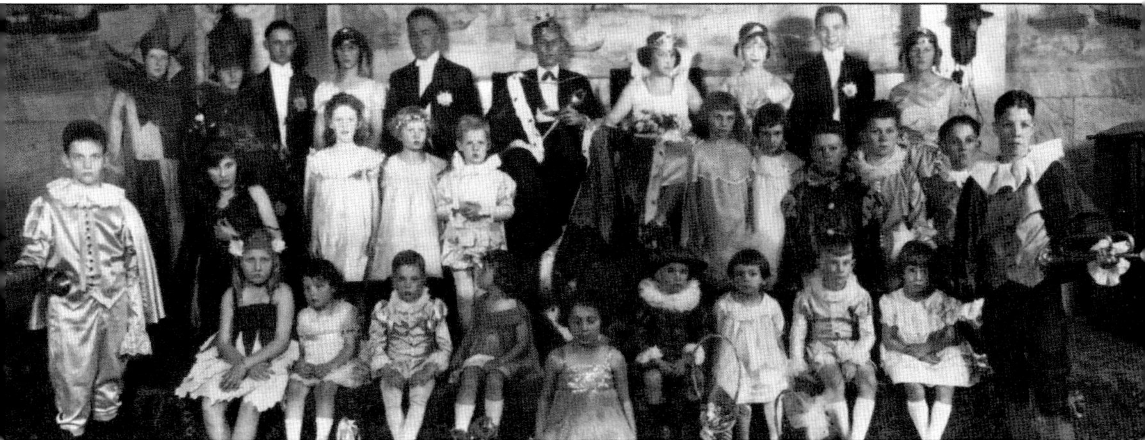

Bolton High School's Mardi Gras Carnival Court of 1922 poses for the camera. Organized by Miss Kilpatrick, the festivities were held in the Venetian Room of the Hotel Bentley. The king was Lynwood Bond, and Minnie Wilson served as queen.

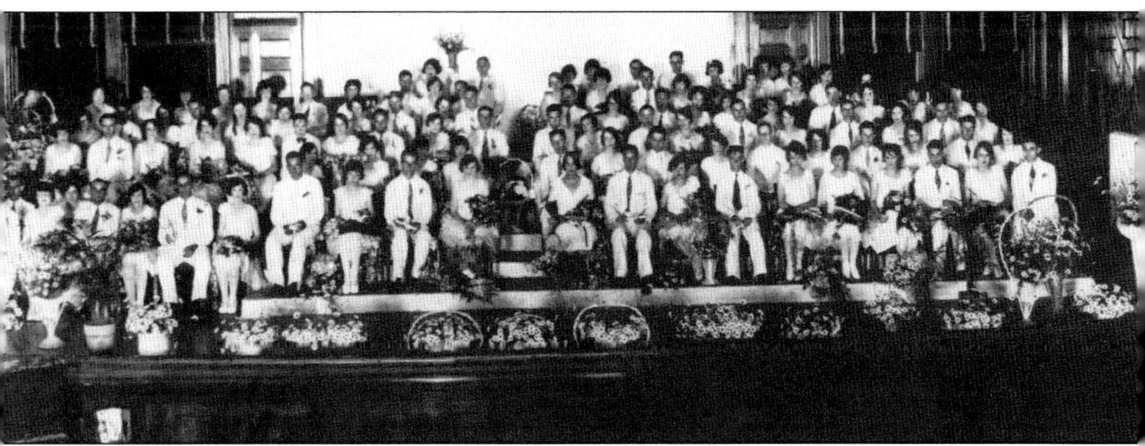

Bolton High graduates of the class of 1927 are pictured here. These students were the first to graduate from the new Bolton High School building on Vance Avenue, which was completed in 1926.

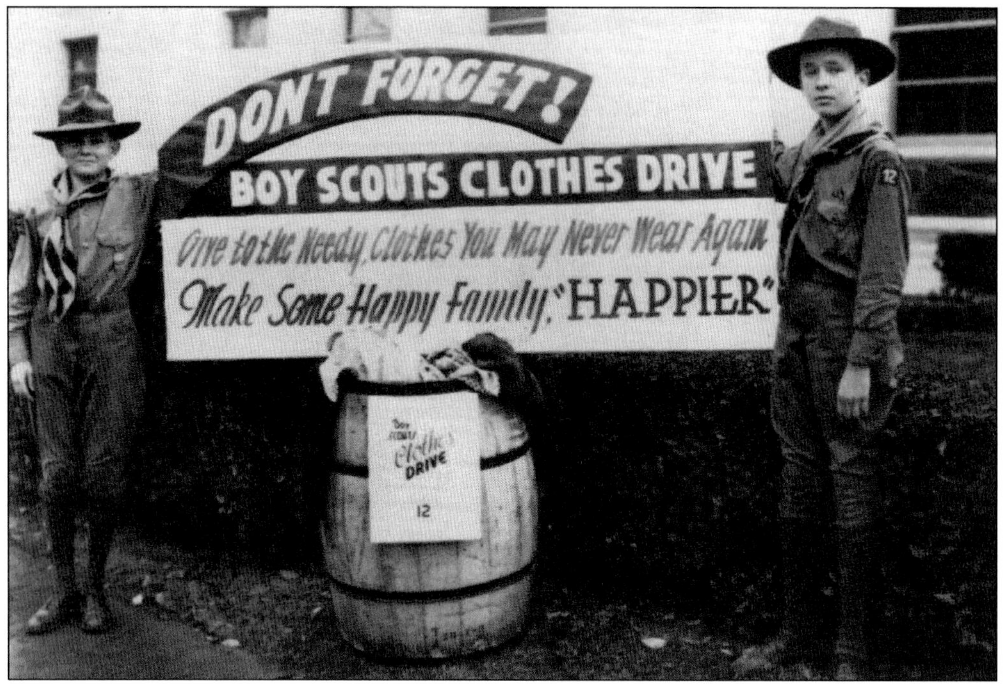

Boy Scouts from Troop 12 conduct a clothing drive during the World War II. Scouting in central Louisiana was largely supported by civic organizations and churches, leading to the establishment of Attakapas Council for central Louisiana.

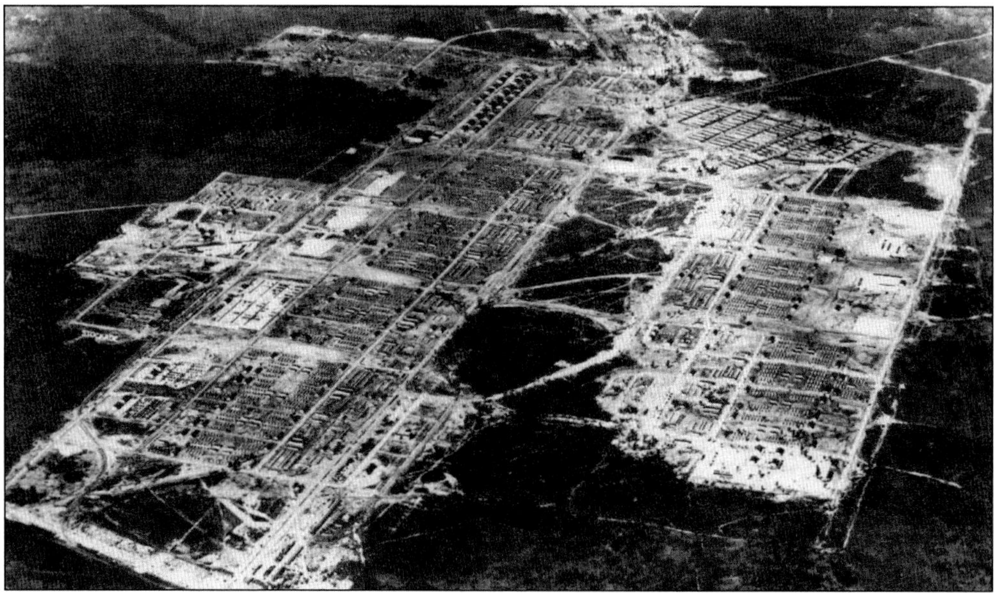

This is a 1941 aerial view of Camp Claiborne, one of the many camps constructed around Alexandria for Army maneuvers in 1940. Over 90,000 servicemen were accommodated in the area, and Rapides Parish became one of the largest troop training areas in the South after Pearl Harbor. Over 500,000 men would undergo training here before the invasion of Normandy in 1944.

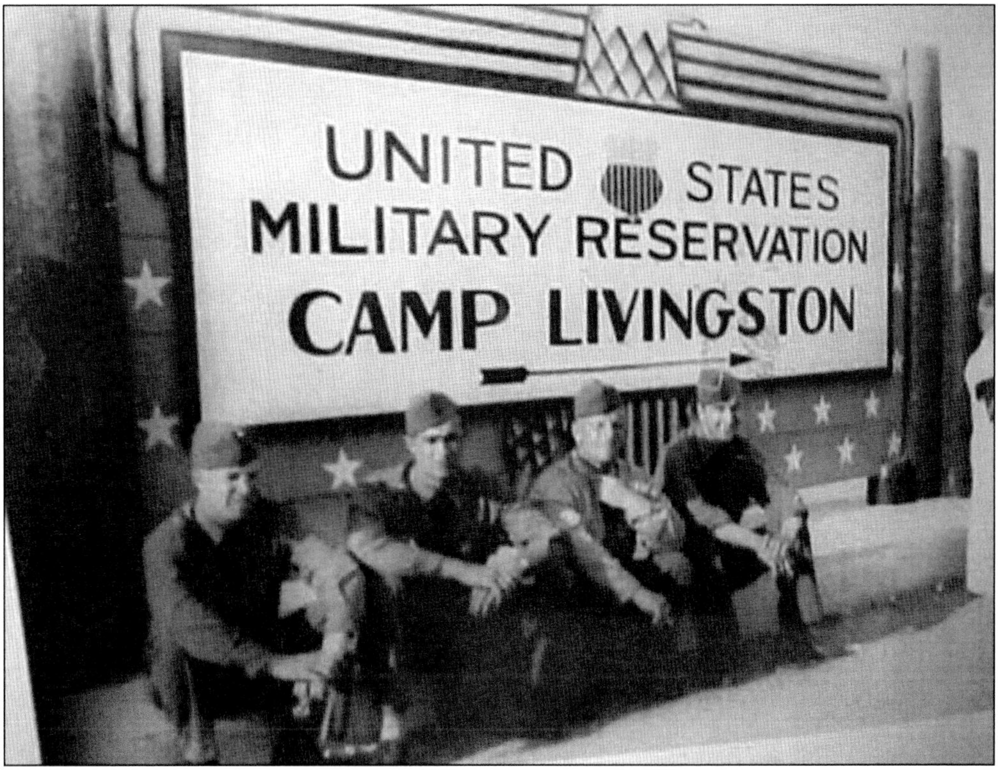

Camp Livingston was one of many established by the Army as training centers after the 1940 Army maneuvers. As the troops departed for war zones, they were replaced by prisoners of war. By June 1942, Japanese prisoners were being interred at Camp Livingston. In 1943, German and Italian prisoners appeared in the fields as farm laborers.

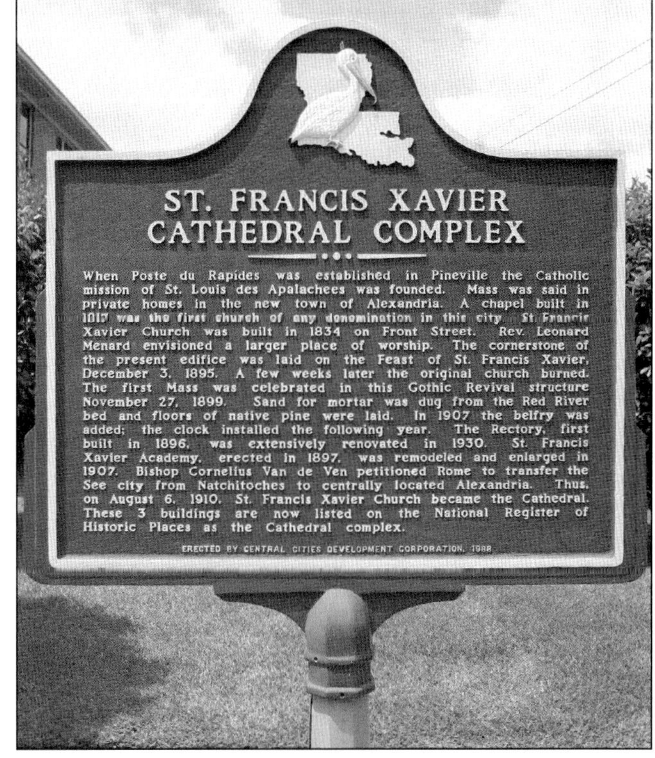

Thanks to the efforts of Msgr. Julius Walle, chancellor of the diocese and rector of the cathedral in Alexandria from 1971 to 1985, and his staff, the cathedral church of St. Francis Xavier was placed in the National Register of Historic Places in 1980. Later, the entire complex was added to the register, as shown by the state marker on Fourth Street.

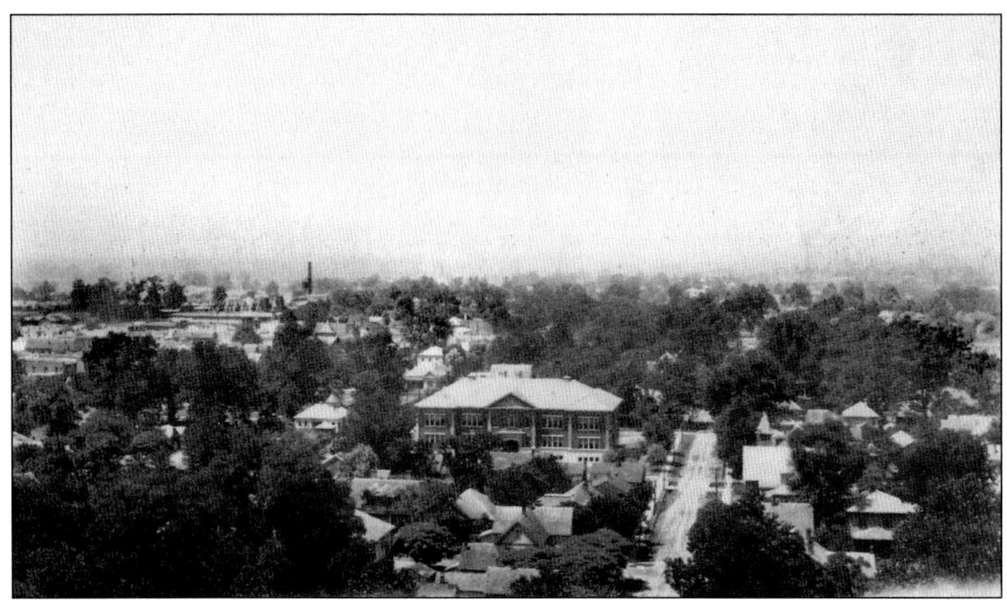

Pictured are the Old West End High School and Bolton Avenue in the first decade of the 20th century. Commercial expansion in the 1950s and 1960s turned the avenue from a prime residential area into a business district.

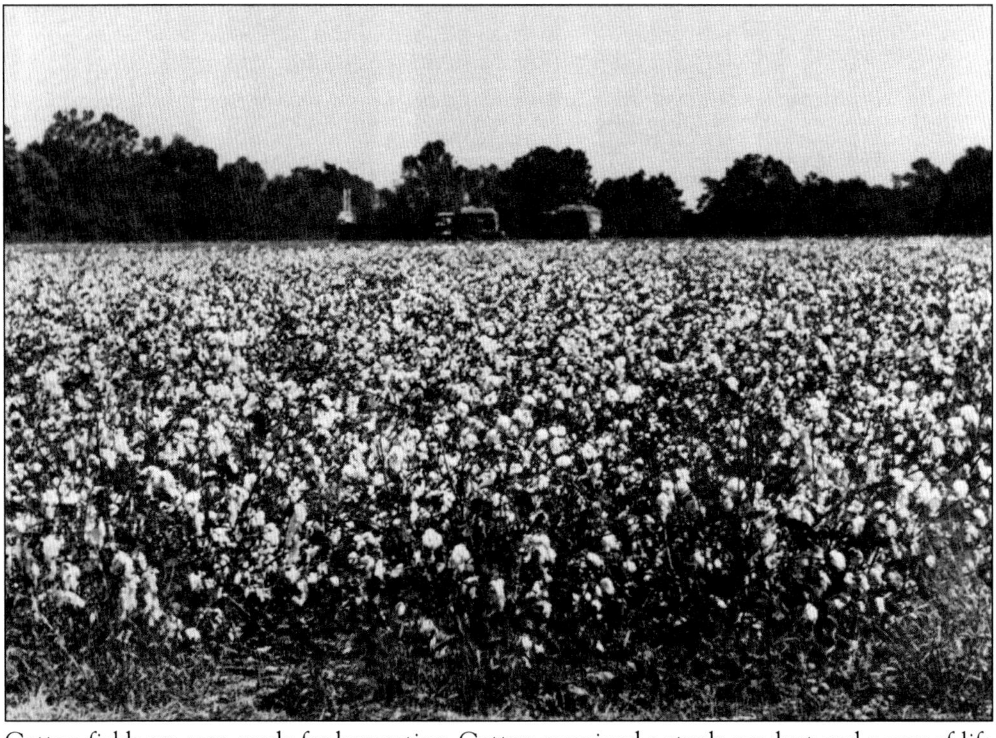

Cotton fields are seen ready for harvesting. Cotton remained a staple product and a way of life for many in Rapides Parish well into the 20th century.

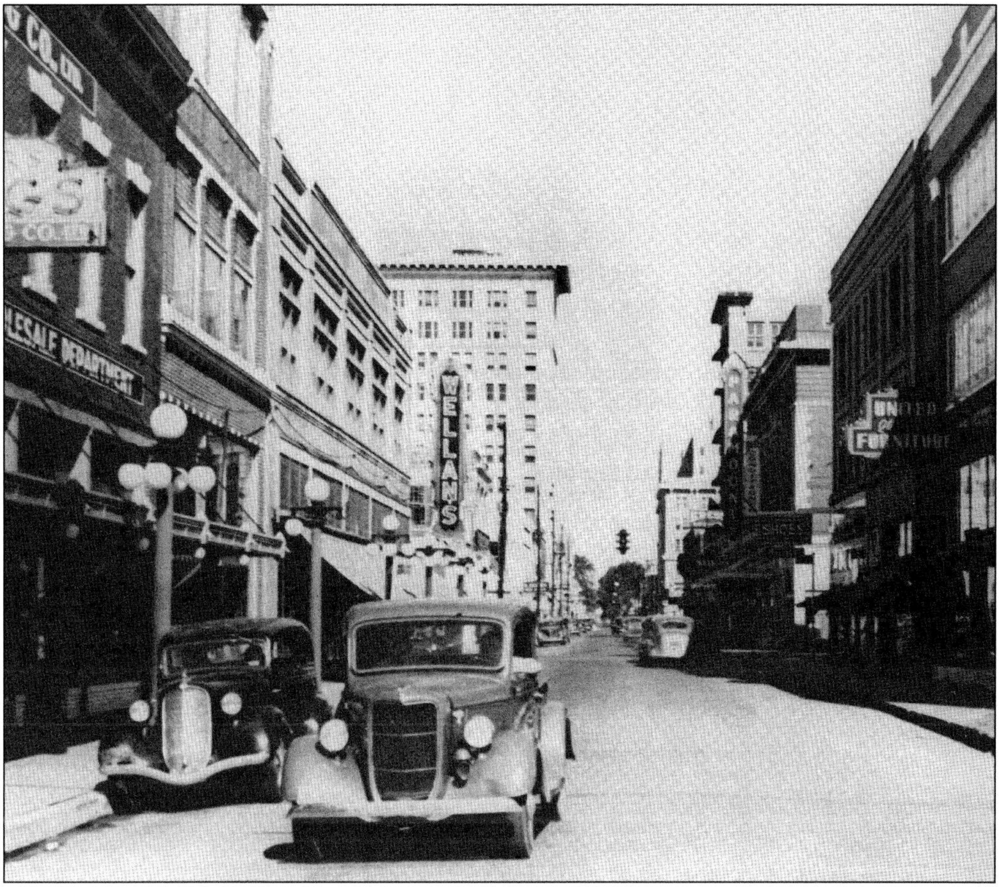

Wellan's Department Store in downtown Alexandria is pictured in the 1940s. One of the many department stores that moved out to the new suburban Alexandria on Masonic Drive in the 1970s, Wellan's was a downtown hot spot for decades.

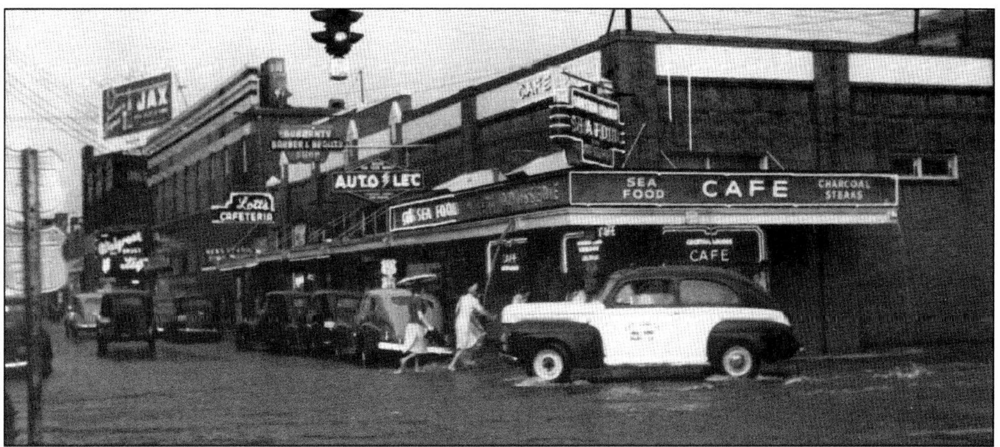

Heavy rains tax Alexandria's drainage and sewer system. This photograph shows the corner of Fourth and Murray Streets in the 1940s.

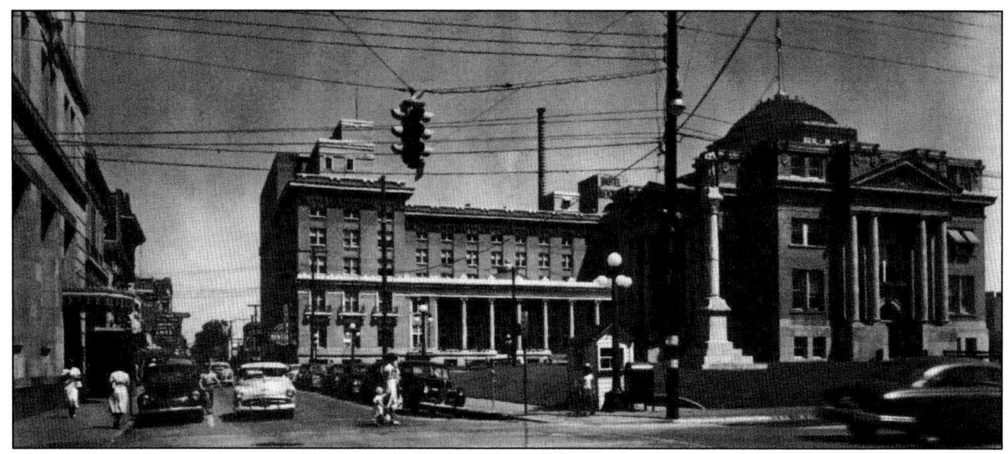

The Hotel Bentley and city hall, with its Confederate Soldiers' Monument, dominate the scene in the 1950s. Today, only the Bentley remains as Alexandria's premier classical Beaux Arts–style structure.

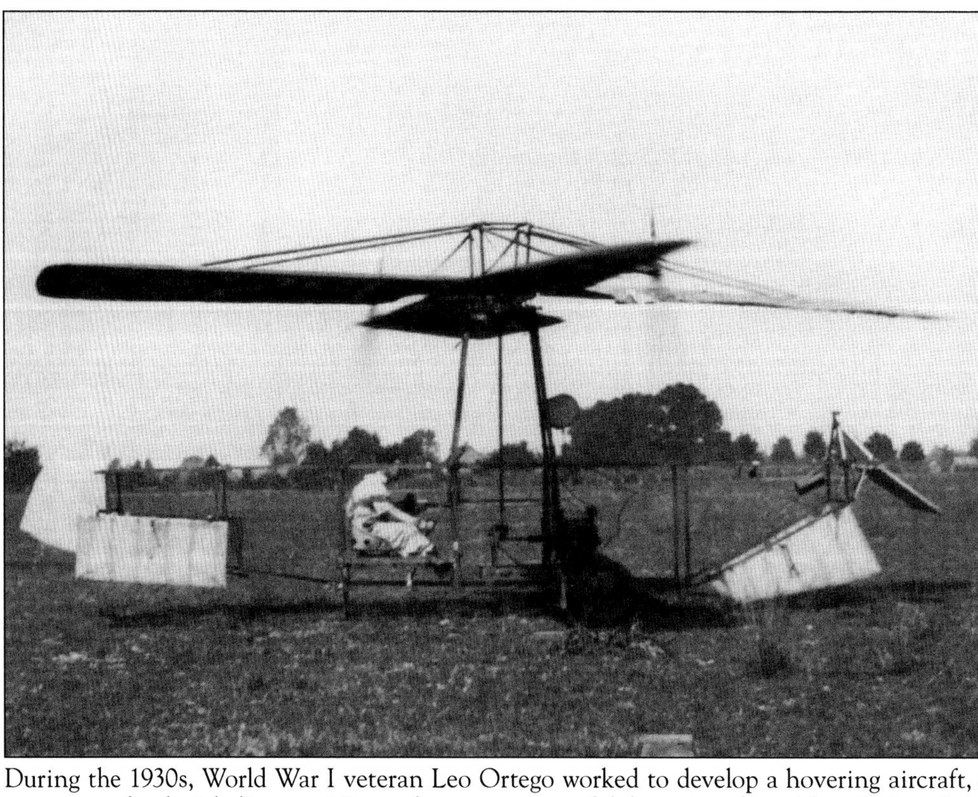

During the 1930s, World War I veteran Leo Ortego worked to develop a hovering aircraft, a prototype of today's helicopter. His machine was successful, hovering about 10 to 15 feet above the ground, and an early patent was given to this Alexandria tinkerer.

Leo Ortego's Alexandria workshop is pictured here. After the outbreak of the World War II, Ortego went west to work for the Ryan Aeronautical Company in California, where he died in 1947.

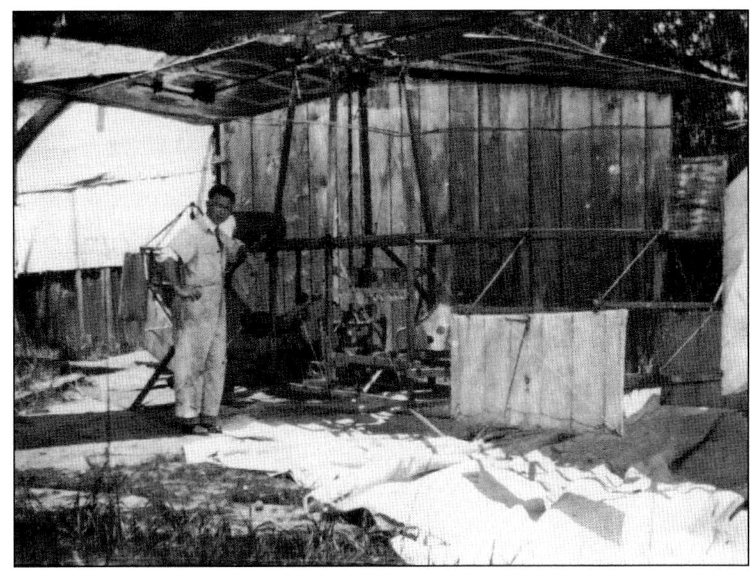

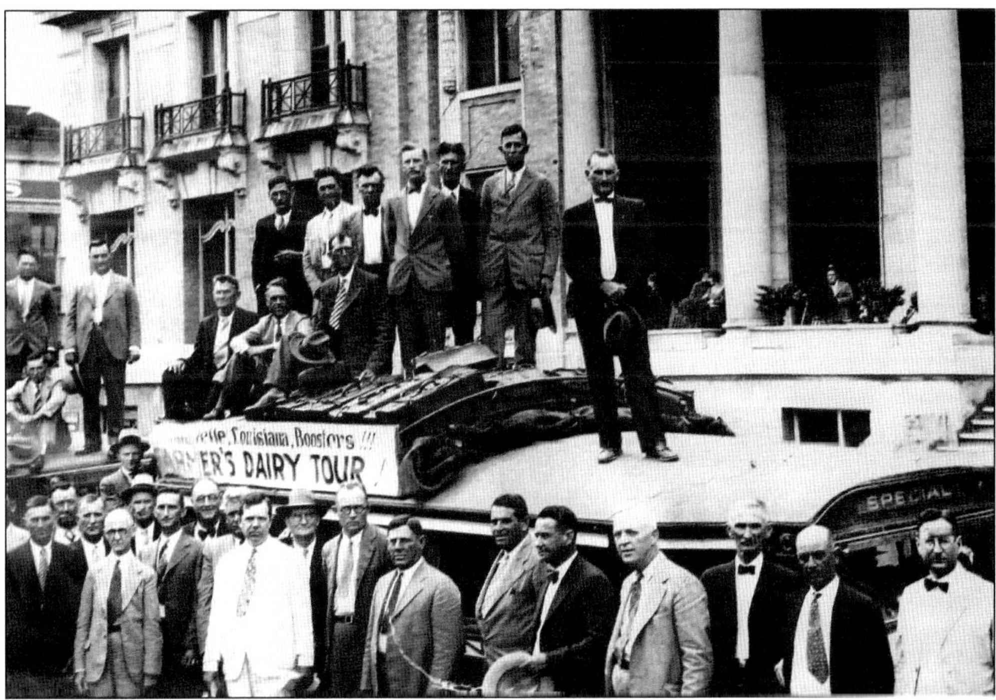

Huey Long, the constant campaigner, launched his second run for the governor's seat at a rally held in the Bolton High School auditorium in 1928. The editors of the *Alexandria Daily Town Talk*, a paper Long called the "Alexandria Bladder," turned against the Long machine and joined in the call for his impeachment in 1929. At a later rally in front of the Hotel Bentley in 1933, Long was forced from the steps and pelted with eggs and rotten vegetables by a hostile crowd. Infuriated, Long removed Alexandria's entire administration and threatened to revoke the city's charter.

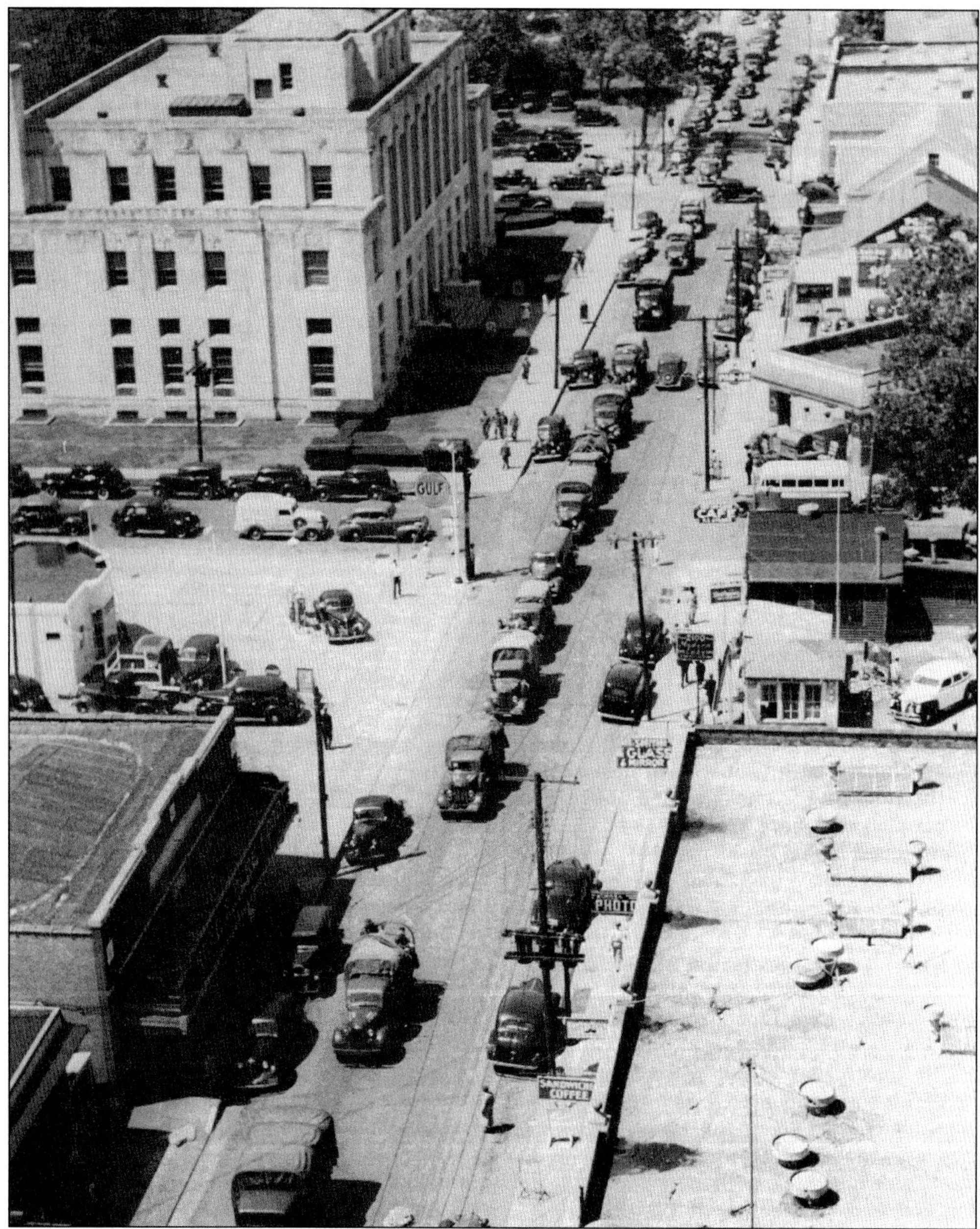

This was a familiar scene in Alexandria during the 1940s. A military convey pushes down Murray Street in front of the new post office building. After the death of Huey Long in 1936, federal patronage began to flow into Louisiana. The new Art Deco–style post office and the new Rapides Parish Courthouse were built during this period.

Downtown Alexandria was the scene of many military parades, as seen here in 1941. With Camps Livingston, Claiborne, and Beauregard in the near vicinity and Fort Polk less than 100 miles to the west, Alexandria was at the very heart of the war effort.

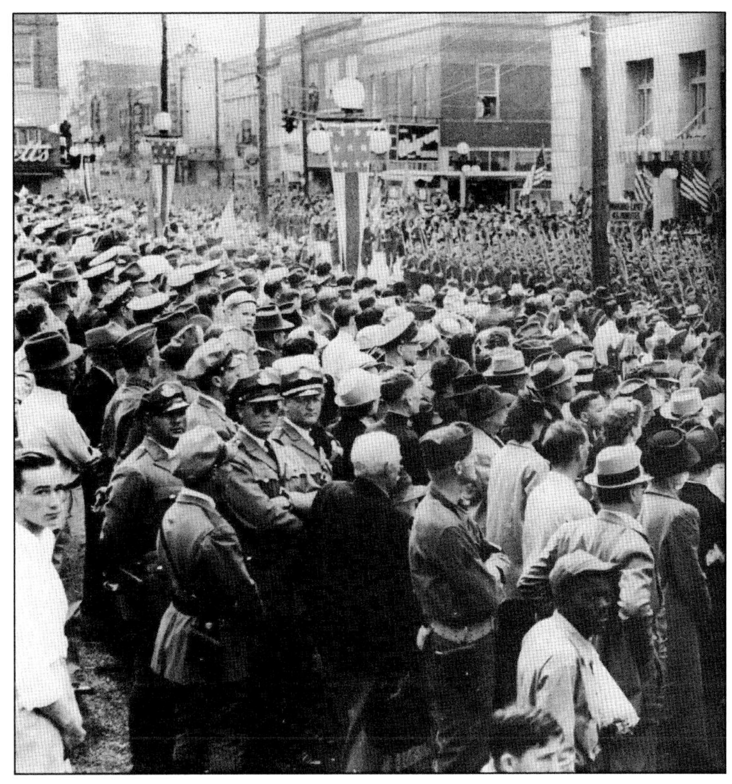

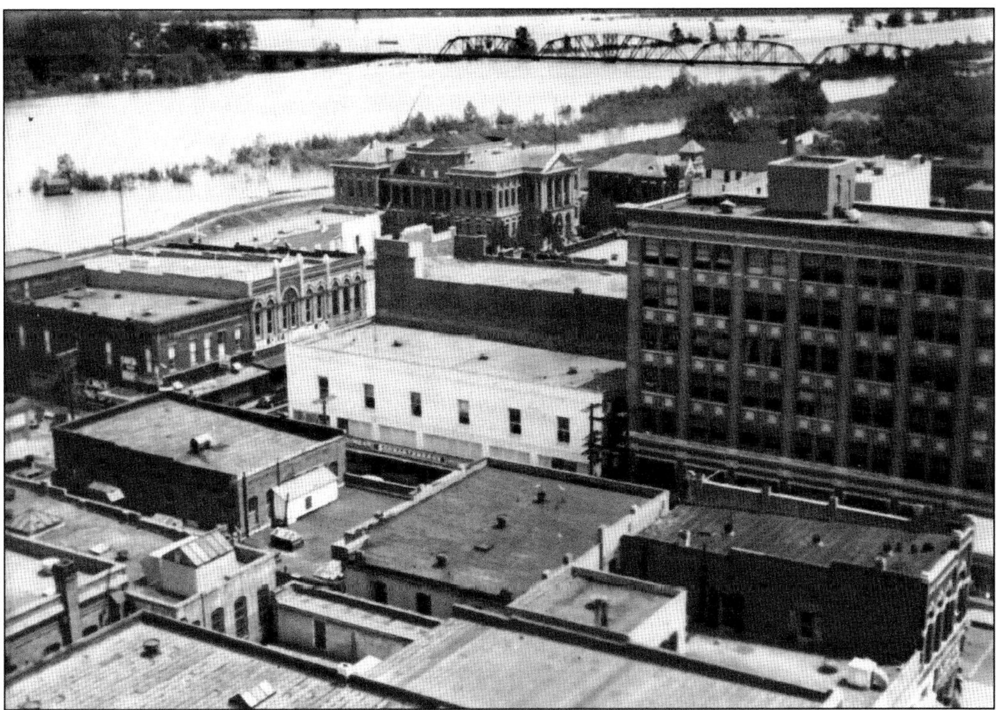

This is an aerial view of high water in the Red River. The old parish courthouse is visible together with the Commercial Building, Alexandria's first "skyscraper."

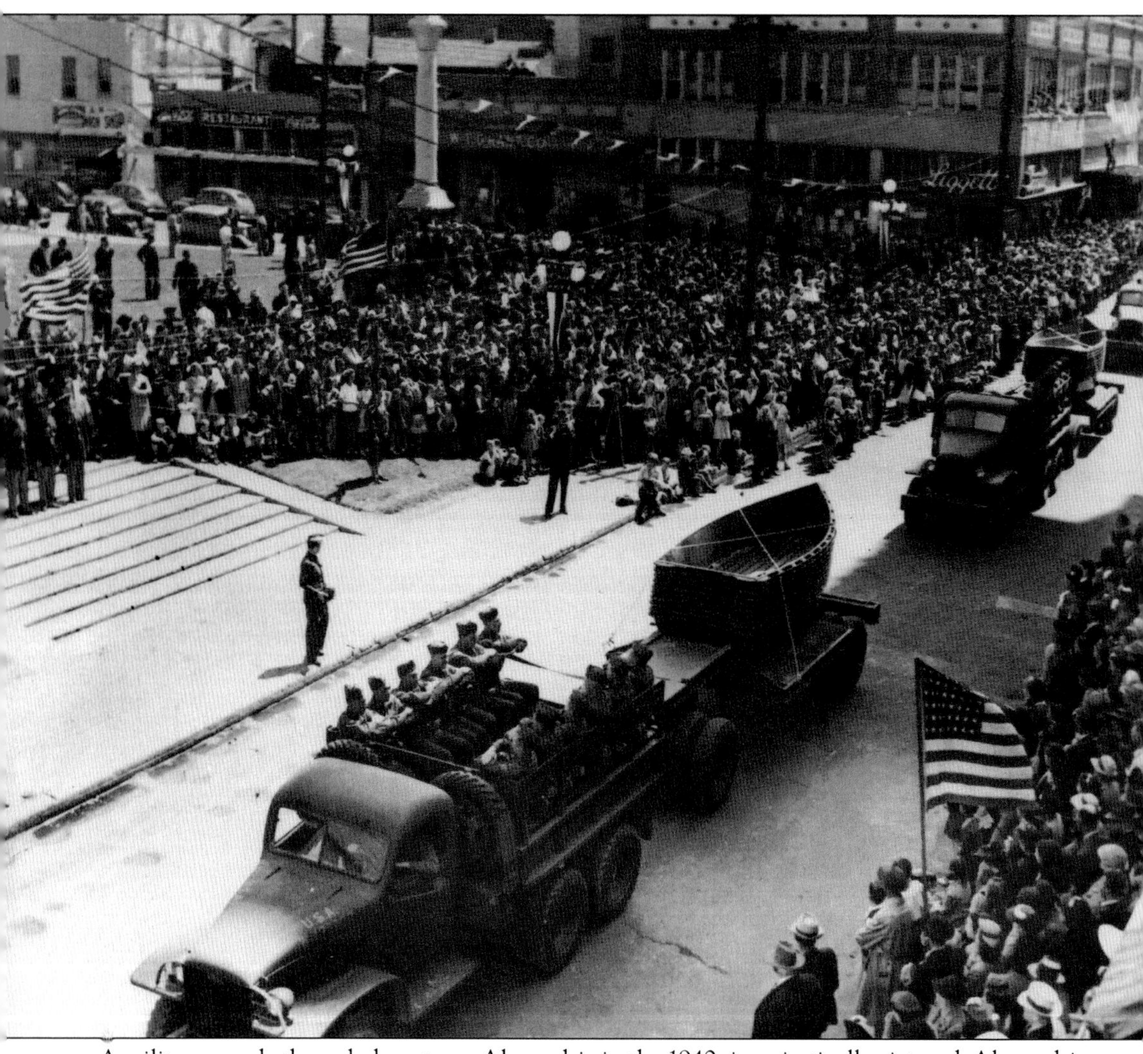

A military parade through downtown Alexandria in the 1940s is majestically pictured. Alexandria experienced great growth and tension during the war years, when the town's population was more than double because of troops and their families.

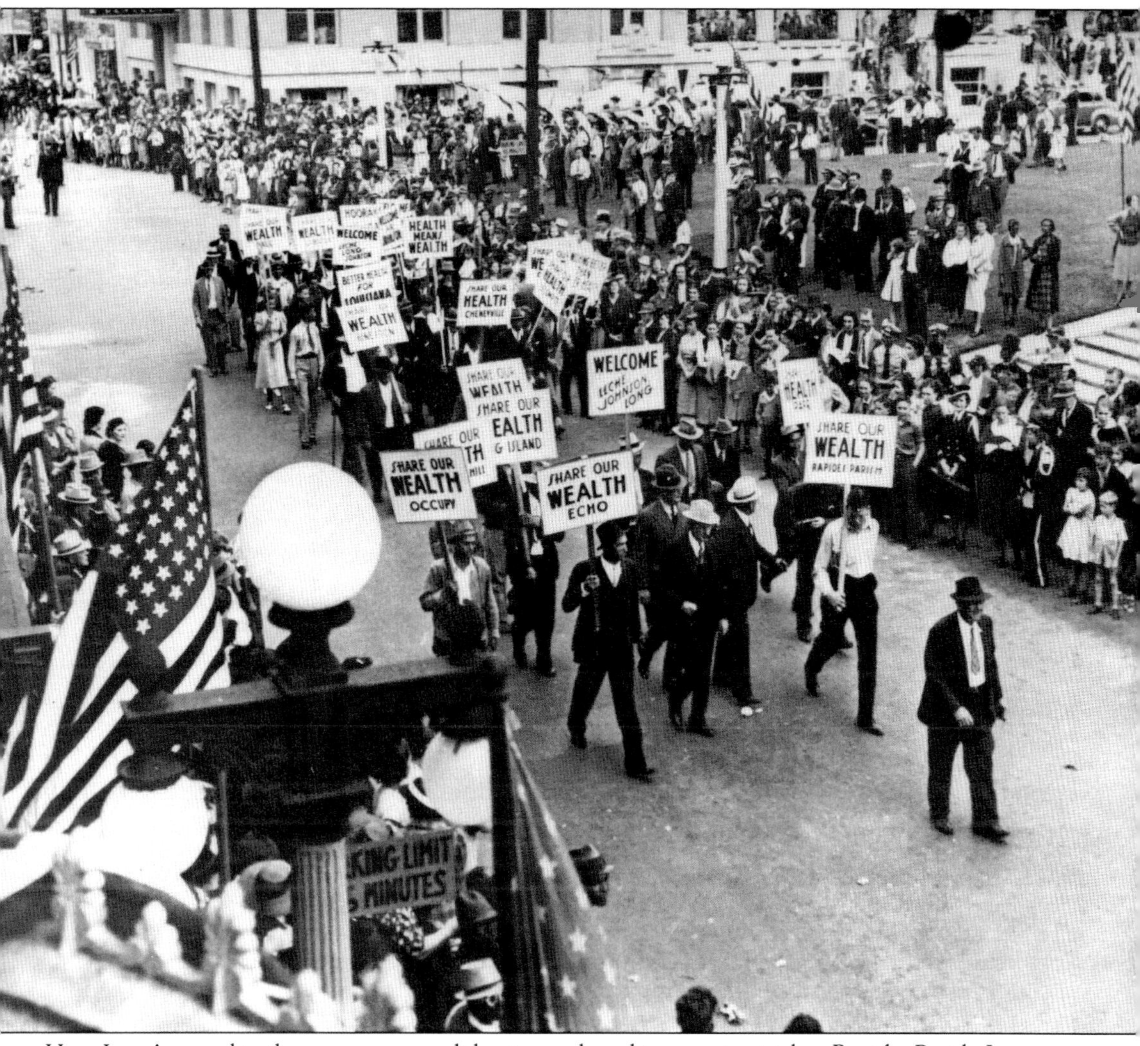

Huey Long's appeal to the common man did not go unheard in poverty-stricken Rapides Parish. Long supporters march here in 1931 in a local "Share Our Wealth" rally in downtown Alexandria.

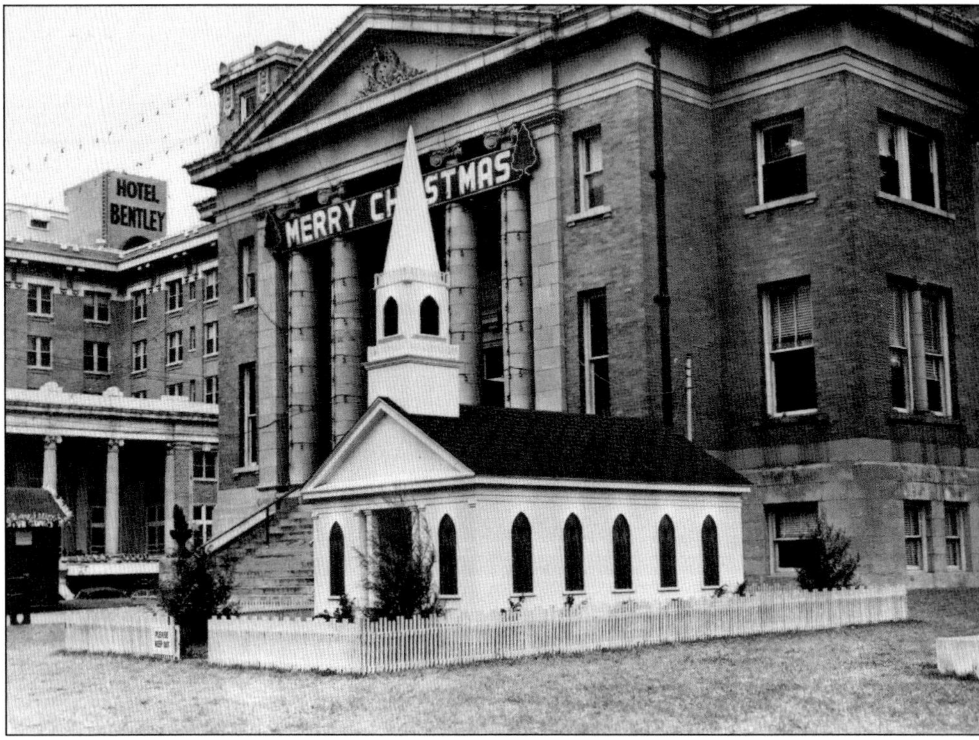

The Christmas decorations are pictured on the City Hall Square. The annual lighting was a local tradition for years.

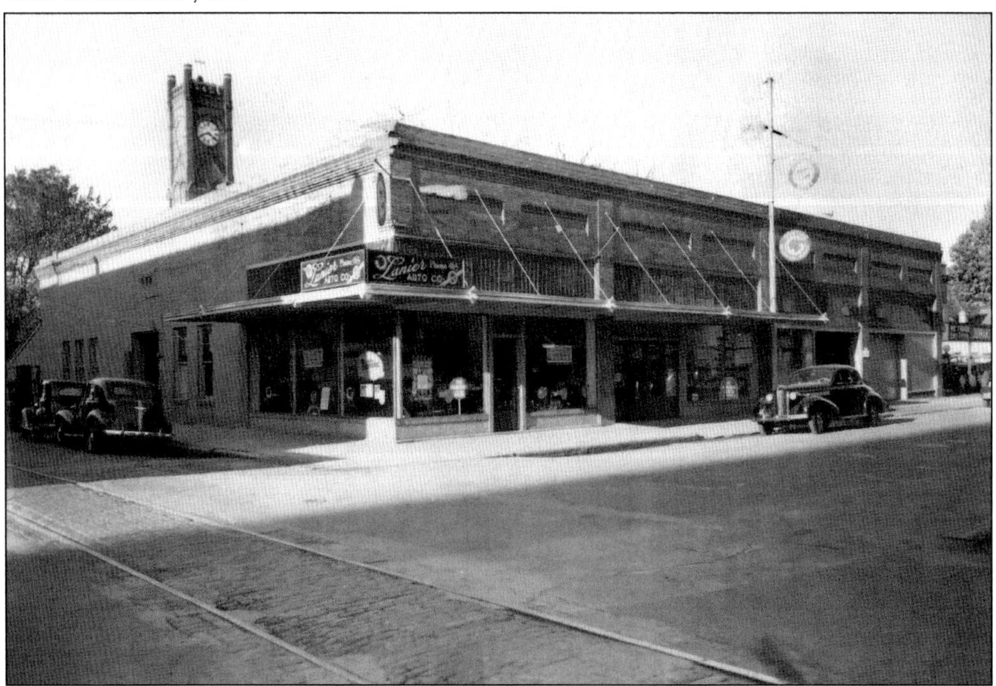

The Lanier Automobile Company is seen on Third and Beauregard Streets in this 1938 photograph. It was one of the first local car dealerships specializing in luxury automobiles.

Pictured here is Hotel Bentley's elegant lobby in the 1940s as it was seen by George Marshall, George S. Patton, Dwight Eisenhower, and Henry Kissinger. The structure is currently owned by Mike Jenkins, who is planning a complete restoration of the grand hotel.

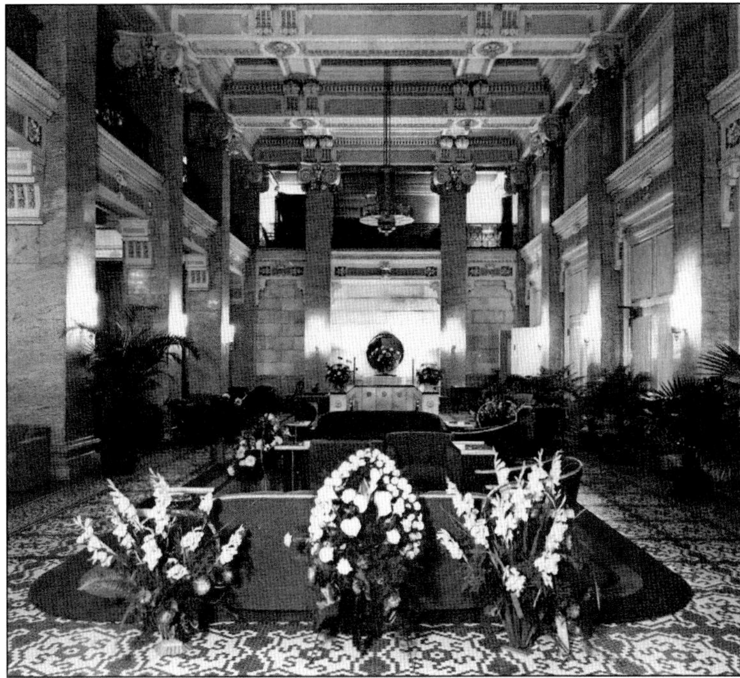

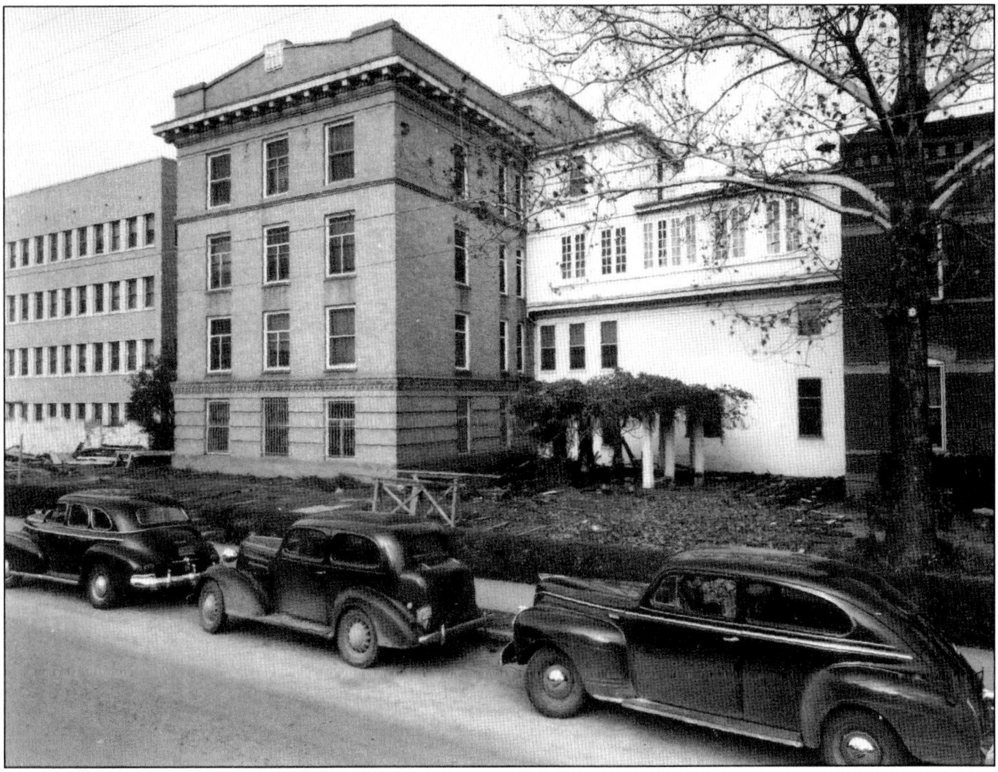

A c. 1948 image captures Baptist Hospital (now Rapides Regional Medical Center). The building on the right is the original brick Alexandria Sanitarium. The center structure is the expansion added after 1917. The structure on the far left was added in 1941.

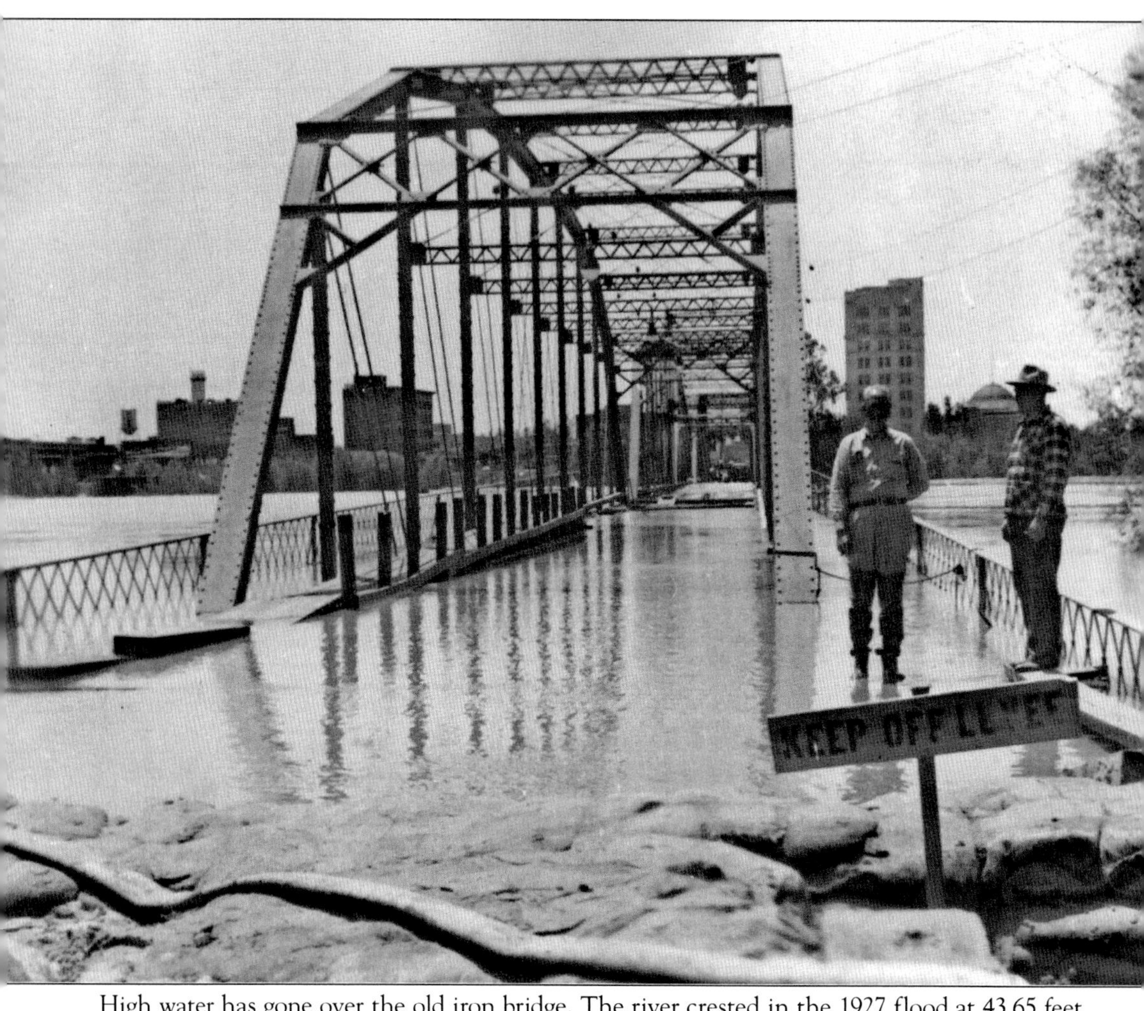

High water has gone over the old iron bridge. The river crested in the 1927 flood at 43.65 feet. The levees at Alexandria held, but they broke just south of the town, inundating the bottomlands with six to seven feet of water spread over 425,000 acres.

The Alexandria Fire Department is ready for a parade. Downtown Alexandria still hosts a variety of parades, including the various local krewes during the Mardi Gras season.

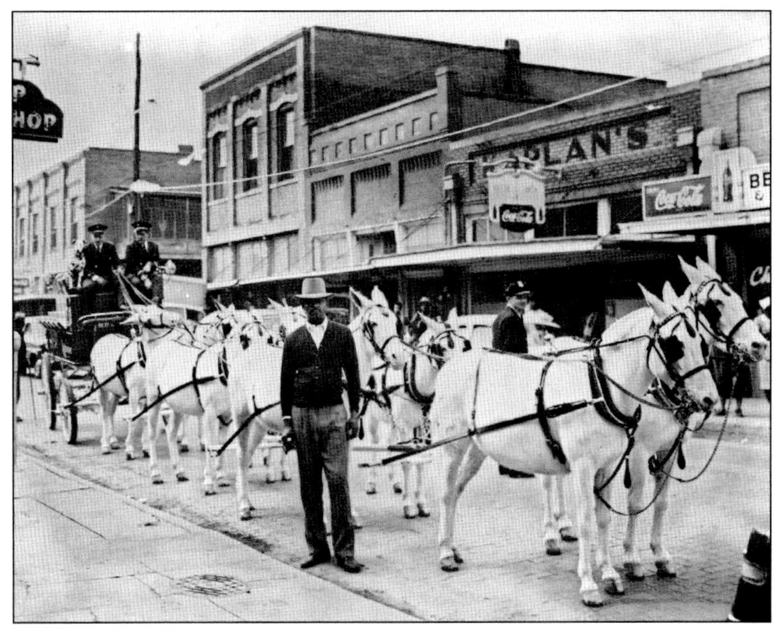

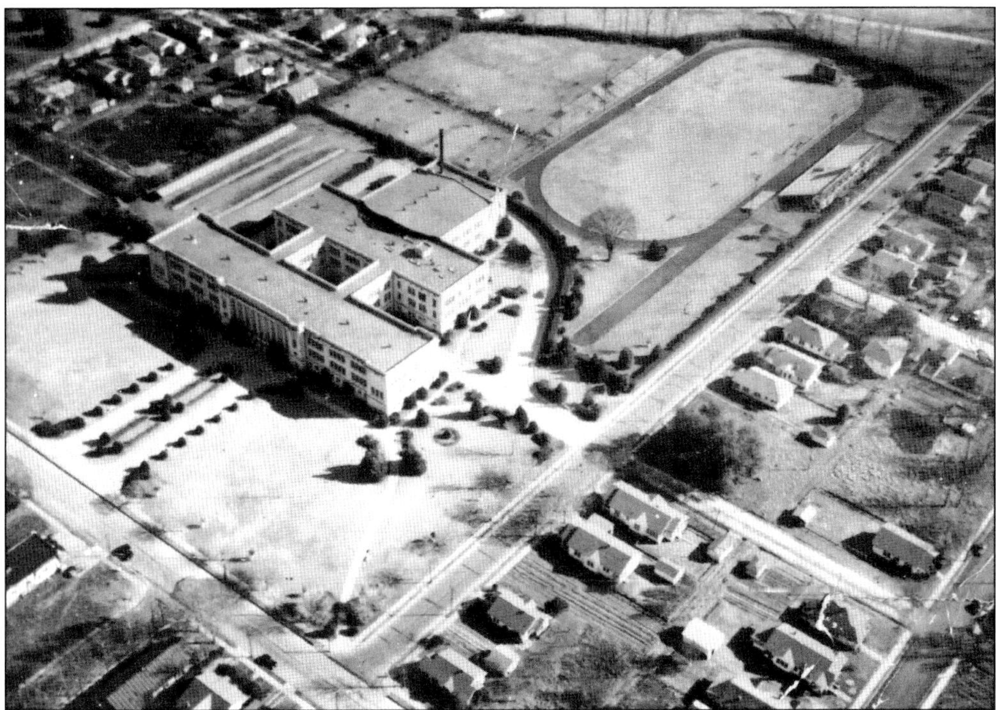

Bolton High School was built on Vance Avenue in 1926. Bolton served as the only high school for white students in Alexandria until the construction of Alexandria Senior High School in 1969.

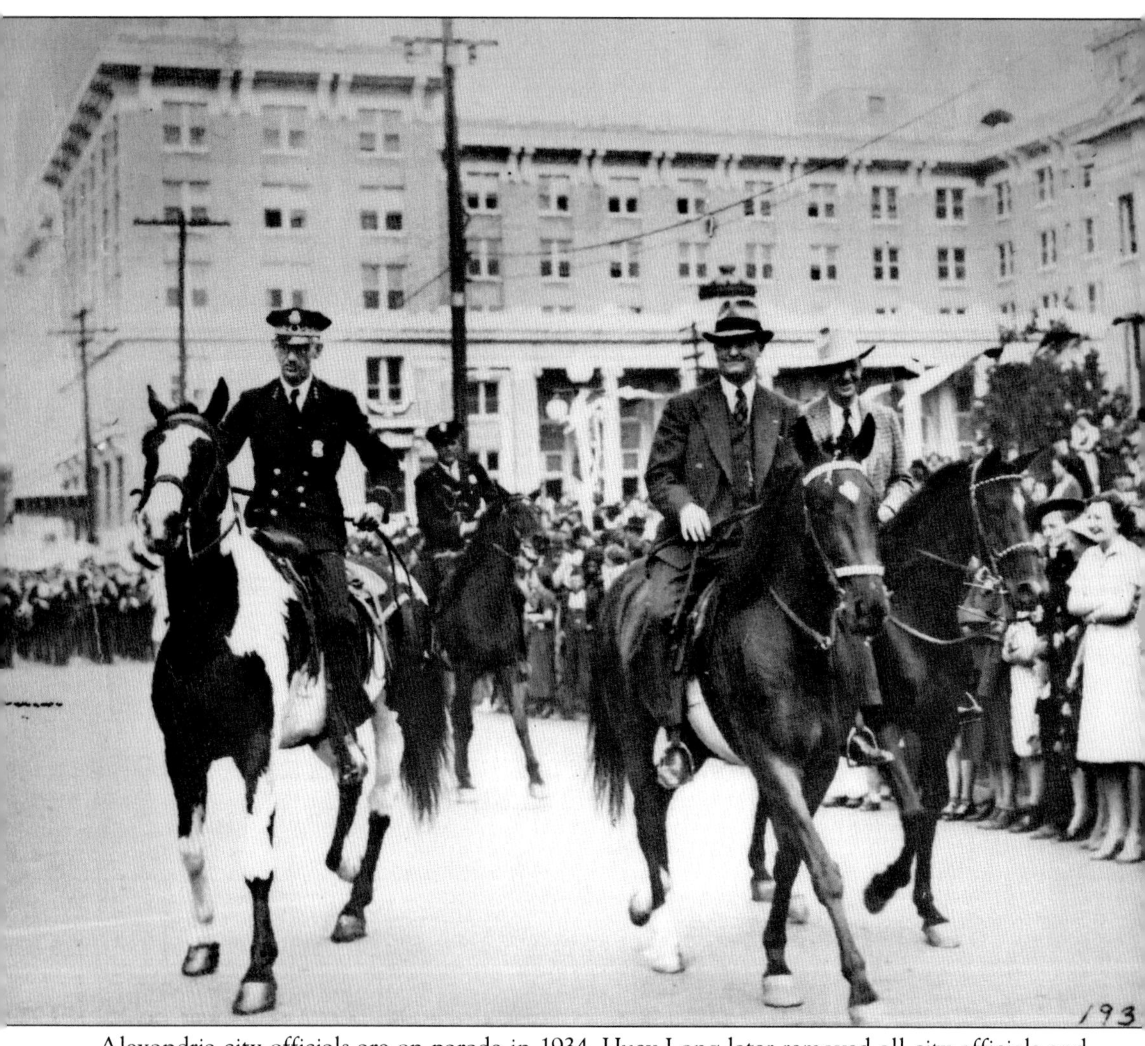

Alexandria city officials are on parade in 1934. Huey Long later removed all city officials and threatened to revoke the city's charter before his death in 1936.

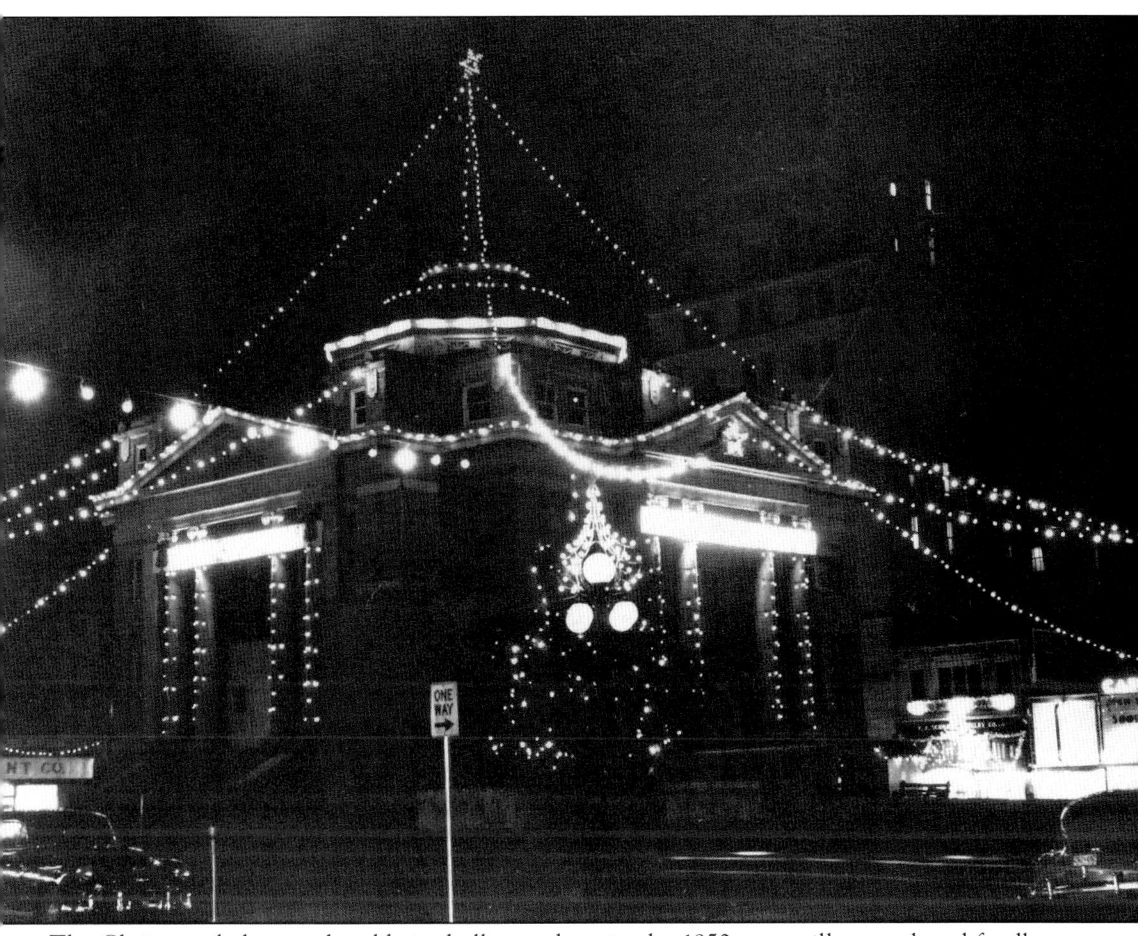

The Christmas lights on the old city hall, seen here in the 1950s, are still remembered fondly by many.

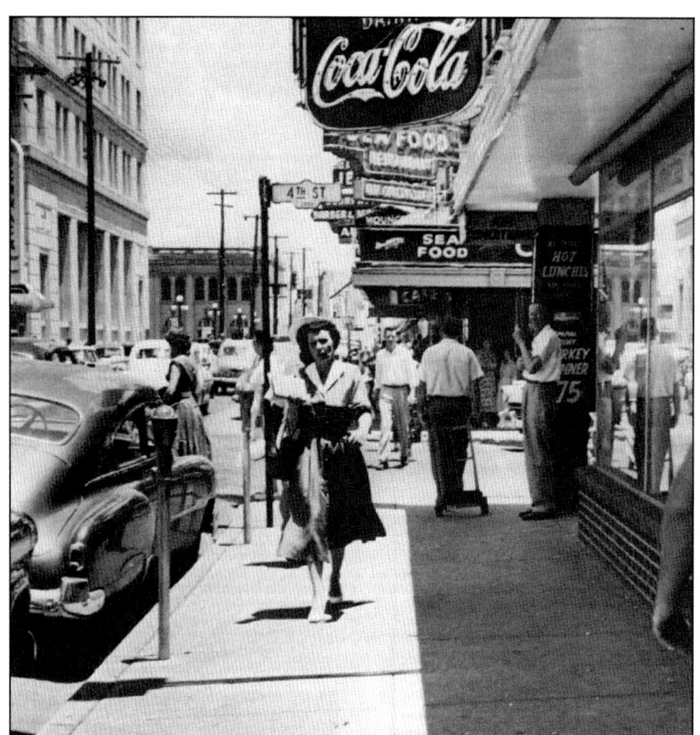

This is Murray Street at Fourth Street in 1955. Streets in Alexandria are numbered starting from the river.

Here is St. Francis Xavier Elementary School, with the old academy building and the brick annex addition. The addition has since been torn down.

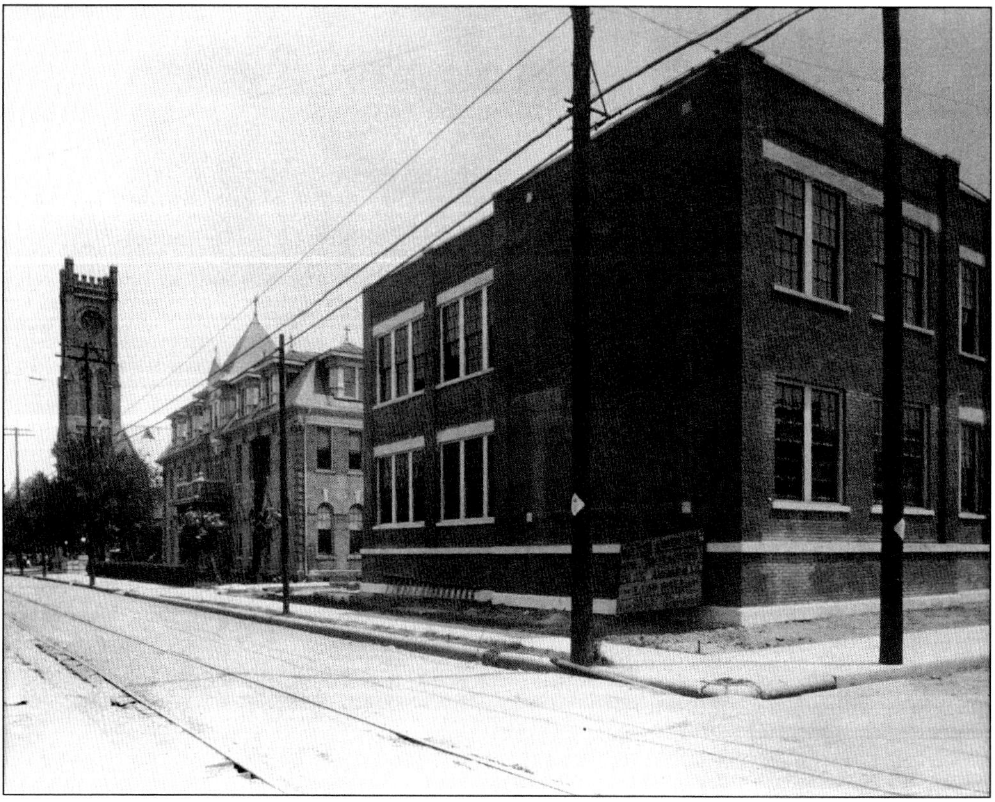

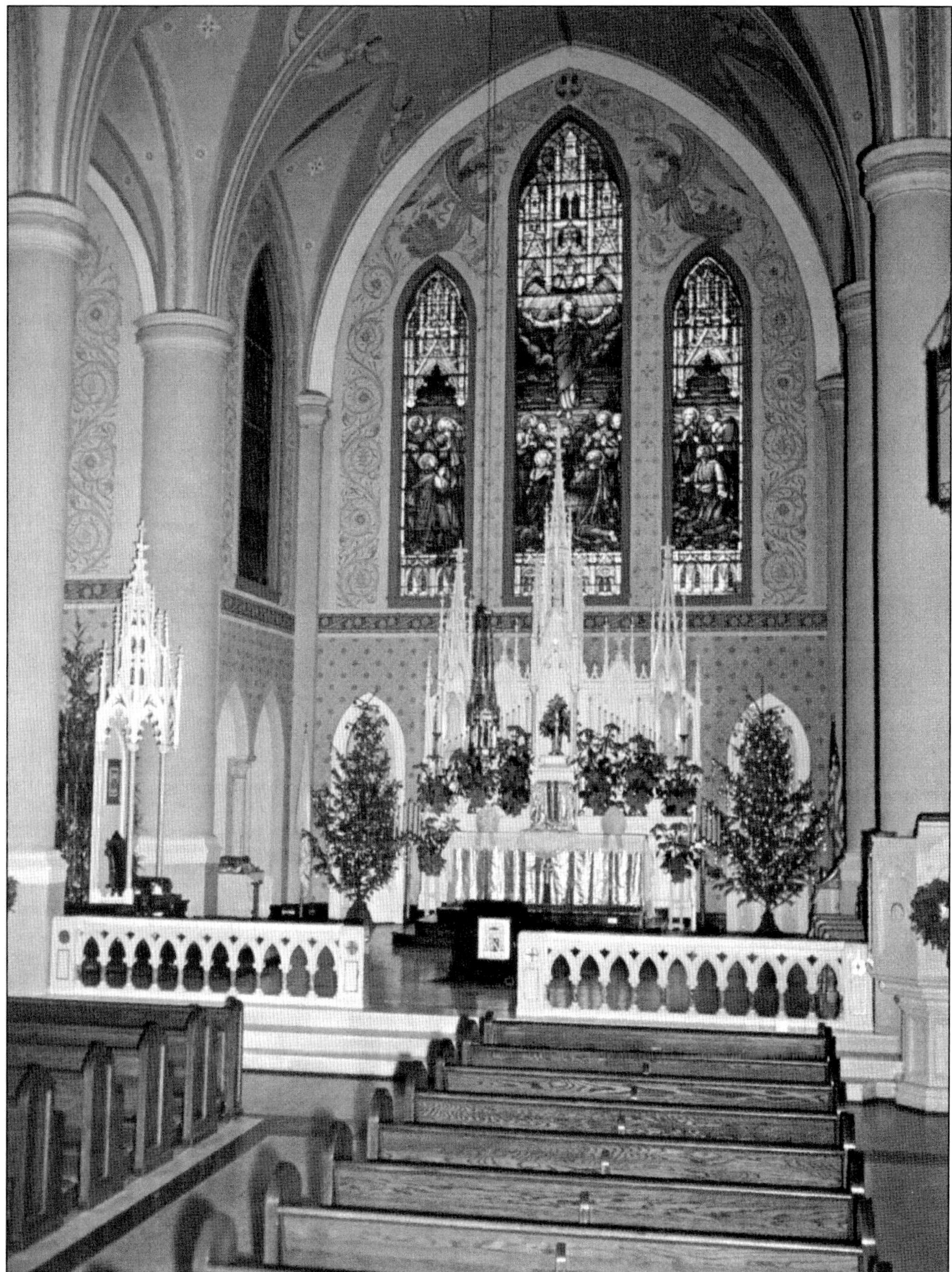

This is an interior view of the cathedral church in the 1960s during Bishop Greco's time. Work on the interior decoration of the cathedral continued through the Depression years, largely through the efforts of Fr. Clement Neulding and Monsignor Francis Putz.

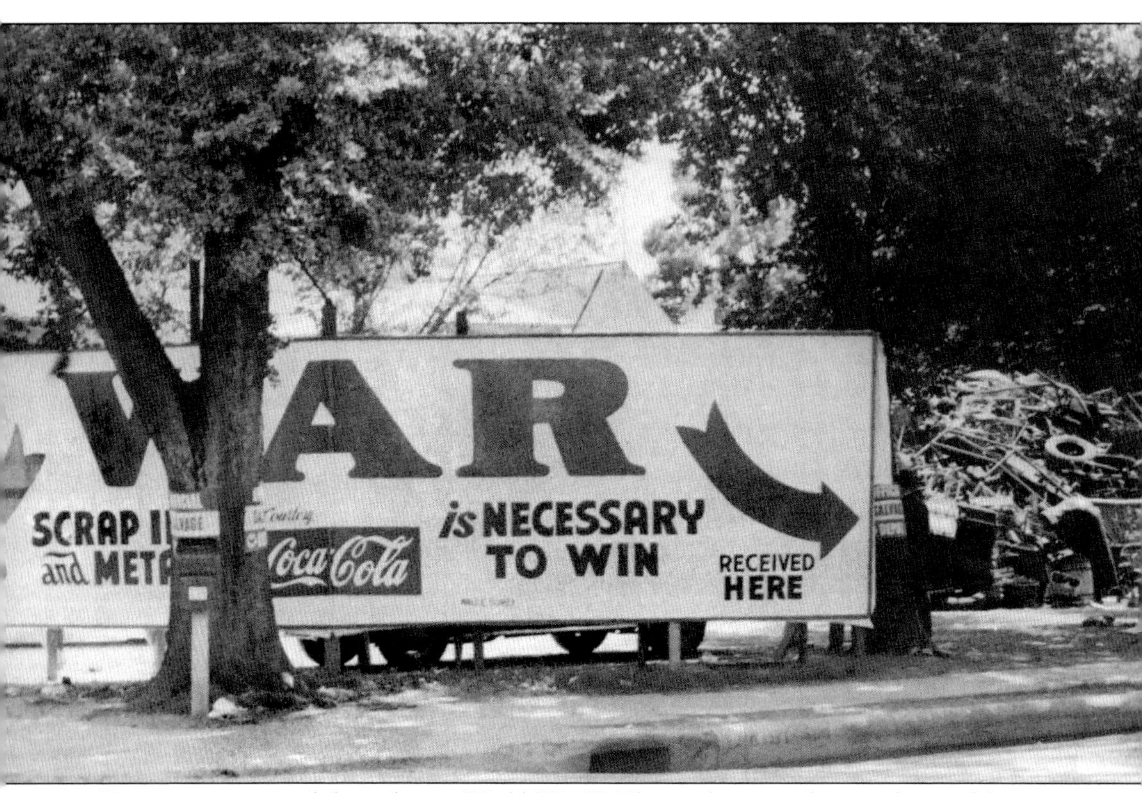

Here is a scrap-metal drive during World War II. The civilian population of central Louisiana was mobilized for the duration of the war.

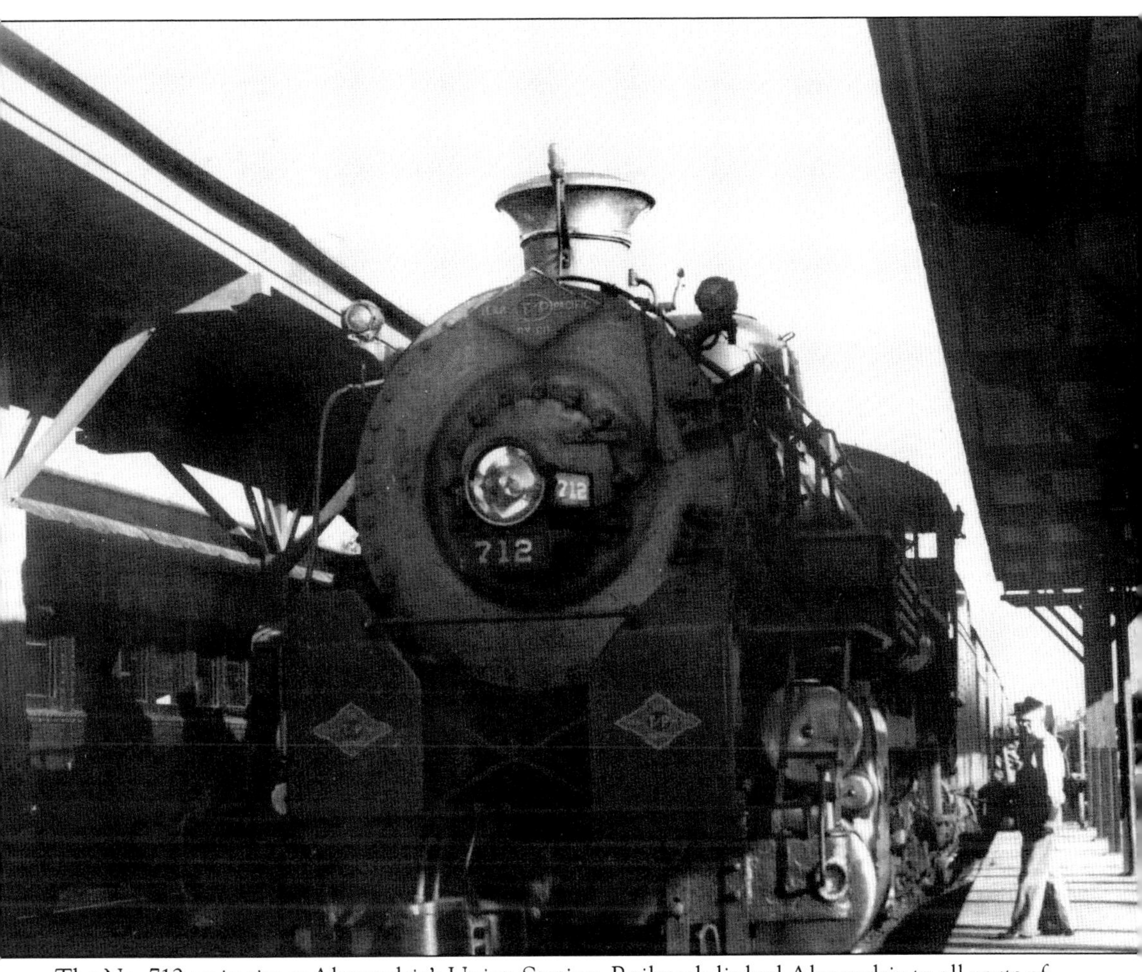

The No. 712 train sits at Alexandria's Union Station. Railroads linked Alexandria to all parts of the state before the construction of the interstate highway system.

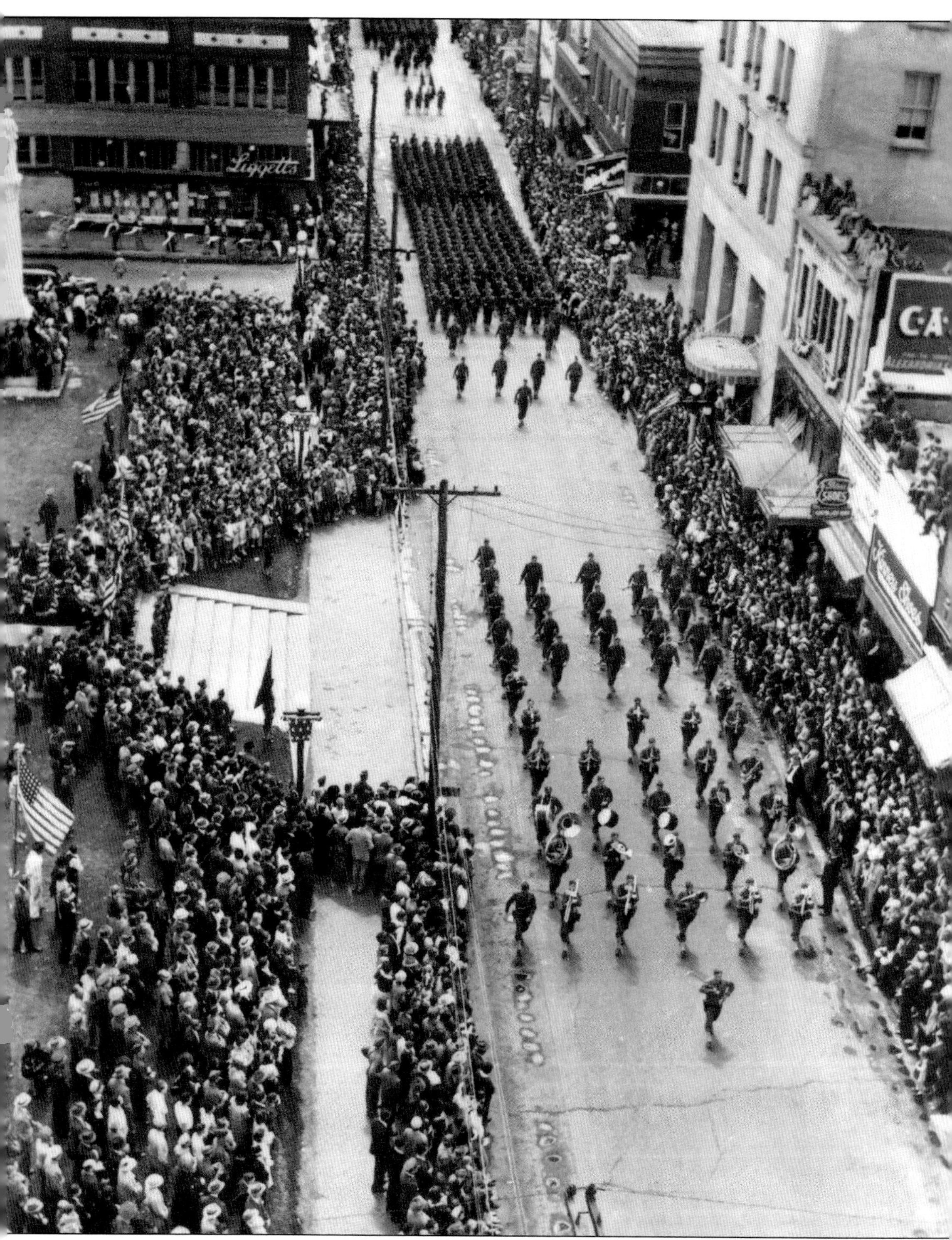

Pictured is a military parade in Alexandria in 1941. Thousands of troops passed through central Louisiana during World War II.

Six

Back to the Future

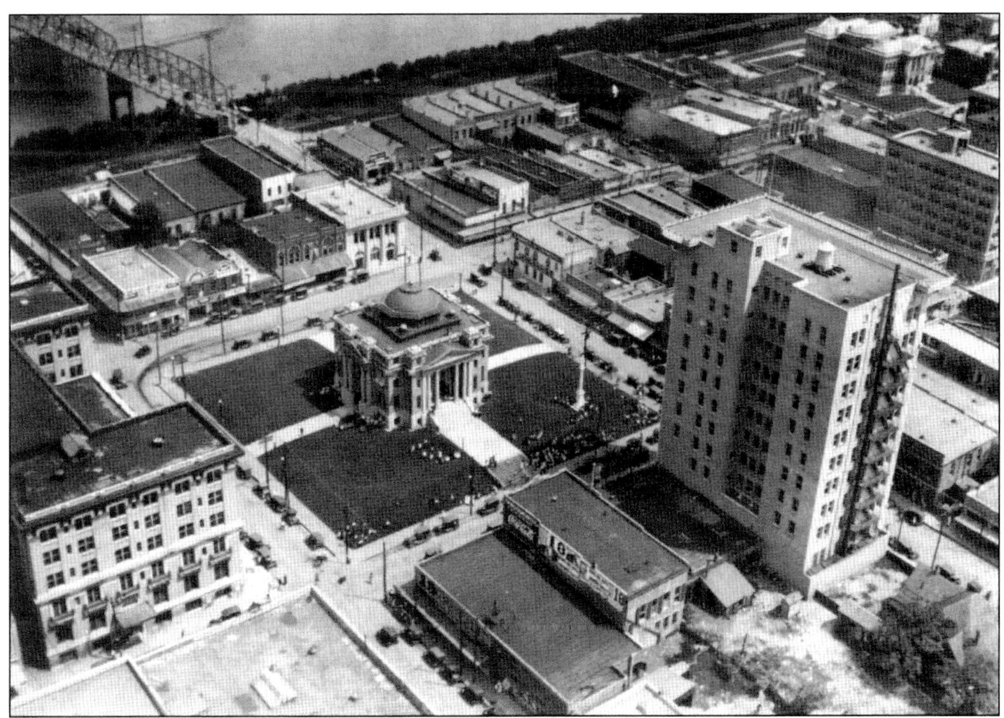

An aerial view depicts downtown Alexandria's City Hall Square and Hotel Bentley at a time when downtown Alexandria was in its finest hour. The iconic city hall was destroyed in 1963 and replaced by a modernist-style city hall and convention center.

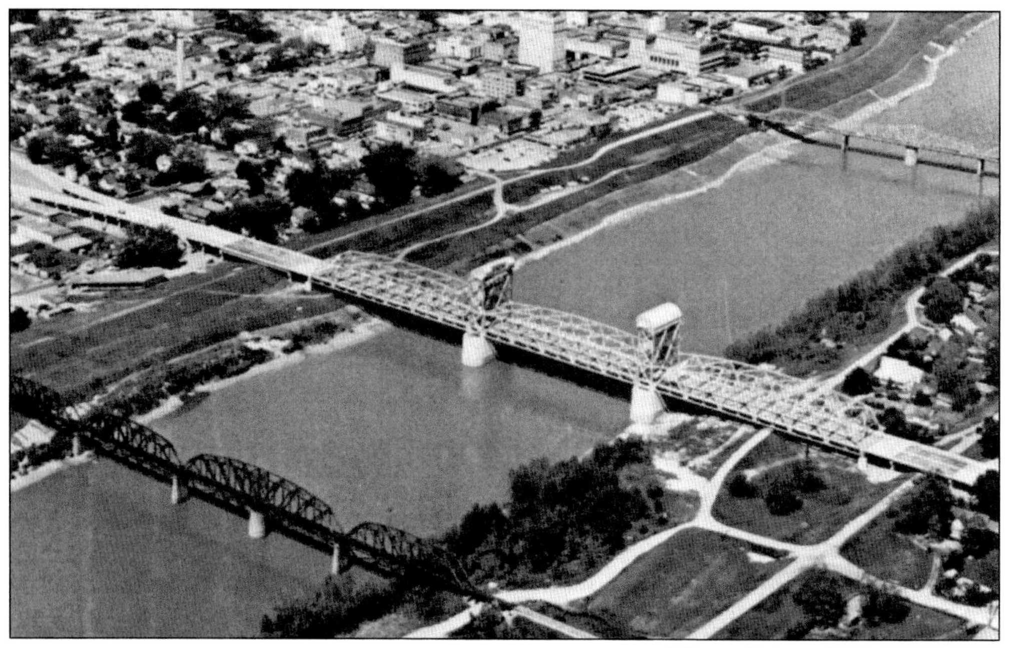

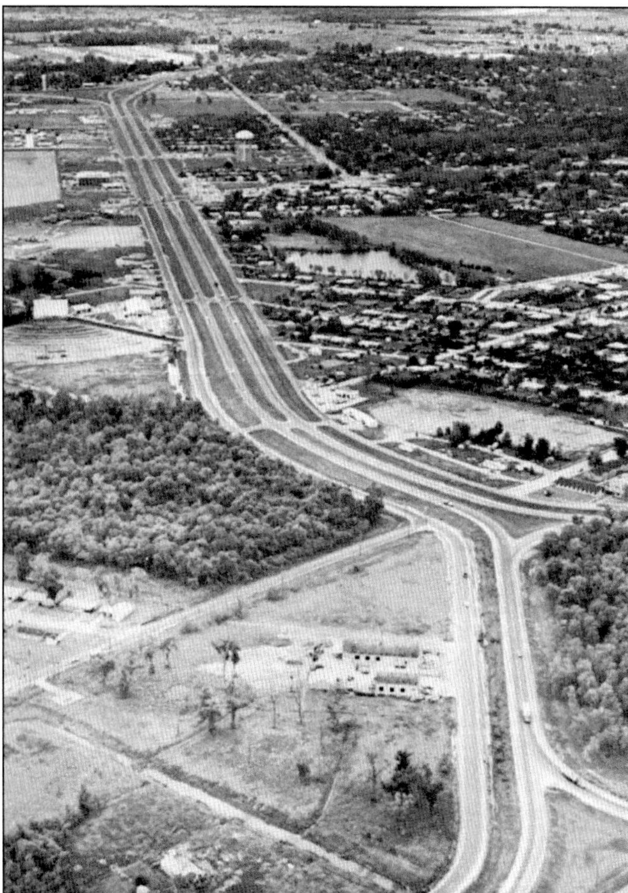

This is Fulton Street Bridge over the Red River in the 1960s. Fulton Street and the bridge are named after Alexander Fulton, the Pennsylvania merchant and Indian trader who laid out plans for the town of Alexandria in 1805.

A 1960s aerial depicts South McArthur Drive. Built by military engineers between 1941 and 1944, McArthur Drive was originally far from the city center. In time, the city expanded to include the drive as a major north-south thoroughfare.

The Confederate Soldiers' Monument sits in front of the parish courthouse on Murray Street. Rapides Parish sent 12 companies of infantry and two companies of cavalry to bolster the Confederate cause. The first resident of Rapides Parish to die in the conflict was George Washington Compton, one of the first cadets at the Louisiana Seminary of Learning in Pineville. He died at the first Battle of Bull Run in July 1861.

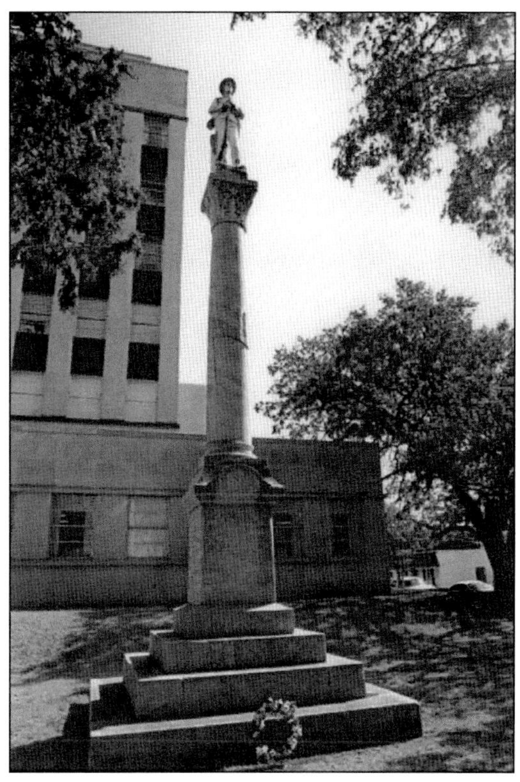

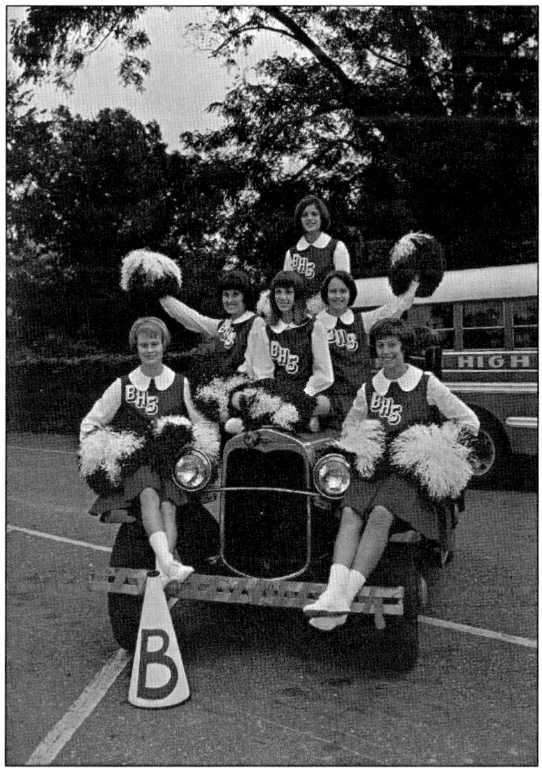

Bolton High School cheerleaders pose in 1966. Bolton, with class sizes of 400 and 500 students, was ranked as one of the top five high schools in Louisiana before the construction of Alexandria Senior High School in 1969.

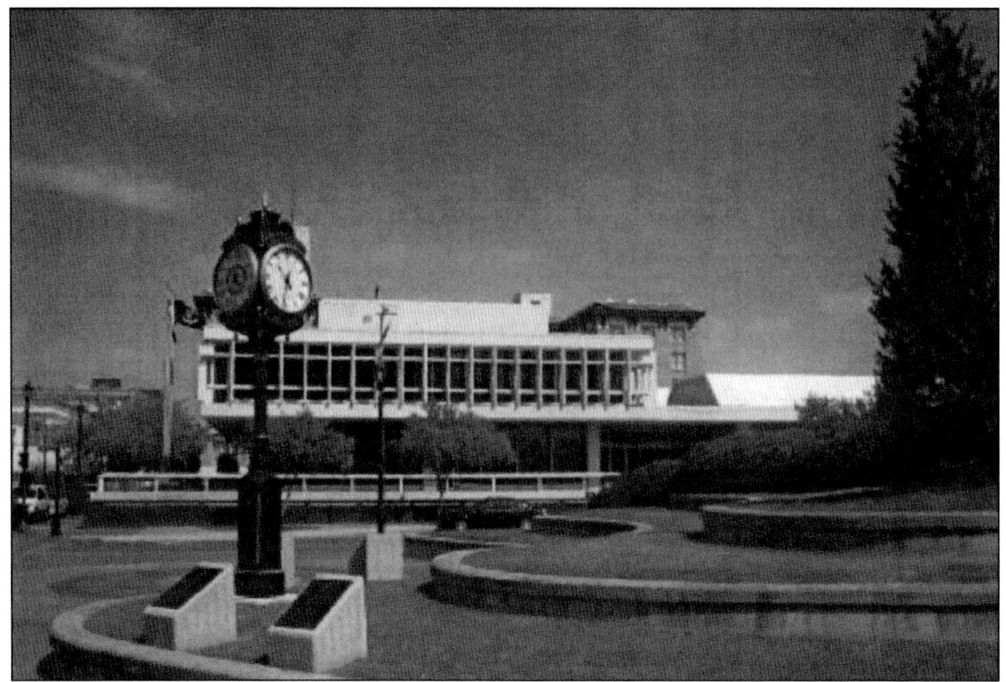

Pictured are city hall and Alexander Fulton Mini-Park. This view shows the bicentennial clock, erected in 2007 to commemorate the 200th anniversary of the founding of the town by Alexander Fulton.

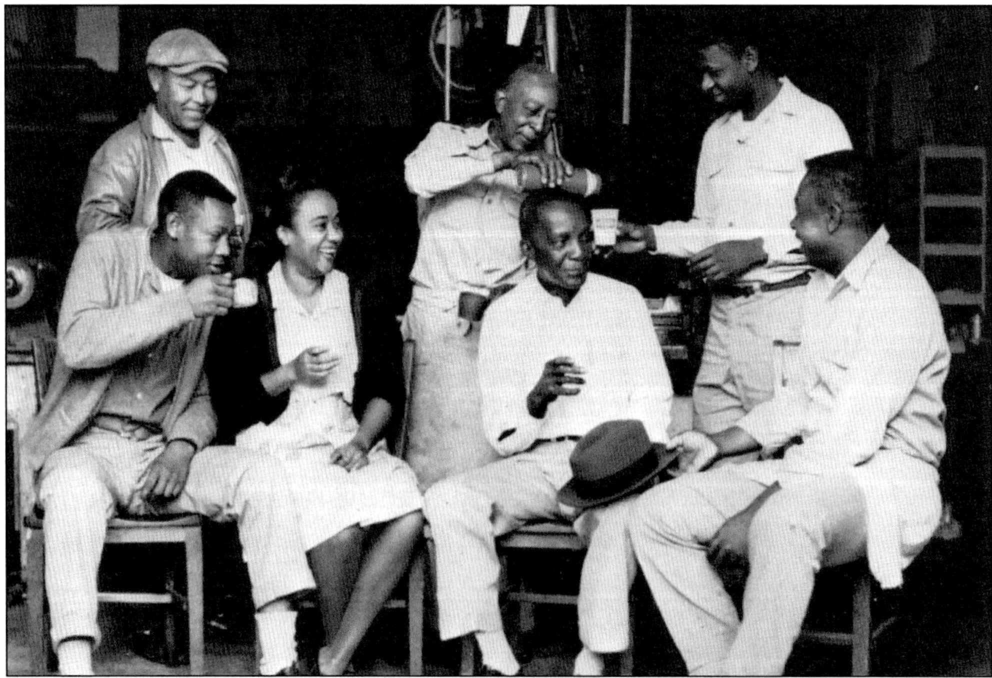

The custodial staff at Bolton High School takes a break in 1966. Because of strict segregation laws, African American students were not allowed to attend the all-white Bolton High School until 1969.

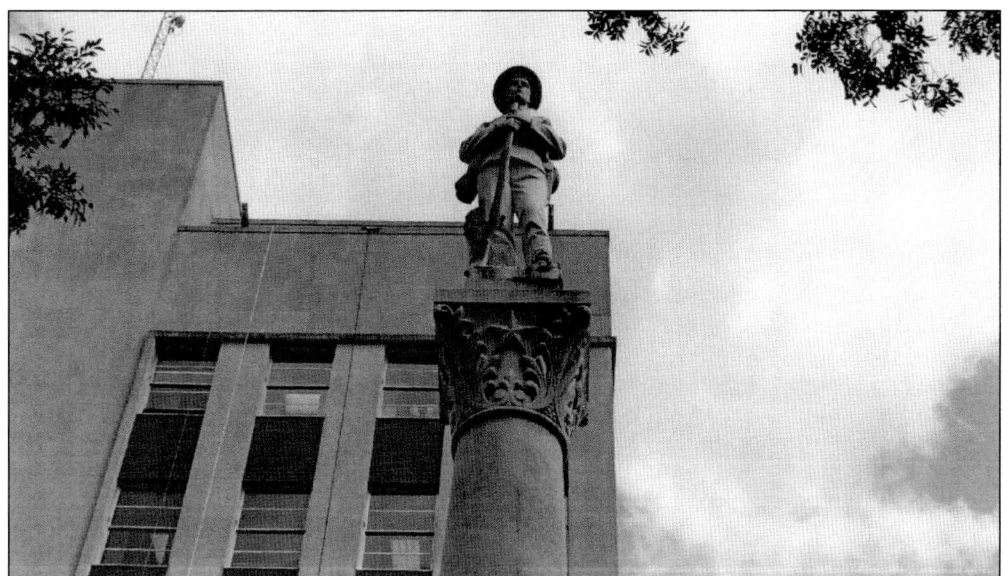

This is a close-up view of the Confederate Soldiers' Monument. Erected by the Thomas Overton Moore Chapter of the United Daughters of the Confederacy, it originally stood at the City Hall Square. After the demolition of the old city hall, the monument was moved to its present location in front of the parish courthouse on Murray Street.

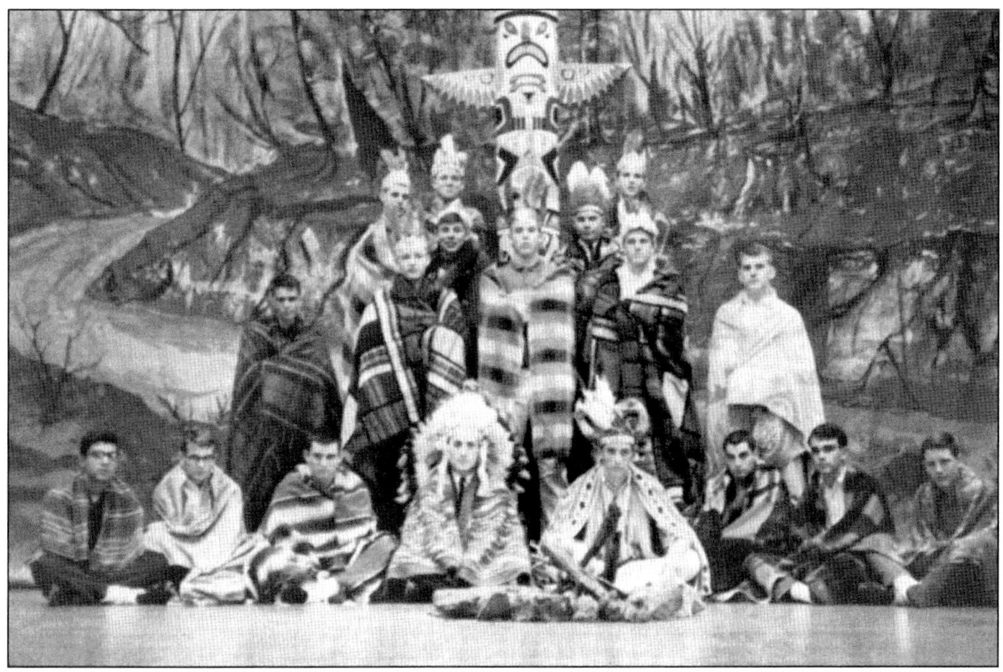

Pictured here are Chief Cumtux and his braves (honor students from Bolton High School) in the 1960s.

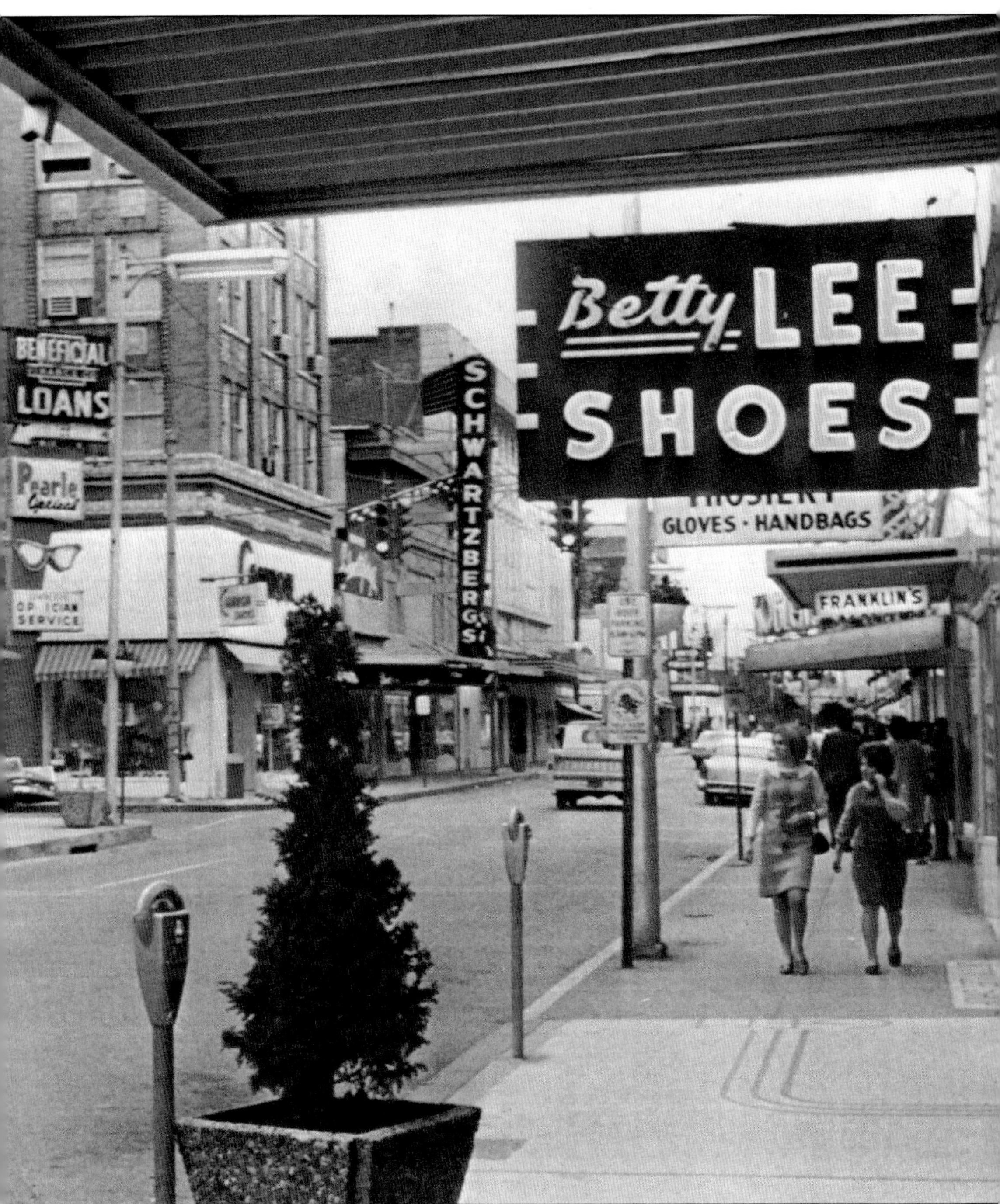

Two ladies walk on the opposite side of Schwartzberg's Department Store in the 1960s. Large department stores like Schwartzberg's, Wellan's, and Weiss and Goldring were a vibrant part of the downtown landscape until the development of the suburban Alexandria Mall in the 1970s.

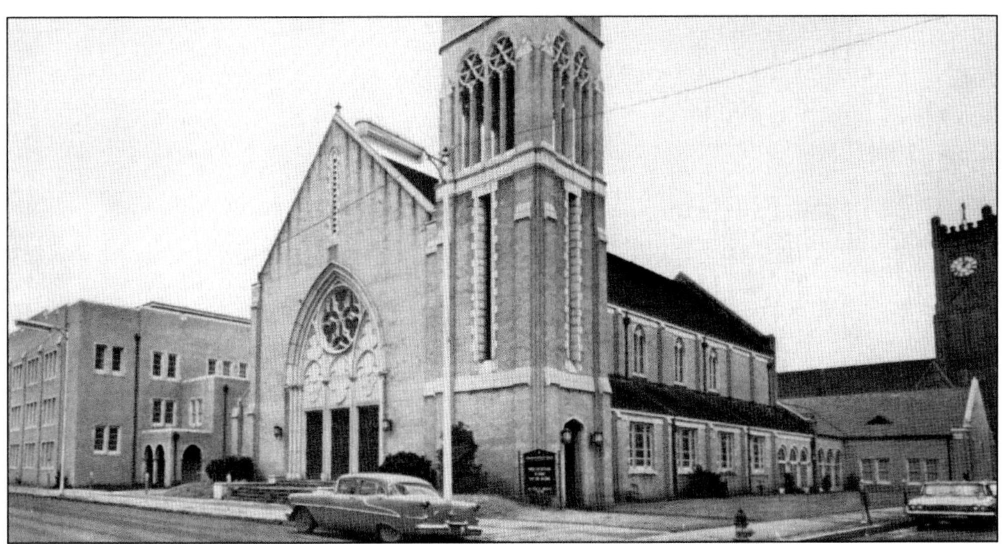

A car is parked out front of Emmanuel Baptist Church on Jackson Street in 1964. Emmanuel remains as one of the principle churches in the downtown district.

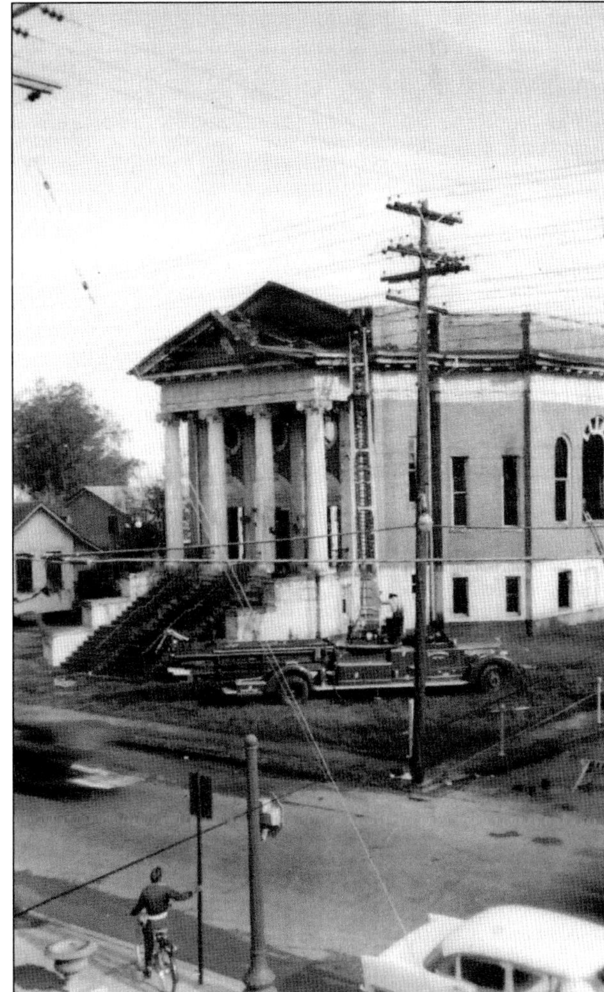

Fire gutted the old Jewish temple after its congregation had moved to a new temple on Turner Street in 1952. Elements of the old temple's sanctuary, including the ark for the Torah scrolls, are preserved in the new temple's historical collection.

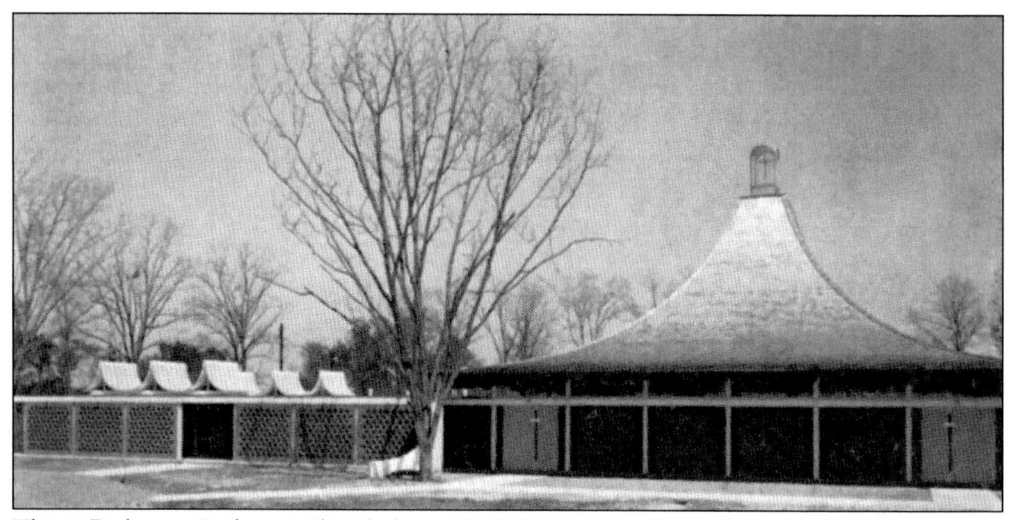

This is Redeemer Lutheran Church, located off the south traffic circle on Masonic Drive.

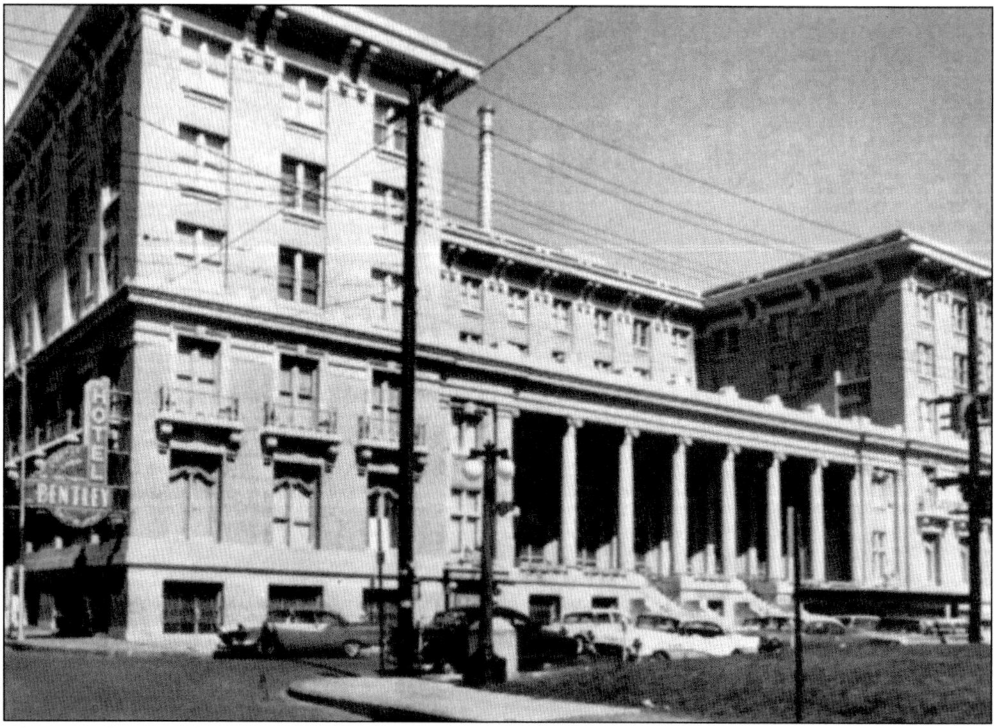

The Bentley Hotel in seen here in the early 1960s. The Bentley's Mirror Room Lounge was a popular nightclub for decades.

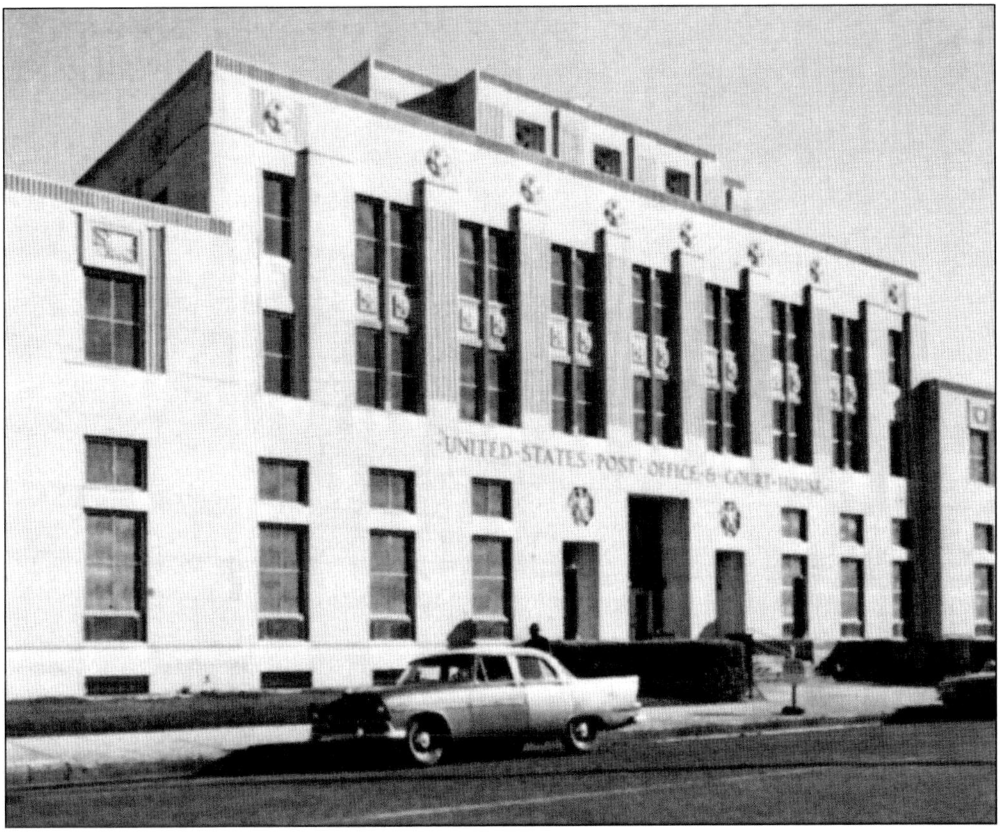

Here is the federal post office and courthouse on Murray Street. Built in the 1930s, it is one of Alexandria's grandest Art Deco–style buildings.

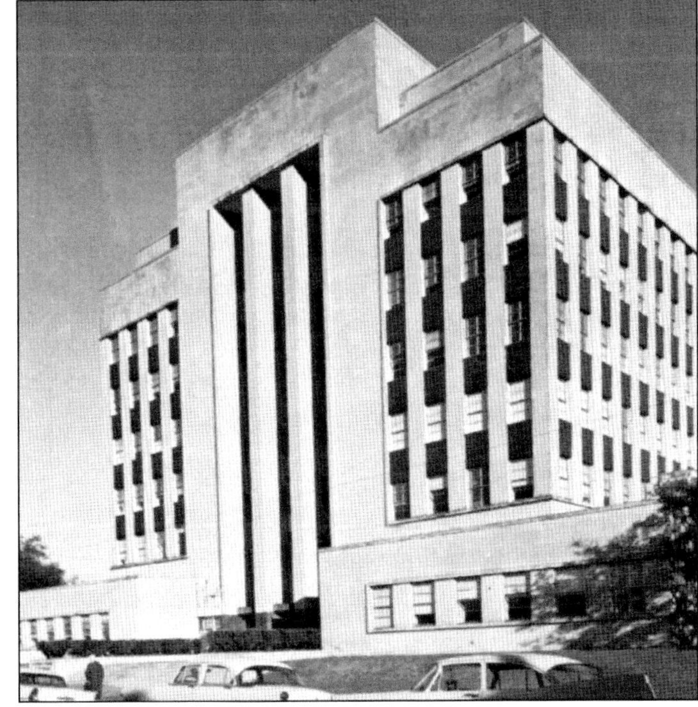

Rapides Parish Courthouse stands on Murray Street. This 1930s structure was built to replace the older 1908 courthouse. It was here that young enlistees made their oath of allegiance after the 1941 bombing of Pearl Harbor. A gas vigil light on the lawn of the courthouse commemorates the dead of all wars hailing from Rapides Parish.

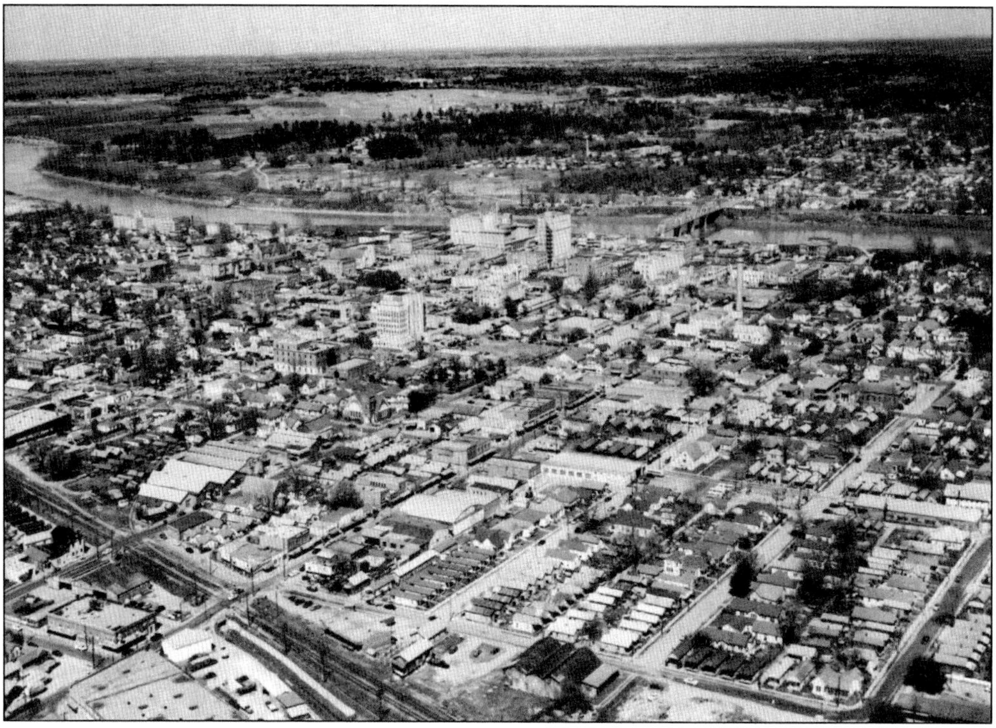

An aerial view shows the development of the city as it moved towards McArthur Drive in the late 1950s and early 1960s.

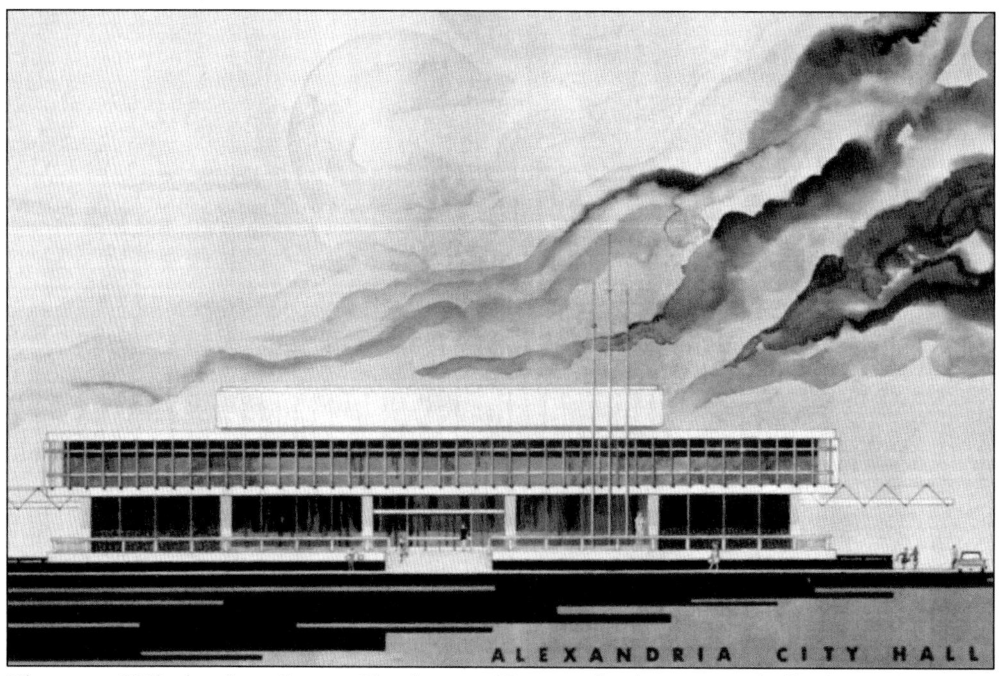

This is a c. 1963 plan from Barron, Heinberg and Brocato for the new city hall. This mid-century, modern building replaced the old classical city hall, which was deemed too small and antiquated for the city's expanding office needs.

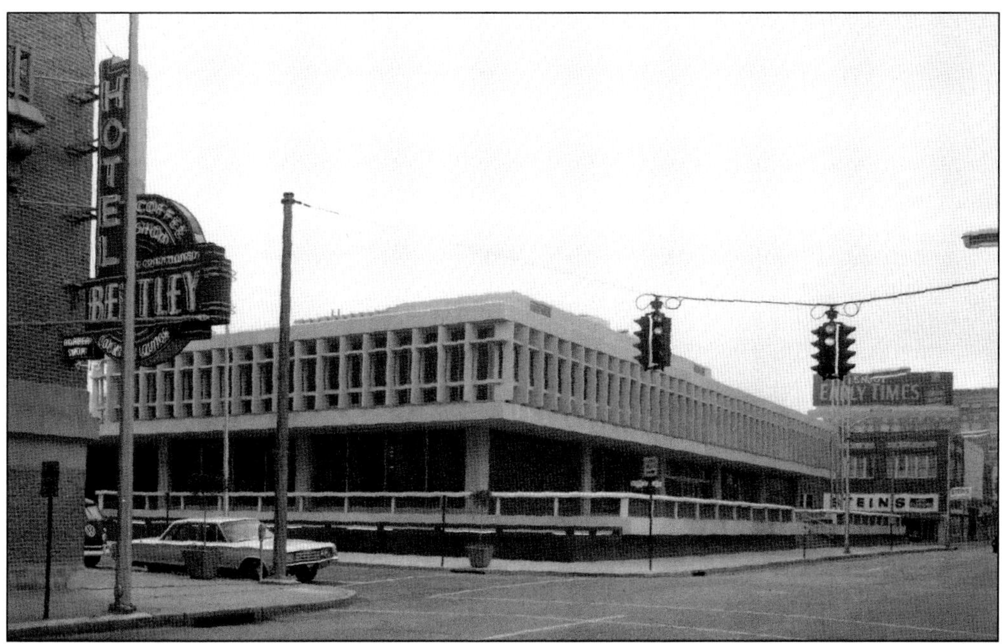

The new city hall and convention center were built under the administration of Mayor George Bowden in 1963 from plans submitted by Barron, Heinberg and Brocato.

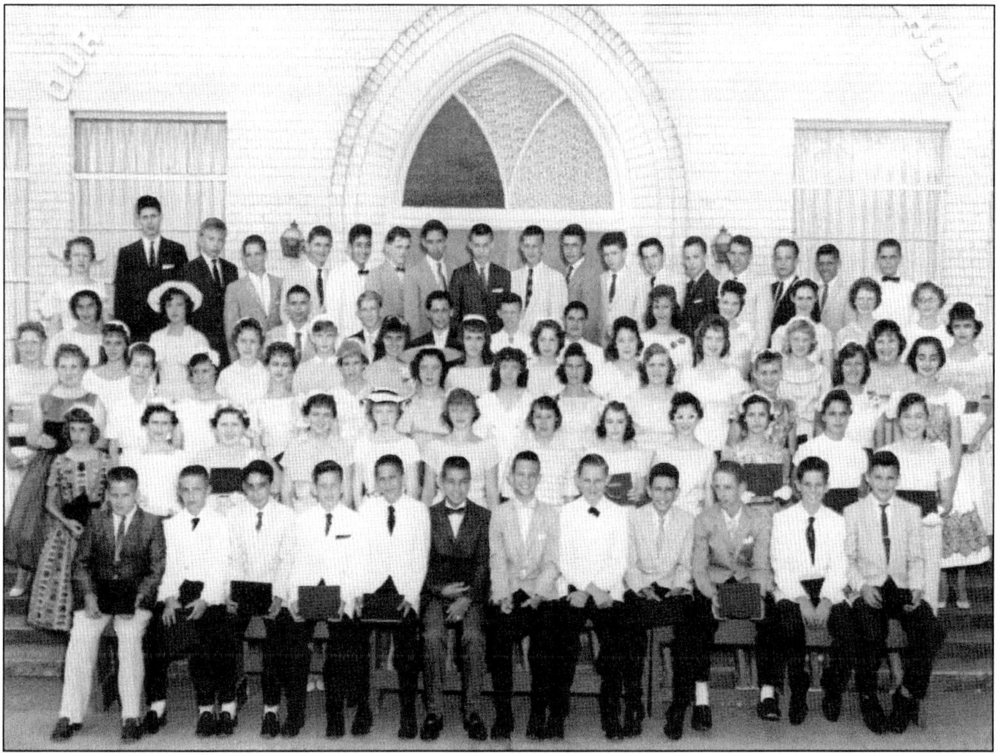

Posing is the 1960 class of eighth-grade graduates of Prompt Succor Parochial School, a Catholic elementary school established by Msgr. Aloysius Olinger and staffed by the Sisters of Divine Providence.

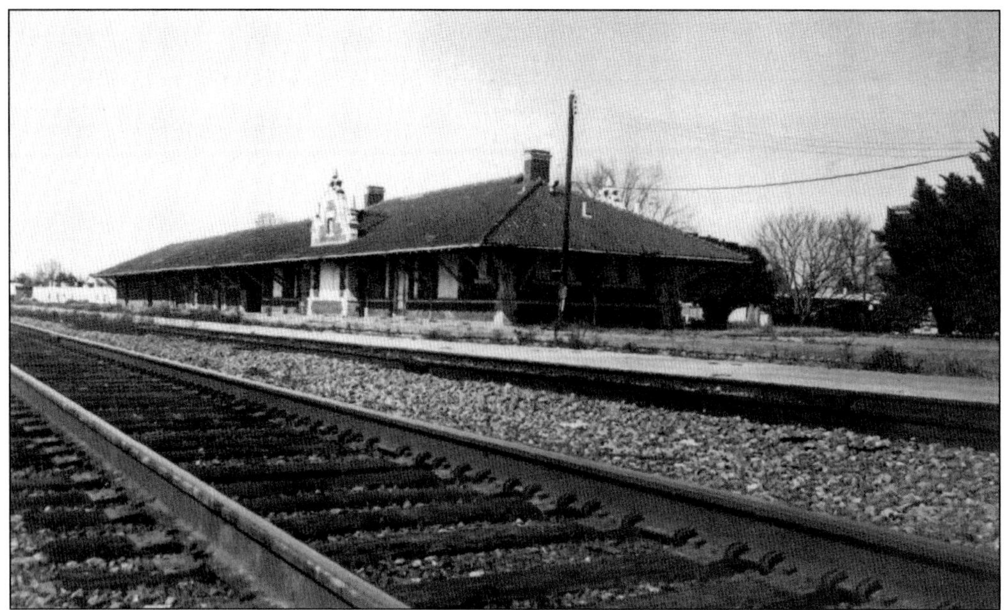

Union Depot was abandoned after the closing of passenger service on the T&P Railway. The station was later torn down to make way for the construction of Interstate 49. Portions of the Jacobean-style building were used in the construction of the city's new bus terminal downtown. Architectural elements of the depot were used in the construction of the city's new A-Trans bus terminal, located opposite Fulton Park.

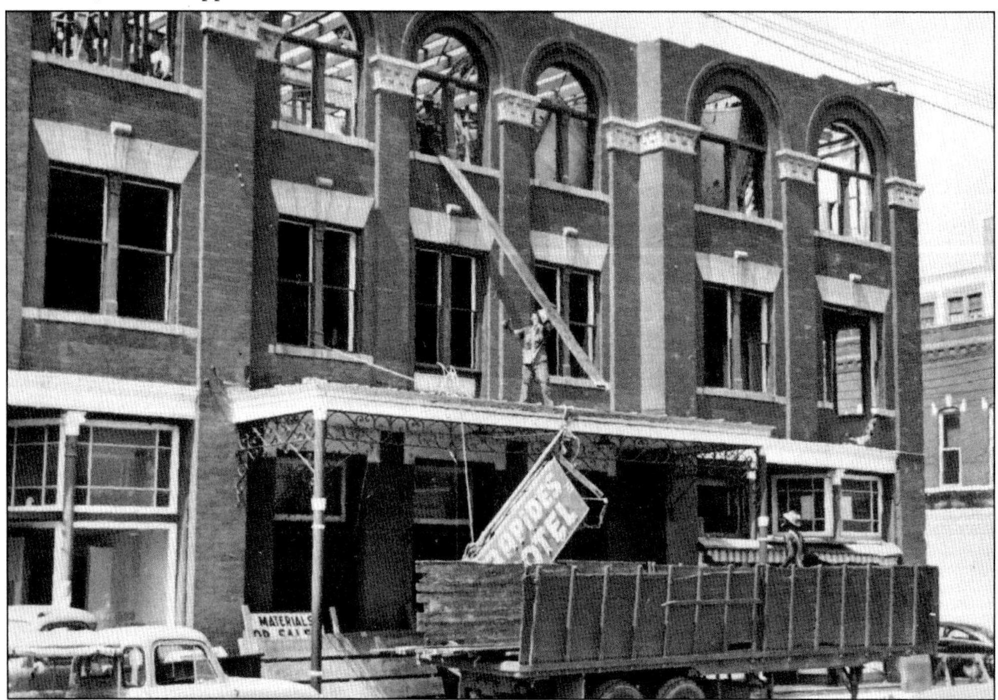

This photograph was taken during the demolition of the old Rapides Hotel. Many of downtown Alexandria's great historic buildings were lost in the late 1950s and early 1960s because of negligence and poor civic planning.

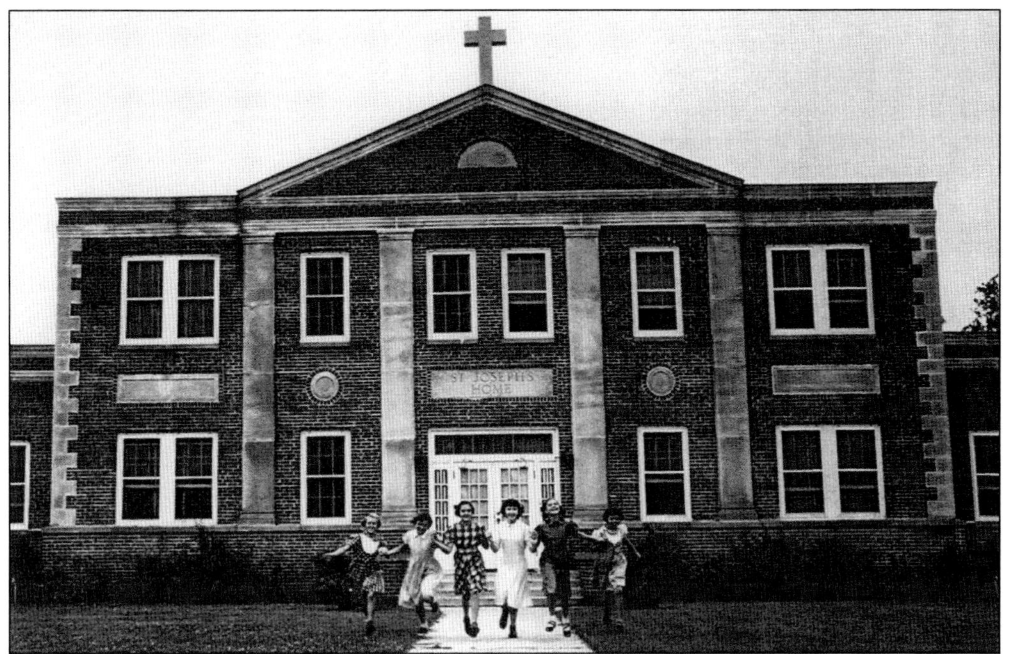

St. Joseph's Orphanage, seen here, was situated on Texas Avenue until its demolition in the early 1990s. Originally founded by Bishop Van de Ven in Pineville, the orphanage was moved to its Texas Avenue location by Bishop Greco. The institute was originally staffed by Sisters of Charity of the Incarnate Word. These same religious still staff Cabrini Hospital today.

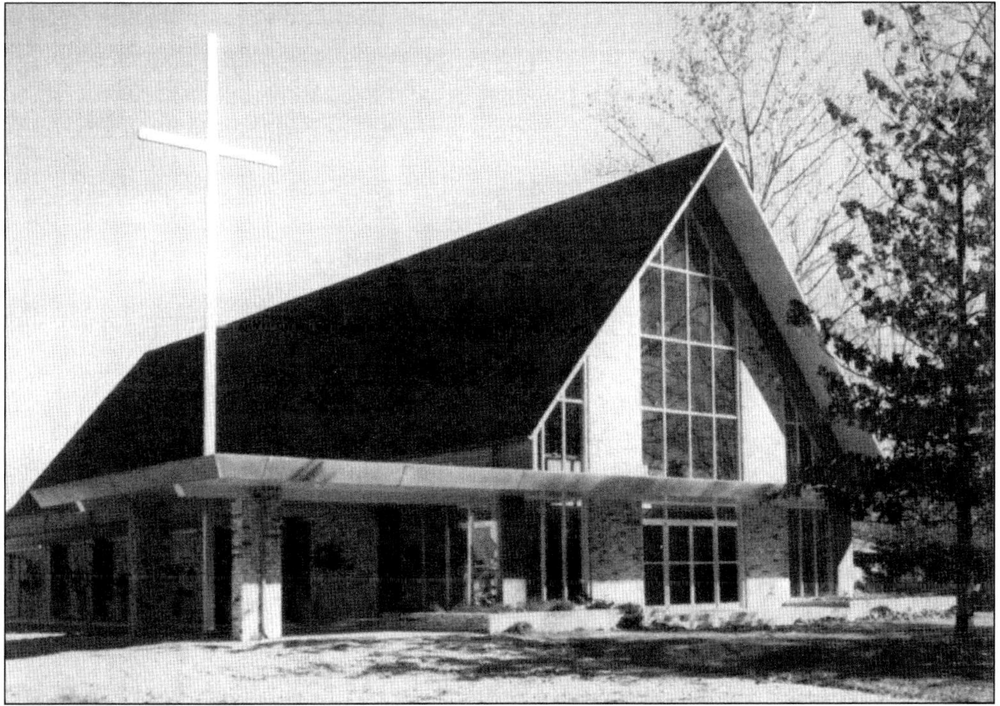

St. Timothy's Episcopal Church on Horseshoe Drive is one of the many new sanctuaries built outside the old city center as the community expanded beyond McArthur Drive in the 1960s.

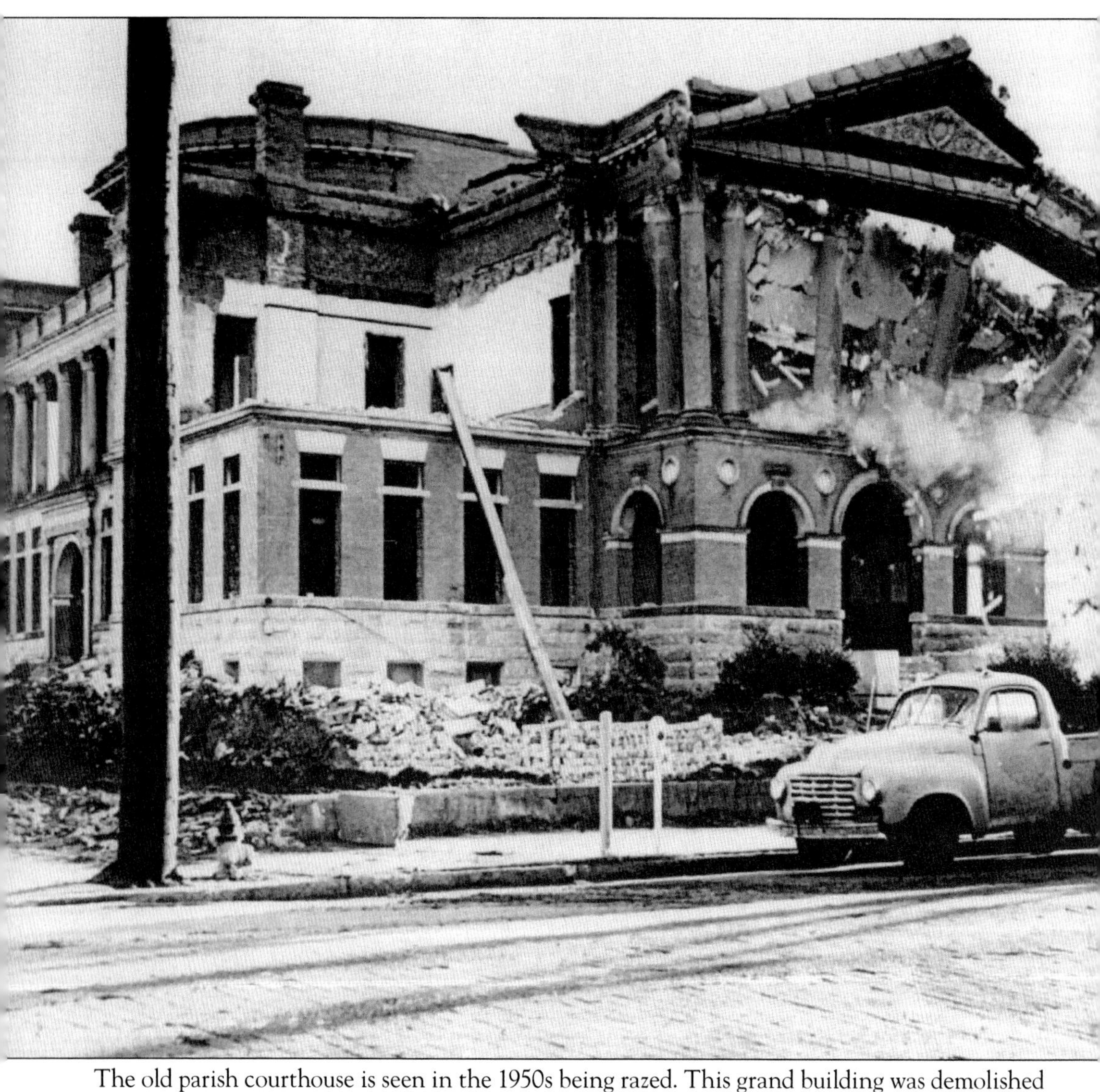

The old parish courthouse is seen in the 1950s being razed. This grand building was demolished to make way for a parking lot.

The Tudor family was largely responsible for returning the Hotel Bentley to its original beauty in 1985. From left to right are (first row) Michael Tudor, Lorraine Tudor, and Sue Tudor Miller; (second row) R.B. "Buddy" Tudor Jr. and Robert B. Tudor. In October 1986, the Hotel Bentley partners were honored for their restoration work with one of 16 national awards for preservation given by the National Trust for Historic Preservation.

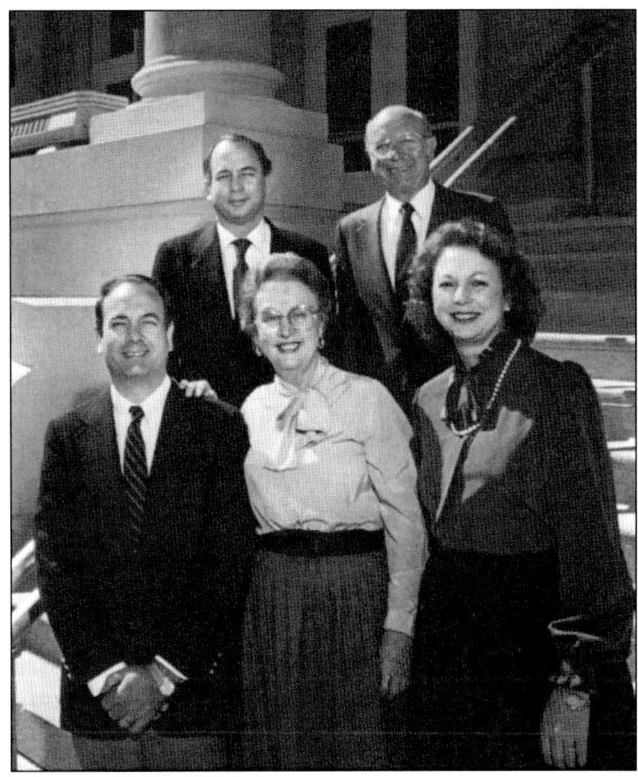

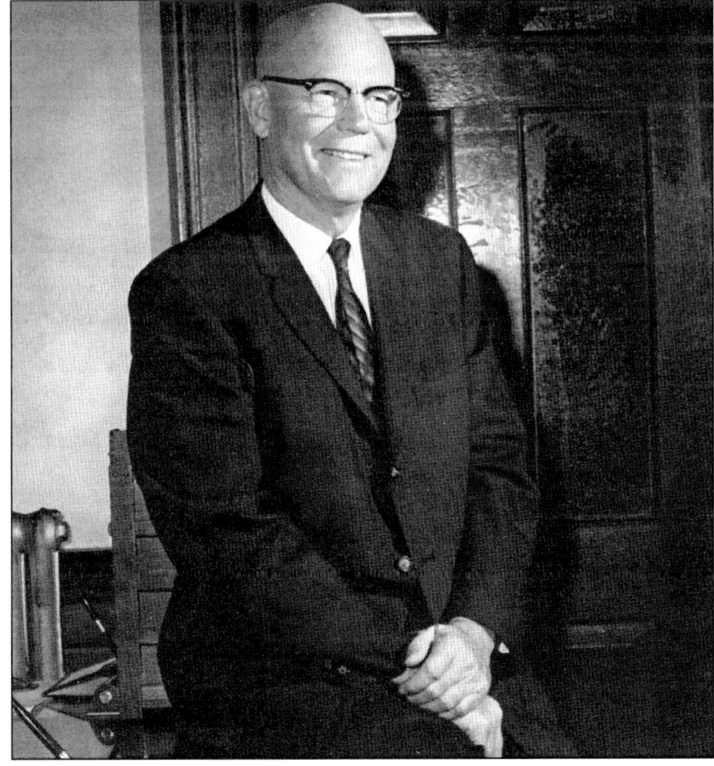

Seen here is James Pate, a longtime educator and revered principal of Bolton High School during its heyday in the 1950s and 1960s.

Discover Thousands of Local History Books Featuring Millions of Vintage Images

Arcadia Publishing, the leading local history publisher in the United States, is committed to making history accessible and meaningful through publishing books that celebrate and preserve the heritage of America's people and places.

Find more books like this at
www.arcadiapublishing.com

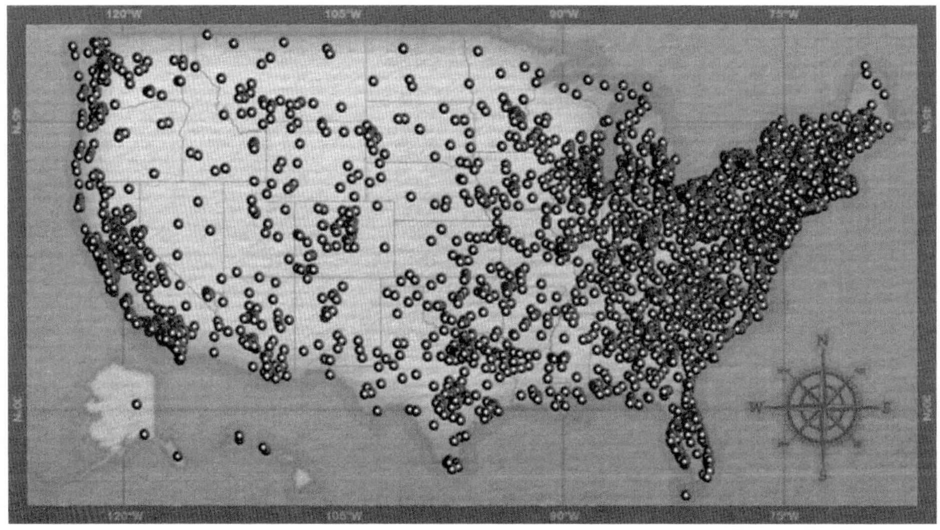

Search for your hometown history, your old stomping grounds, and even your favorite sports team.

Consistent with our mission to preserve history on a local level, this book was printed in South Carolina on American-made paper and manufactured entirely in the United States. Products carrying the accredited Forest Stewardship Council (FSC) label are printed on 100 percent FSC-certified paper.

MADE IN THE

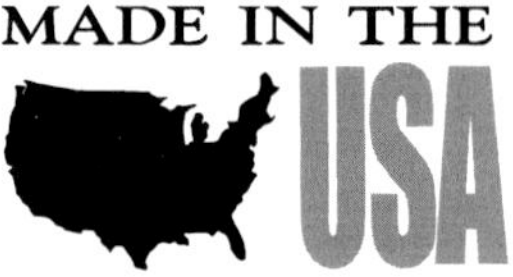